The Essential Guide to Pensions

A Worker's Handbook
THIRD EDITION

Sue Ward

PLUTO  PRESS

London • Winchester, Mass

First published 1981 by Pluto Press
345 Archway Road, London N6 5AA
and 8 Winchester Place, Winchester
MA 01890 USA

British Library Cataloguing in Publication Data
Ward, Sue
 The essential guide to pensions : a
 worker's handbook.
 1. Great Britain. Occupational
 superannuation schemes
 I. Title
 331.25'2'0941

 ISBN 0-7453-0395-1

Typeset by Stanford Desktop Publishing Services, Milton Keynes
Printed in Great Britain by Billing and Sons Ltd, Worcester

Contents

Contents *vii*

Preface and Acknowledgements

This is the third edition of *Pensions: a Worker's Handbook*, first published by Pluto Press in 1981. Since then a great deal has changed in the world of pensions, especially with the new framework of 'Personal Pensions' introduced by the government under the Social Security Act 1986.

The new edition follows the pattern of the original version, but has a substantial amount of new material. In order to create the space for this, some of the earlier text has had to be taken out or compressed.

As with the first and second editions, this is not intended as a book for experts. It is a handbook for shop stewards, union representatives and full time officials, to help them to understand and negotiate company pension schemes, and to see behind the new 'Personal Pensions' now being sold by the financial institutions. It cannot cover everything; the framework of taxation and administration, in particular, has only been summarised briefly, and in some cases I have simplified complex processes in a way that may offend pensions professionals.

I owe thanks to all the employers and pension professionals who have taught me so much about pensions over the last few years, and to all the editors who have had me writing, extensively and in many different places, about the subject. Also my previous employers, the GMWU (as they were then) who allowed me to write the first edition, and the TUC who enabled me to write other material, especially the Trustee Handbook during my time there. With their permission, I have quoted extensively from the National Association of Pensions Fund Survey, but I did not ask them to comment on the use to which those extracts have been put, or on any views or conclusions drawn from them.

I should also like to thank personally Myles White, Bryn Davies, Frances Bennett and Jim Moher for reading and commenting on the first edition of the manuscript; Colin Lever, John Prevatt, Brian Mead and Don Warren for commenting on parts of it; and Michael Cunningham for discussing it exhaustively with me. For the subsequent editions I received considerable help from Bryn Davies (again) and John Cullen, and am very grateful to them. I should also like to thank Elsie Denham, who did a very considerable amount of typing, checking and correcting for this third edition.

Sue Ward
March 1990

Part I

1

What is a Company Pension Scheme?

'Company pension schemes' are agreements made by an employer to provide a certain amount of money:

- when the worker retires, as a pension or a lump sum;
- when the worker dies, as a lump sum; and/or
- as a spouse's or dependant's pension.

The most usual way of calculating these benefits is for the amount of money to be provided to be stated as a fraction (1/60th, or 1/80th, for instance) or a percentage (1.66%, 1.25%) of the worker's wage, at or near the time when they retire or die. It doesn't have to be; it can be a flat sum of money for each year you are in the scheme, or it can depend on how well the cash has been invested.

Many employers refuse to regard pension schemes as negotiable, and it's rare for them to be included in the same collective agreement as everything else. But they will normally be:

- written down, in a pension scheme booklet that any member of the scheme must be given; and
- backed up by a trust deed and rules, which are legal documents that the members have a right to see.

Various names are used for these arrangements. They can be called:

- company pension schemes;
- occupational pension schemes;
- superannuation – this is the name often used for local government, central government, or nationalised industry pensions;
- retirement benefit schemes. This is the name used by a number of US companies.

They are all different names for the same thing. In this book, they are called either company pension schemes, or employer-provided schemes, except where schemes in the public sector are meant, when they'll be called superannuation.

They can be paid for entirely by the employer, or the employee can also pay a contribution. The money goes into a fund which is administered by trustees.

The trustees are responsible for investing this money. They may do it themselves, employing an investment manager directly, or they may get a merchant bank, or some other financial institution, to do the work on a contract basis; or they may buy policies with an insurance company. Whichever of these things happens, the money will be used to buy shares in companies, government stocks, property, and various other things.

In 1975 the Social Security Pensions Act became law. Under this, all employed people had to be either members of SERPS, the State Earnings Related Pension Scheme, or they had to be members of a contracted-out employer's scheme. If they were contracted out, the employer had to guarantee to give at least as good a pension as they would have had from the State.

In 1986 a new Social Security Act was passed, which allowed employees to contract out by themselves after July 1988, by taking Personal Pensions. These are not related to your pay; what you get depends on how much money goes into the scheme. They are covered in detail in Chapter 6. It is possible to 'mix and match' different types of pensions, so that it can get extremely complicated.

For any contracted-out scheme, there is a special set of rules that must be followed, and these are laid down by an organisation called the Occupational Pensions Board. There are other rules, laid down by the Inland Revenue (the tax people) which apply to all schemes. These cover the maximum levels of contribution you can make, and of benefits you can get from these schemes.

The rules, and the way pension funds work, are explained in detail later on. Although they may look very different and complicated because of these various rules, pensions are as much a negotiable item as anything else, so far as we are concerned, although the employer may well think differently. You do, though, have to treat pensions negotiations in a rather different way from wage negotiations, as explained in Chapter 25.

Your employer may want you to think of the pension scheme as something he provides out of the goodness of his heart, and therefore as something you have no business arguing about. Don't let the employer get away with this. Even if your pension scheme is 'non-contributory', you still have rights. The employer is putting in all the contributions, but where does he get the money from, except from the value you add by your work? The alternative would be for him to add it to your wages, and then to take it away from you as a pension contribution.

Why Should We Negotiate Pension Schemes?

In the past, trade unions did not take much part in negotiating or running employer-provided pension schemes. In fact there was often a strong wish not to become involved. We believed that pensions should be provided by the State, as part of the Social Security system.

At the moment the State pension is far too small. It has been around a fifth of the average industrial wage since the war, or about a third for a married couple. The TUC, and the pensioner organisations, have been asking for years for the pension to be increased to a half of the average wage for a married couple, or a third for a single person.

No government has done this and since 1979 the real value of the State pension has fallen. Pensioners who only have the basic State pension to live on have seen their standard of living drop compared to that of the working population.

Because of this, many people in the trade union movement have felt that if we go for better employer-based pensions for some, we will be contradicting the TUC aim of better State pensions for everyone. After, all, even if the standard of living rises, there must be some limit on the amount of cash that can be distributed from the working population to the non-working population. We know that there is a limit on the amount that people are willing to see go in deductions from their pay packets, before they take them home. So the more we pay into company pension schemes, which give much more to the better off than to the poor, the less we may be willing to pay to the State, who give the same basic pensions to everyone. By tying up so much in company schemes, we may be making it impossible to achieve the TUC aim.

If we were redesigning things from scratch, we probably wouldn't want to have company pension schemes in their present form, nor Personal Pensions. It would be better if we could rely more heavily on each other, via paying taxes to the government to provide a decent pension. We might want to enforce an obligation on all employers to look after their retired workers, rather than making it discretionary so that some had extra privileges.

Pension schemes are not very efficient at doing the job they claim to be doing. They work pretty well for the small group of people who stay 40 years with one company, and have their best earnings, in real terms, at the end of their working lives. But even while still doing the same job, they can find that suddenly they have much reduced expectations, if their firm is taken over or the scheme wound up and a new one started.

Pensions schemes work badly – though thanks to some reforms, not quite as badly as they did – for people who change jobs, for whatever reason, and for those who have a break in their working lives, perhaps in order to bring up children.

People who are already well paid tend to have the most generous pension schemes, so that the system as a whole takes money from the poor and gives it to the rich. For many people the schemes make promises which turn out to be misleading when you look at the small print.

So why get involved at all? Why have a workers' handbook about pensions?

We can't now avoid them. In 1975 the State went into 'partnership' with private pension schemes, so that whether we like it or not, all employed people have been building up an earnings related pension, whether from the State or from their employers. Eleven million people are now in employers' pension schemes, and the people who run them have a huge vested interest. And ordinary people also now have a vested interest.

The tax relief on pension contributions, and the fact that the lump sums payable on death and at retirement are tax free, means that even people on quite low incomes now get their tax bills reduced if they are members of a pension scheme.

On top of this, many people may find themselves with a poor deal from the new 'Personal Pensions', unless the unions are alert to what is going on and ready to advise their members. If we ignore all this, millions of trade unionists will still belong to schemes, and they won't thank us for walking away and allowing management and the financial institutions to get away with more. So if we are going to put up with them at all, we ought to do the job properly and understand what pension schemes are about, so that we can get the best possible deal. That is what this book is all about.

2

The State Pension Schemes

Before thinking about the pensions you get from your employer, or buy for yourself, it is important to understand the framework of the State system. The benefits you get from the State are the basic 'building bricks' on which the employer's pension scheme is based. So this chapter looks at first the State Basic Pension, and then the State Earnings Related Pension Scheme, commonly known as SERPS or the State Additional Pension.

The State Basic Pension

Most people will get this when they retire, and most pension schemes have this assumption built into them. But to get a basic pension, you must have paid, or been credited with, the right number of National Insurance contributions at the right time.

Until 1975, for each week during which you earned enough, a stamp went on your National Insurance card. In 1975, the system changed, though the old contributions still counted. Contributions are now collected through the PAYE system like income tax, and passed on by the Inland Revenue to the DSS.

The contributions are all earnings related, but the percentage rate you pay varies according to what category you are in. For some women, there is a reduced-rate contribution (covered in more detail on page 9). The reduced rate is what used to be called the 'small stamp', and it does not count towards the basic pension. A married woman who is paying this, or who has not paid enough full rate contributions to have built up a pension in her own right, is given a 'dependant's pension' instead, at 60% of the full rate, but only when her husband starts drawing his own State pension.

To be paid a full pension in your own right, you need to have paid, or been credited with, full rate contributions for about nine-tenths of your 'working life'. This is always assumed to start at 16, except for people retiring over the next few years, who were over 16 when the National Insurance system started in 1948. For most of them, their working life is assumed to have started in 1948, except for those in 'insurable employments' before that date, whose 'working life' may be counted as having started earlier.

For a year to count, you must have paid, or been credited with, contributions on earnings of 52 times the Lower Earnings Limit (LEL) or more. This LEL is set each year by the government in April, and is roughly the same as the National Insurance basic pension. So in

1990–1 it is £46 a week. If you earn less than this, you do not pay contributions at all, and the National Insurance system treats you as if you do not exist. As soon as you earn more, you pay contributions on all your earnings. The rate you pay depends on whether or not you are contracted out of SERPS (explained on page 32) by your employer. If you are in SERPS, or if you have an Appropriate Personal Pension of your own (these are explained in later sections), you pay 2% of your earnings up to the Lower Earnings Limit, then 9% of your earnings above that.

(These are all the 1990–1 figures; they will go up when the Lower Earnings Limit goes up.)

There is also an Upper Earnings Limit, the UEL, and if you earn more than that, you don't pay any extra National Insurance contributions. In 1990–1 this is £350 a week.

For people paid monthly, there are equivalent monthly figures. The contributions are always deducted from your gross pay, at the rate that's appropriate for that level of pay.

People who are 'contracted out' via their employer's pension scheme pay 2% of their earnings up to the Lower Earnings Limit, and then 7% on the rest.

Paul, earning £226 a week, will pay 2% of the first £46, which comes to £0.92, plus 7% of the remaining £180, which comes to £12.60, making a total of £13.52.

This 2% saving is called the National Insurance Rebate, and is meant to pay for the pension you are getting from your employer's scheme.

If at the end of the year it's found that because your earnings have varied a lot at different times you've paid too much or too little, the employer makes an extra deduction or gives a refund, all on the Inland Revenue's behalf.

If the employer goes bankrupt still owing National Insurance contributions which have been collected from you but not handed over yet, the DSS will try to reclaim them. If they do not succeed, you are 'deemed' to be covered for that period when it should have been paid in, but it may take some time to sort out.

For complete weeks when you are signing on as unemployed, or off sick and receiving State sickness benefit or invalidity benefit, or when you are receiving Maternity Allowance, you get a credit. This counts for National Insurance as if you had earned exactly the amount of the LEL. Sick pay and maternity pay from your employer are dealt with under the PAYE system anyway, so you automatically pay PAYE contributions on them.

If you are getting money 'out of the till' on which you are not paying PAYE, you are committing an offence, and you are also likely to lose out in old age, because you won't qualify for State pension. Having a few years of illegal work is one way in which people tend to fall through the holes in the system.

The DSS decide whether a year – always a tax year, April to April – counts as a 'qualifying year' for you after the end of it. They take the figure for your PAYE earnings, and any credits, and calculate whether you have earned or had credits of as much as the minimum. In 1990–1, this minimum is £2,392. If you meet this figure, 1990–1 will be a qualifying year for you. So a high paid person qualifies much more quickly than a low paid one. If you are earning right up to, or above, the UEL you qualify in about six weeks. But you have to carry on paying the contributions, and you can't use extra NI contributions in one year to make up a shortfall in another. You can pay 'voluntary' contributions in some rather limited circumstances.

DSS leaflet NP.32 gives a scale for the number of 'qualifying years' you must have, depending on the length of your working life. So, if it is 41 years or more, you have five years' leeway. With a working life of 31–40 years, you have only four years' leeway; 27–30 years, only three years. If your 'working life' is shorter than that, every year matters.

You can find out what your contribution record is, and whether you are likely to receive the full pension or only a proportion of it, by getting form BR19 from your local DSS office, and sending it to RPFA Unit, Room 37D, Central Office, Newcastle upon Tyne NE98 1YX.

The Married Woman's Contribution

Before 1977, any married woman or widow could opt to pay a special reduced rate contribution. When it originally started this was an old fourpence a week; it's now 3.85% of all your wages if you earn more than the Lower Earnings Limit.

The idea originally was that once a woman got married, she would rely on her husband for income. Even if they paid the full rate, married women were paid a lower level of unemployment benefit, for this reason, until 1975. There was a special extra qualification called the 'half test', which they had to fulfil before they could get a pension in their own right.

The reduced rate is gradually being phased out. No-one has been able to start paying it since 1977. A woman who has a break in employment for two complete consecutive tax years, whatever the reason, must pay the full rate when she returns. So if for instance you left in July 1989, and went back to work at any time up to April 1992, you could still pay the 3.85%. But at any date after April 1992, you'd have to pay the full amount. If you have been paying the reduced rate and then get divorced, you have to pay the full amount immediately. A widow who stops receiving widow's pension (explained on page 11) must also start paying the full rate, but only at the beginning of the next tax year.

Many people paying the reduced rate might do better to change over. You can do this by filling in a form in leaflet NI.1, or NI.51 if you are widowed. You can send in this form at any time during the year.

If you pay the full rate, you build up benefits in your own right, and can therefore qualify for a pension of your own. (Widows' pensions, though, depend on the husband's contributions.) There's a sliding scale if you only have contributions for a limited number of years, though there is a cut-off point of about ten years below which you don't get any benefit. There's a chart showing this in DSS leaflet NP.32.

If you are wondering whether to change over or not, the points to think about are:

- whether you can build up enough pension, by the time you retire, to take you above the rate of a dependant's pension, which is 60% of the full rate;
- whether you will retire before your husband does. If you count as his dependant, you will have to wait until he starts drawing his pension before you can collect yours. And if he works on after retirement, you will have to wait still longer;
- whether you will have to pay the full rate sooner or later anyway. Are you going to be away from work bringing up children for a period in the future? You will have to start paying the full rate then, so it might be as well to start now, and build up the maximum benefit.

Younger women are most likely to benefit from changing over. If you are over 45 or 50, it's worth considering only if you had several years of full contributions in the past, before you got married. But if you are about to take a break in paid employment, and know it will be longer than two years, then elect to pay the full rate before you leave – it won't take effect until you get back, so you won't see any more money going out of your pay packet. But it will qualify you for home responsibilities protection, explained in the next section.

Home Responsibilities Protection
Since 1978 there have been special arrangements for people who are at home looking after children or sick and disabled relatives.

You qualify if you were paying, or had told the DSS you intended to pay, NI contributions at the full rate. You must build up, through your whole working life, at least 20 years' NI record, though these years need not follow on from each other. When you retire, the DSS check if there are any gaps in your 'contribution years'. If during those gaps child benefit was payable, or you were receiving a benefit for caring for an invalid, the number of qualifying years you need for full benefit is reduced.

This only works for complete years, which is a disadvantage. It's best to try to arrange, when you return to work, that you can pay enough contributions in the first year for it to qualify you.

Widows and Widowers

For widows' pensions, there are different contribution conditions. The wife qualifies for a widow's pension if her husband has paid the right amount. In the tax year before the calendar year of his death, he must have paid, or been credited with, contributions on at least 52 times the Lower Earnings Limit (explained on page 7). But even if he did meet this condition, you will only qualify for the full rate of widow's pension if you have dependent children, or are aged over 55 (after April 1988). If you are between 45 and 55 when your husband dies, you get an age-related widow's pension, which can be much smaller. For a widow of 45, for instance, it's 30% of the full rate, and it remains at that level whatever age you reach.

There's no basic widower's pension from the State. A widower who has to look after children might well have to claim Income Support, which is the new name for Supplementary Benefit.

Retiring Early

If you have to retire early because your health is too bad to continue working, you should be able to claim invalidity benefit from the State. This follows on from sickness benefit after six months. You must have qualified by having actually paid contributions of 25 times the Lower Earnings Limit in one tax year since you started work *and* having paid or been credited with contributions on 50 times the Lower Earnings Limit in each of the last two tax years before the current calendar year – and you must also be signed off as 'unfit for work' regularly by your doctor.

If, though, you retire at your own or the firm's request without a health problem, you cannot draw your State pension any earlier than 65 for a man, 60 for a woman. For a person aged between 55 and 65, with an employer's pension or a personal pension of £35 a week or more, unemployment benefit is deducted £ for £ above that level. Men over 60 are automatically credited with contributions for the years up to 65, even if they are not signing on as unemployed. People under 60 need to sign on to receive credits; if there is nothing to come from UB because of their pension, they can sign on for 'contributions only'.

Unemployment benefit lasts a year. If after that you do not have enough to live on, you have to claim Income Support, which used to be called Supplementary Benefit.

You also have to show that you are 'actively seeking work'. This means that you have to be able to prove that you have taken 'reasonable steps' each week to find a job. If you are 'voluntarily unemployed' you can have the benefit suspended for up to 26 weeks. This penalty should not be imposed on people who take voluntary redundancy, but it will be if you simply leave when the job was going to remain open to you. You have a right of appeal against any decision to suspend your benefit, and if in doubt you should use it.

If You Retire Late

If you carry on working after State retirement age, you are allowed to draw your State pension in full. Your earnings will be added to your state pension when working out your tax, and all the tax taken off the earnings. Alternatively, you can 'defer' your pension until you do retire, and this means that it increases while it is waiting for you. It would be about a third larger at 70 for a man, or 65 for a woman, than at 65 or 60.

The Graduated Scheme

The old Graduated Scheme was the first attempt at getting an earnings-related State pension in this country, but it was not inflation proofed at first. It came to an end in 1975, and the benefits that are frozen in it have been increased in line with the main pension since 1978. Since they were very small originally, they have simply remained small in real terms, and not shrunk any further. The pension from this is paid at the same time as the main pension.

After 1975 there were special arrangements for people whose employers had 'contracted out' of this scheme to buy them back in. You should have been informed at the time, if you were affected; if not, ask the DSS now.

The State Additional Scheme

This gives you an earnings-related pension, and so is often called by the initials SERPS, which stands for State Earnings Related Pension Scheme. It started in 1978, and has been altered by the Social Security Act 1986. But as most of these alterations do not come into effect for many years, this section looks first at the current position, and then at the changes being made.

The scheme was brought in by Barbara Castle in an Act passed in 1975. It was the fourth attempt at producing an earnings-related State scheme to go on top of the basic pension. The old Graduated Scheme was the first, and then two governments in succession had tried – with Crossman's scheme in 1969 and Keith Joseph's in 1973 – to bring in something else, but had been prevented by election defeats. When the Castle scheme was brought in, the Conservative Party said that they would not change it again; but they have done so, because they claim that we cannot afford the pensions promised under the 1975 Act.

Everybody in employment started contributing to the new State additional pension in April 1978, and the first pensions were paid out to people retiring in 1979. It's now possible to get £20 or more from this, on top of your basic pension. The scheme was designed to build up slowly until the first full pensions were paid in 1998–9. With the government changes, though, it is only people retiring in that year who will get the full planned amount. After that, it gets phased down.

What the Act Says

Even if your employer's pension scheme is contracted out, you are still entitled to SERPS benefits in some cases. If you are drawing invalidity benefit, for instance, you get the earnings-related addition on top of it for years up to 1991. With the original arrangements for contracting out, the employer had to guarantee that the pension you'd get would be at least as much as you would have had from SERPS. With the new Personal Pensions, though, and the new employers COMPS (contracted-out money purchase schemes, explained on pages 37–9) this is not the case; instead you give up your SERPS rights. So it is very important to know what those rights are.

To calculate what you are entitled to, the DSS take the earnings between the LEL and the UEL (explained on pages 7–8) for each tax year since 1978. They then recalculate them to take account of the increase in National Average Earnings, between the date you earned the money and State retirement age. Then they pay you 1/80th of the average of all those years' earnings, for every complete year you've been in the scheme. So if you retired in 1988–9, you'd have ten years in the scheme, and therefore 10/80ths of your earnings between the Lower and Upper Limits.

The original idea was that once the scheme had been running for 20 years or more, people retiring after that (in 1998–9) would not build up any more 80ths. The most you could get would be 20/80ths of your revalued average earnings. But it was planned that the DSS would revalue each year's money, and pick out the best 20 years – which could come from any part of your working life, a few years when you were young and the rest when you were older – and average those.

This has now been changed, and the amount of SERPS pension is being reduced for anyone retiring after 5 April 1998. There's a complicated formula that safeguards to some extent the pension already earned before the changes in 1988. But eventually, the maximum that can be built up will be one-fifth (20%), rather than the planned one-quarter.

Under the new formula, the revalued average earnings (explained above) for the years 1978–88 are added up, and 25% is calculated. Then the figure you reach is divided again, by the number of years in total between 1978 and the date you retire.

For people who retire in tax year 2008–9 or later, the revalued average earnings for the years starting in 1988–9 are added up, 20% is calculated, and then divided again by the number of years in total between 1978 and the date you retire.

For people retiring during the ten years' 'phasing down period', between these two dates, what matters is the exact year in which they retire. At the start of that period, the figure in the formula is 25; at the end it is 20. So for each year in between, it drops by 0.5. So someone retiring in the middle, in 2004–5, uses 22.5 as the figure in the formula, while someone retiring a year later uses 22.0.

The best 20 years' arrangement has never come into force, because no-one has yet had 20 years in the scheme. But it has now been abolished altogether, and all your years' earnings will count in the calculation. The only exception to this is years you spend at home and covered by Home Responsibilities Protection (covered on page 10) or years when you are sick. These are not counted when the averaging is done. But years when you are unemployed, or only working part time or on low wages, will be counted, and so the average will be lower.

Working Out Your SERPS Pension

The formula explained above is too complicated to use for yourself, but you can work out roughly what you would get as SERPS pension, based on your earnings today. It's important to realise that in doing this, you're making the assumption that earnings will not rise between now and the date you retire. This is not a realistic assumption – but it means you can see what you'd get in terms of today's spending power.

Step 1: Take your PAYE earnings for last week, and deduct the Lower Earnings Limit (£46 in 1990–1). If your earnings are above the Upper Earnings Limit, use that figure instead (£350 in 1990–1) as the earnings figure.

Step 2: Work out the number of years from 1978 to your State retirement age. The maximum entitlement is 20 years, so ignore any years over 20.

Step 3: Work out which year it is in which you retire, because under the new Social Security Act 1986 this affects how much you get. If you retire in or before 1998-9, you build up pension at 1/80th of your earnings for each year. So we'll take that first as an example:

Jim will retire in 1992, with 14 years in the scheme since it started in 1978. His earnings are £206 a week. So he starts by deducting the Lower Earnings Limit from these, giving £160. This is called 'band earnings'. He then divides that by 80, because his pension is building up at 1/80th a year. This gives him a figure of £2. Since he has 14 years in the scheme, he multiplies that figure by 14, which gives him £28. So that would be his weekly SERPS pension, on top of the basic amount, if his earnings were going to stay the same until 1992.

For someone retiring after 1998–9, the changes in the scheme mean you can only do a rough-and-ready calculation, ignoring the safeguards for the first ten years in the scheme. Everyone then will have their 20 years' maximum in the scheme, and as explained above, those going after 2008–9 will have a pension of 20% (a fifth) of the band earnings. So let's take another example, of someone earning the same amount as Jim, but much younger.

Eva will not retire until 2010–11. Her band earnings are £160 also. To find out roughly what she would get, in today's money, she divides this by 5, which gives £32.

During the transitional years, between 1998–9 and 2008–9, the proportion of your earnings drops by $1/2$ a per cent a year. So Edward, retiring in the year 2000–1, gets 24% of his band earnings.

To find out your SERPS entitlement from the DSS using the proper formula, get leaflet BR.19 from your local DSS office; this includes a form to fill in and post to the main DSS office in Newcastle. Within a few weeks, they will send an 'additional pension' statement showing:

- the amount of SERPS pension earned up until the end of the last tax year (always 5 April), at today's values;
- an estimate of what SERPS will be as pension if the person carries on working up to normal State pension age; and
- an estimate of the SERPS pension at that date, if future earnings increase faster than prices.

Like the arithmetic you have just done on your own pension, this is a set of guesses. They'll still be useful for giving you some idea of what you will have from the State.

Widows and Widowers

The additional pension is also paid to widows, so long as they are eligible for a basic widow's pension. It is based on the husband's earnings. For anyone dying before 5 April 2000, the widow gets the whole of the accrued additional pension, added on to the basic widow's pension.

Peter Williams dies in May 1991, after the scheme has been running for 13 years. His wife gets the basic pension, because she has small children, plus 13/80ths of his revalued average earnings between the limits.

If the husband is a dependent invalid, and his wife dies, then he gets a widower's pension in the same way. But there is no widower's pension for a healthy man before retirement age, whether or not he has children.

After retirement, the pension becomes a survivor's pension. Whichever one of the couple dies first, the other inherits the additional pension. But the survivor cannot receive more than the maximum s/he could have had from the State anyway, if both of them had had earnings at the top limit.

Eric Walters has an additional pension of £30, and his wife an additional pension of £15, in her own right. The most that anyone could have had out of the scheme is £30. So when Eric dies, his wife can inherit £15 of his pension, to bring it up to £30. If she died first, he could not inherit any of her pension.

Another government 'reform' affects these pensions. For anyone who dies after 5 April 2000, the widow's or survivor's pension is only half the deceased partner's pension. It doesn't make any difference when you retired; what matters is the date of death.

Invalidity

If someone is sick for more than six months, and therefore goes on to invalidity benefit, then whatever additional pension s/he has earned is added on to that, for as long as s/he is an invalid. It's offset against the 'age-related' addition to invalidity benefit, which is intended to give more to the person who becomes an invalid when s/he is young. You get whichever is the higher of the two.

Eva is 37 when she has to go on to invalidity benefit. Her 'age related' addition is £10, the highest rate because she was under 40 when she started on the benefit. But her earnings-related pension is £13. So she gets that instead.

This 'offsetting' is a change made by the government in 1984. Before that, an invalid had both. A further change is being made under which no SERPS pension built up after April 1991 will count.

Inflation

One of the ideas behind SERPS is that pensions will be protected against inflation. Up to retirement, they are protected because the earnings on which they are calculated are revalued. This is done by the government issuing a table each year, based on the rise in National Average Earnings over that year. So, for instance, the announcement of the 1989/90 figures said that earnings in 1987–8 would be increased, for people retiring in tax year 1990, by 20.5%. Earnings in 1978–9, the first year in which the scheme was running, would be increased by 211.5%.

Think back to what you were earning in 1978. The average was £80 a week. To bring that figure up to date, another 211.5% is added to it. This makes it £249.20. A similar sum will be done for each year's earnings figure; in the end, when the scheme has been running for half a century, there could be 49 different sums to take into account.

After retirement, the pension is protected against increases in prices only. It is increased by the Secretary of State's estimate of the rate of inflation since the last time. Except in occasional bad years, for instance during the 1970s when inflation was high and the economy doing poorly, you expect wages to rise faster than prices – that's what having a rising standard of living means. But pensioners do not have the chance to share in this rise; their buying power is protected, but does not increase as the rest of the population's does.

If you are contracted out of the State scheme, the employer's pension scheme now has to take some responsibility for part of the increases.

So Why the Changes?

The Tory government's changes to SERPS, under the 1986 Social Security Act, are estimated to cut its value, over the long term, by about half. The reason for them, according to Norman Fowler, who was in charge of Social Security at the time, is that the original SERPS scheme was 'too generous'. They want to change the balance, therefore, between State provision and the benefits that people pay for themselves, and build up on their own account, through the new Personal Pensions explained in Chapter 6.

As the Minister of State Tony Newton put it, in the debate in Parliament on the Bill,

> It is not responsible to make promises for a generation ahead when we cannot be certain that that generation will be able to fulfil them. This is not because of the burden we might be imposing on people who might not be able to sustain it, but because it is not right to make promises to pensioners about what they will be paid and risk not being able to pay it when the time comes.

It's certainly true that if you have more pensioners, and pay them better pensions, your costs go up. But the unions, led by the TUC, are convinced that SERPS could be afforded in its original form, with better benefits for future pensioners emerging in the long run.

The government argues that, because there is a rising proportion of pensioners and a falling workforce, the cost will impose too great a burden on that reduced number of people. But what we can afford does not depend just on the number of pensioners, but on the overall standard of living, and on what we choose to spend our money on. Since the turn of the century, each generation has been able to pay better pensions than the last, because of economic growth. The government has assumed, for the purposes of this argument, a low level of growth in the economy. But for other sets of forecasts, it has assumed a much higher rate of growth.

With a reasonable level of growth in the economy, everyone's standard of living can go up. To give more to one group of the population (pensioners) will only mean that living standards of other groups rise a little less fast, but they will keep rising.

The real reason for the change was political. Right-wing political philosophers like Milton Friedman do not like State provision of benefits, where there is no fund and where today's benefits are paid out of today's contributions. Friedman says that, 'this one sided "compact between the generations" foisted on generations that cannot give their assent, is a very different thing from a "trust fund". It is more like a chain letter.'

Instead, therefore, they want each person to provide their own benefits, to 'stand on their own two feet'. This idea, of relying on yourself rather than on the payments of the next generation, sounds superficially attractive to many people. But looking at it logically, there is no reason to think that having your private pot of gold is any more secure than being promised your pension through the State. There is a danger of poor investment returns, people running off with your cash, or inflation wiping the investments out. The cost of pensions really always arises when they are paid out, whether they have been allowed for in a fund or not. When you are saving for a pension, you are not saving the loaves of bread and the tins of baked beans you need to live on. You're saving the promise that the loaves of bread and tins of baked beans will be available when you need them. If there are none in the shops, or if the working population muscles ahead of the pensioners in the queue, or if prices have risen faster than the value of pensions, these promises would be valueless whether they come from State or private sources.

3

The Different Types of Pension Scheme

This chapter goes through the different types of pension scheme, in broad terms. You need to know this before understanding how the different sets of rules outlined in Chapter 4 apply. We're also dealing here with integrated schemes – where the benefits have something deducted to take account of the State benefits. These are covered after 'final earnings' schemes, as they are the sort that are most likely to be integrated.

There are five main types of pension scheme. Some designs mix more than one, but you'll be able to see in each case what the basic framework is. They are:

- final earnings;
- career average, also sometimes called salary grade;
- revalued career average;
- money purchase; and
- flat rate.

Of the schemes available, 95% are 'final earnings'. If your scheme has been negotiated or renegotiated in the last few years, it is almost certainly final earnings. But the other sorts do have their followers also.

So the first thing is to work out what type your pension scheme is. Find your scheme booklet; it will be helpful to have it beside you while you are reading the rest of this book as well. In most booklets there will be a list of 'definitions'. This is probably at either the very front or the back. If this mentions:

- final pensionable earnings; or
- final pensionable pay; or
- final pensionable salary; or
- retiring pensionable pay/earnings/salary; or
- final remuneration; or
- retiring pay/earnings/salary; or
- Final pay/earnings/ salary

or a phrase which means the same, then your scheme is a final earnings scheme.

If there is no list of definitions, then look in the rest of the booklet, and see if there is a page which says 'How to calculate your pension' or something similar, and look for the same words there.

Career average earnings schemes are much rarer. They can also be called 'salary grade' schemes. Again, look at the definitions of your booklet. Do they say something about 'pensionable earnings' or 'pensionable pay' or anything of that sort, without including the term 'final' anywhere? If so, it's quite likely career average earnings. If you can't tell from the definitions, find the paragraph which says 'How your pension is calculated' or something similar. If it says something like:

> A unit of pension for each year's contributory service from joining the scheme up to 24 July before the normal retirement date. The units vary according to the salary grade, as shown in the table on page ...

or:

> The total pension at normal retirement date is the total of the pensions thus earned by each year's service ...

or there is a table showing different salary or wage grades, and a pension earned in each, then it is a career average earnings scheme.

But look out for any mention of 'revalued' or 'indexed'; if there is one, it's probably the next sort of scheme.

As a slight variation, it could say that 'your pension is £1 for each £2.50 of contributions' or something similar. But as a lot of final earnings schemes also have a guarantee about the pension you get back from your contributions, make sure you haven't missed a 'final' anywhere.

If you've decided it definitely is a career average scheme, read the section on that. But look also at the sections on final earnings and revalued average earnings schemes. They give you a much better pension and you ought to try to change your scheme to one of these.

If you have come across the words 'revalued' or 'indexed' in your booklet, it is probably a revalued career average scheme. There are not very many of these around, so check harder. Look for a phrase like 'revalued earnings' or 'revaluation factor' or some mention of the Retail Prices Index. Or there could be some statement like:

> Your yearly pension at your normal retiring date will be £1 a year for each £2 that you contributed to the scheme, increased to take account of changes in the Index of Retail Prices up to your normal retiring date

or:

> The pension is based on your earnings for your whole working life uprated to take account of inflation.

If it is one of these, turn to that section.

If you've had no luck so far, you could be in a money purchase scheme. If yours is a 'Personal Pension' or one of the new COMP schemes (both explained in Chapter 4) it will certainly be money purchase. These schemes are being sold vigorously by people like insurance companies, banks and building societies. Even if your main pension scheme is based on final earnings, it's quite likely that any additional contributions you are making are to a scheme of this sort. Does your booklet say something like this:

> For each member of the plan his/her contribution and the company's contribution on his/her behalf will be paid into an individual account with the ABC Life Insurance Society. The Society will invest these moneys so as to obtain interest and capital growth. The earnings will then be credited back to individual accounts by way of interest and bonus ...

or:

> Each contribution made by you is invested in the XYZ Managed Pension Fund, which is divided into units. When you retire, the value of the pension account at the time determines the amount of pension benefit you receive ... The level of the pension benefits will depend on the size of the contribution, the investment performance of the Managed Pension Fund, and annuity rates at retirement.

Then it's money purchase and you need that section. Read the section on final earnings as well, to give you ideas about a better scheme.

Finally, there's the flat rate scheme. This is pretty simple to spot; it might say, for instance, that benefit is £20 per year of service, or 'pension is 10p a week for each year you have been with the company,' or it might give you a lump sum only, at the same rate however long you have been there.

If you're in doubt, look for a money figure for each year of service, without 'estimated' or a similar word in front of it. And if it is this sort, again look at final earnings and revalued average earnings schemes, since they are better.

There are two further points:

(1) Any of these schemes can give you a pension, or a pension plus a lump sum, or a lump sum alone. In the past, only a final earnings or revalued average earnings scheme could be contracted out of the State scheme (explained on pages 32–6); since 1987, a money purchase one can be also.

(2) It may sound obvious or patronising, but if your scheme appears to be career average or flat rate, check that you've got the up-to-date booklet. Personnel departments have been known to hand out old ones, and the slips of paper that amend them have been known to get lost!

The Different Types

Final Earnings

Three things are taken into account:

- final earnings – your earnings when you reach retirement age, or when you retire or die early. Often these are averaged over several years, perhaps the last three or the last five;

- pensionable service – how long you've been in the scheme; and
- accrual rate – the rate at which the pension builds up.

The accrual rate will be a fraction, or a percentage, of your final earnings. It might be 1/80th, or 1/60th, or 1/45th. This means that you get one of these fractions for each year you are in the scheme. After 5 years in the scheme, you'll have 5/80ths, or 5/60ths, or 5/45ths. So you start by dividing the final earnings by 80, 60 or 45, and then you take that figure and multiply it by the number of years in the scheme.

Jo Evans has final pensionable earnings of £6,000 a year. Her scheme's accrual rate is 1/60th. So for each year she is in the scheme, she accrues £6,000 divided by 60, which comes to £100. As she has been in the scheme ten years, she gets 10 times that, which is 10/60ths, £1,000.

If the figure is written in percentage terms, you can either turn it back into a fraction – 1/60th, for instance, is 1.67%, or you can do the sum on that basis. That would mean, in Jo's case, that she divided the final earnings by 100 and then multiplied them by 1.67, and then multiplied them again by 10. The figure will come out very slightly different, because you have rounded the decimal point, but not enough to matter.

Because it's final earnings, you can't know how much your pension is going to be, as money, when you retire. Before that, you can estimate what proportion of your earnings it will be. If you did a full working life with the one company, for instance, then your pension would be 40/60ths, or two-thirds, of your final earnings, whether they were £6,000 or £60,000 by then.

Integration
This is the term that is used when a certain amount is deducted to take account of the State pension, before your employer's pension is calculated. There are two main ways in which this is done:

First, the scheme can deduct something from your earnings before it uses them to calculate your pension. It will usually be a figure related to the Lower Earnings Limit (explained on page 7) or to the State pension for a single person, which is roughly the same. It could be, for example:

- 1.5 times the lower earnings limit; or
- the same as the lower earnings limit; or
- three-quarters of it; or
- a fixed money figure, perhaps based on what the pension was a few years ago.

Here's an example of how it works:

Harold Smith has final earnings of £6,000. But an amount equal to the Lower Earnings Limit is deducted from them, before the pensionable earnings are calculated. The LEL, as a yearly figure, is £2,392, and so what's left is £3,608. As he's been in the scheme ten years, and it's a 1/60th scheme, he gets 10/60ths of £3,608, which is £601.33. As you can see, this is a good deal lower than Jo's pension based on the same original earnings.

The alternative is for your scheme to build the integration into your pension, so that for each year you are in the company scheme a fraction of the State pension is deducted. It's usually arranged so that when you have worked for the maximum number of years in the scheme, the whole of the State pension is deducted.

This then means you have to do a second sum – having worked out the company pension for each year, you then have to deduct the appropriate slice of the State pension, before you get the final result. For example:

Suni's scheme gives 1/60th pension, minus 1/40th of the Lower Earnings Limit for each year she is in the scheme. As before, her final earnings are £6,000 and the Lower Earnings Limit is £2,392. So she must divide £2,392 by 40, and multiply it by her years of service – which we'll assume as 10, as with the others, to find out her pension. £2,392 divided by 40 is £59.80, and if you multiply that by 10 you get £598. So that's the deduction from her earnings before the pension is worked out. It leaves her with £5,402, and 10/60ths of that is £900.33. This is much better than Harold's, though worse than Jo's.

According to the 1988 National Association of Pension Funds Survey, 52% of schemes are integrated. It's especially common with hourly paid schemes, and with those that sit on top of SERPS, rather than being contracted out (explained on pages 32–6). Companies based in the US are particularly fond of this idea.

Career Average Earnings Schemes

The idea of a career average scheme is that all your earnings, throughout your working life, are added together and then averaged to work out your pension. This isn't quite as stupid as it sounds. It was a method of calculation developed in the days before inflation took off, when earnings in money terms could go down as well as up. There are various ways in which it can be worked out.

One is to take three separate things into account:

- your average earnings, which means the total amount you've earned with the employer from the year you start until the date you retire, divided by the number of years you've been there;
- your pensionable service: the number of years you've worked for the company;
- the accrual rate: the rate at which your pension builds up. The accrual rate will be a fraction, or a percentage, of these average earnings. It might be 1/80th, or 1/60th, or 1/45th. For each year

you are in the scheme, you collect one of these fractions. So after five years in the scheme you might have 5/80ths, or 5/60ths, or 5/45ths. Then you divide this into the average earnings, and there's your pension.

Ghulam Mayet retires at the end of 1989. He has earnings over the last five years of:

1984 £5,000
1985 £6,000
1986 £7,000
1987 £8,000
1988 £9,000

Added together, these make £35,000. So his average earnings are that figure divided by 5, which comes to £7,000. Now you divide that again by 60, the accrual rate in his scheme, which makes £116.67, and multiply it by 5, which comes to £583.

The second method is almost the same mathematically, but it looks different. This is to say that the pension is, for instance, 1/60th of lifetime earnings, or in percentage terms 1.67%. If you look at the sum above, you'll see that we have divided by 5, and then multiplied by 5 later on. This method shortcuts that – you simply add up all the earnings and then divide by the accrual rate, and there's the pension. So in Ghulam's case, £35,000 divided by 60 comes to £583.

The third method is a variation of the other two. Here, the pension is expressed as a proportion of the contributions paid in, rather than a proportion of earnings. The booklet will say something like 'you receive £1 pension for every £2.50 paid in contributions.' You need then to find the contribution rate, and you can work backwards from that.

James Curran's contribution rate is 5% of earnings. 5% of his total earnings in the scheme is £1,750. For each £2.50, he gets £1 pension, so £1,750 divided by £2.50 comes to £700, and that's his pension.

The final variation is the salary grade system. In this, the scheme members are divided into grades or 'classes' each covering a specific range of earnings. In each year a member is credited with a 'brick' or unit of pension that depends on his/her current earnings, and is fitted into bands according to the company's salary structure. The pension depends on how many bricks you have accumulated, and how much they are worth.

Hilary Jones is in a scheme that has a table of grades like Table 3.1:

Table 3.1 Salary Graded Scheme

Salary Grade	Annual Salary	Pension	Contributions	Life Ins
A	Less than £8,000	£208	£395.20	£4,000
B	£8,001–£10,000	£260	£444.70	£5,000
C	£10,001–£12,000	£312	£494.20	£6,000
D	£12,001–£14,000	£364	£543.70	£7,000
E	£14,001–£16,000	£416	£593.20	£8,000

Hilary gradually gets promoted through the salary grades. Her pension builds up like this:

2 years in grade A   2 x £208 =   £416
5 years in grade B   5 x £260 = £1,300
5 years in grade C   5 x £312 = £1,560
5 years in grade D   5 x £364 = £1,820
5 years in grade E   5 x £416 = £2,080

So Hilary's pension is calculated by adding all those figures together, coming to £7,176.

What all these versions have in common is that they do not give a very good pension, because they do not take account of inflation. They are cheap for the employer – which is why s/he would have carried on with the scheme. If you are stuck with this sort of scheme, then before looking for any other improvements, you need to get it changed to a final earnings or revalued average earnings scheme. Try to ensure:

• that the changeover is backdated as far as possible, and paid for by the employer. It's his/her fault that it hasn't been changed before for something more suited to modern conditions; and
• that for the first few years after the changeover, a check is kept on people retiring, to see that no individual is worse off as a result. The only people likely to be are those with short service, whose earnings have fallen in money terms in the few years before they retire. Anyone affected should get a pension calculated on the old rather than the new method.

Revalued Average Earnings

If you've read Chapter 2, you'll know that this is the way in which the State calculates the additional pension. It's possible for an employer's scheme to calculate in almost the same way.

First, your earnings are listed for all the years that you've been in the scheme. Then each year's figure is increased by the amount earnings – or sometimes prices – have increased since the earnings were paid. Then these new figures are averaged. Finally, the pension is calculated from them, on the basis of the accrual rate, and the number of years you've been in the scheme. We'll use the example of Ghulam Mayet again, and the earnings index used by the government for its pensions, to show how this works.

Ghulam Mayet's earnings over the last five years were:
    1984   £5,000
    1985   £6,000
    1986   £7,000
    1987   £8,000
    1988   £9,000

When the pension calculation is done, at his retirement date, these figures are increased by these percentages:
    1984   50.2%
    1985   41.0%
    1986   29.4%
    1987   20.5%
    1988   10.8%

So the earnings figures now read:
    1984   £5,000 increased by 50.2% = £7,510
    1985   £6,000   41.0% = £8,460
    1986   £7,000   29.4% = £9,058
    1987   £8,000   20.5% = £9,640
    1988   £9,000   10.8% = £9,972

making a total of £44,640. This is then divided by 5 to give a revalued earnings figure, of £8,928. He then gets 1/60th for every year he's been in the scheme. As he's been in 5 years, that is £8,928 divided by 60 and then multiplied by 5, which is £744.

In this sort of scheme, when someone leaves that employment, the earnings figures normally continue to be revalued – though sometimes in line with prices rather than earnings – so that when the person retires he or she has not lost out by leaving.

Money Purchase Schemes
The idea of 'money purchase' is that the pension you get depends on:

• The contributions you pay
• The contributions the employer pays; and
• What interest they earn, or investment results are achieved.

It does not relate at all to your earnings – simply to the amount that has been put in, and how well it has been invested. It may be put in stocks and shares, and so depend on the fortunes of the stock market, or it may be in a deposit account, with the interest rate perhaps related to the mortgage rate, and so depend on that.

In the past schemes like this have been run by insurance companies, and it's likely that they will still run most of them, but banks, building societies, and unit trusts are now also allowed to run them. The people selling these tend to make optimistic statements about the way the funds will grow, so that you can see astronomical figures as 'projections', but there is usually no guarantee. This is the method that is used in the new Personal Pensions, explained in Chapter 6.

The younger you are, the more pension your contributions will earn, because the longer they have to build up interest or dividends. But schemes like this give a much worse deal to older people. Here is an example from an insurance company's sales brochure, trying to persuade people to take out a pension policy with them as soon as possible. A person putting in £1,000 a year from age 35 to retirement date could expect, if the fund grew at 12% each year, to have £226,000 by the time he or she retired at 65. But if they only started at 37, the brochure says, they would lose £47,084 of this.

The pension for a person with 20 years' service ahead of him or her could be less than a quarter of the pension of the person with 40 years to go.

These schemes also give a worse deal to women than to men. Since women are expected to live longer, the contributions are going to have to buy a pension spread over a longer period. So if the contributions of men and women are the same, the women's pensions will be less.

The benefit can't be predicted. It depends on general investment conditions, and on how well the particular firm looking after your money manages to do the job.

Of the top ten firms providing individual pension fund management over the ten years to May 1987, Target, the best performer of all, had seen its funds grow by 1,102% in ten years. The fund that was number ten on the list, Imperial Life of Canada, had seen its money grow by only 454% – a difference of nearly two and a half times.

When you reach retirement, the money in the fund for you at the time is used to buy an annuity. This means that an insurance company guarantees to pay you so much a year, for as long as you live – perhaps with some increases on a fixed percentage basis, and perhaps with a spouse's annuity attached. The insurance company wants to make a profit, and so it looks closely at the interest rates available, if it invests the money it gets from you. These can vary wildly, so that, for instance, a person retiring in January 1986 could have got an annuity 11.5% higher than someone retiring in July, though each had accumulated exactly the same size of fund.

Flat Rate Schemes
These are extremely simple – which is the problem.

A booklet for a flat rate scheme will say something like 'For every year you are in the service of the company, you will get £x pension.' One scheme, for instance, offers £18 a year pension for each year you were in it.

Schemes like this usually give a very low pension, and do nothing to protect even that pension from inflation. They take no account of your actual earnings.

Lump Sums

Any of the types of scheme explained above can provide:

- a pension only; or
- a pension, some of which you can give up to get a lump sum (the most usual arrangement); or
- a pension together with a lump sum.

Or you can have a scheme which provides only a lump sum on retirement, with no pension at all. Some of the schemes of this sort give a fraction, which is often 3/80ths of your final earnings for each year in the scheme. Others give only a flat amount for each year.

4

The Rules for Schemes Run by Employers

General Points for All Employer-Provided Schemes

All pension schemes are bound by sets of rules, laid down both by Acts of Parliament and in codes by the Inland Revenue and the Occupational Pensions Board who regulate them. This section goes through some of the main issues, although there are others that are dealt with later.

The Way Schemes are Set Up
In order to have the tax advantages explained on pages 36–7, private sector pension schemes must be set up as funds separate from the employer's money, and must have trustees.

What these do, and how they operate, is explained in Chapter 28.

The exception to this rule is pension schemes in the public services, which are set up by Act of Parliament instead of a trust deed. They are covered on page 233.

Scheme Membership
The Social Security Act 1986 says that after April 1988, any clauses of the pension scheme, or of the contract of employment, which make membership compulsory 'shall be void'. So they cannot be enforced, and this means not only that new people cannot be made to join, but also that any existing scheme member can leave the scheme if s/he wishes. The only exception to this is schemes which provide only death benefits, and are non-contributory. An employer is allowed to set up the scheme so that people are assumed to join unless they positively opt out, though.

The implications of this for the unions are covered on pages 57–8.

Discrimination between Men and Women
This section covers discrimination both in pensions, and in retirement ages.

Taking pensions first, the Social Security Pensions Act 1975 gives equal access to pension schemes, but nothing else. It says that:

> membership of pension schemes, whether contracted out or not, must be open to both men and women on terms which are the same as to the age and length of service required for becoming a member, and as to whether membership is voluntary or compulsory.

A scheme must not discriminate except by 'category of employment'. Neither the Equal Pay Act, nor the Sex Discrimination Act, covers pensions, so there is no way under British law of taking a claim for indirect discrimination.

This is why employers can get away with excluding part timers. Almost all of the 4.4 million part timers in employment in this country are women, but only half a million of them were members of pension schemes when the Government Actuary did his last survey in 1983.

Pension schemes are also allowed to discriminate in the benefits they give, and many do. Sometimes the pension builds up at a lower rate, but more often the differences are in the extra benefits, especially in the way that dependants are treated. Women are generally assumed to be men's 'natural' dependants, and the men the 'natural' breadwinners'.

From April 1988 there will have to be a small pension for widowers in contracted-out schemes, as explained later in this chapter, but it will take a long time to build up to any size. Widowers' pensions are beginning to be introduced in the public service schemes, like the Civil Service one, and are now quite common in the private sector. Often, though, they demand that the widower prove himself 'dependant' on his former wife, while no such requirement is imposed on the widow.

It's also standard practice, when setting the rates at which you can swap part of your pension for a lump sum, or buy an annuity, to have different rates for men and women. These rates are worked out by actuaries, and how they do this is explained in more detail in Chapter 28. They say they have to discriminate because women live longer than men, on average. But that does not mean that any particular woman will live longer than any particular man doing the same job, and who retires at the same time. Women's longer expectation of life is only an excuse for discriminating against them. The real reason is that pensions are a tool of personnel management, intended to help with recruiting, and keeping, valuable employees. Women are valued less, and seen as temporary employees on whom it's not worth spending money.

Any employer could set up a pension scheme which did not discriminate. Mecca Leisure, for instance, has done so, since it is in an industry where women make up a very large proportion of the workforce.

European Law

In due course, things will have to change because of our membership of the Common Market. When we joined this, we signed the Treaty of Rome, which is a long document composed of Articles. Two of these cover the principles of Equal Pay, and of Equal Treatment. The rule in the European Court of Justice is that, where an Article is sufficiently clear to be interpreted without any extra legislation, any individual can go to the Court and ask for a ruling on whether someone else is breaking the law – either their government, or some other private individual or body like their employer.

The Articles get expanded and more details added by Directives, which are issued by the European Commission and require member governments to bring them into law in their own countries. When they don't do so, private citizens can go to the Court and enforce these as well, either against the government as employer, where that's relevant, or as the law-making body that hasn't done its job.

Article 119 of the Treaty of Rome says that 'each member state shall ... ensure and subsequently maintain the application of the principle that men and women shall receive equal pay for equal work.'

It defines pay not just as wages but also to include 'any other consideration, whether in cash or in kind, which the worker receives, directly or indirectly ...'

Because of this wide definition, a West German woman shopworker, Karin Weber von Harz, was able to take her employers to the Court about her pension scheme. The case is called Bilka Kaufhaus v Weber, and she said that the company were breaking the Treaty of Rome by excluding her from the non-contributory pension scheme because she was part time. The Court agreed with her, finding that membership of the scheme was part of 'pay'. Since the vast majority of part timers were women, she was receiving unequal pay on grounds of sex.

As a result, any part timers can now challenge their exclusion from pension schemes. There are several more European Court cases due to come up in the next few years which will establish more clearly what the law is. One is called Clarke v Cray Engineering, and another is Barber v Guardian Royal Exchange. They are both being taken by men who lost out when they were made to take early retirement. If they win, it is possible that a very large number of men will have a claim for back payment from their schemes.

There are also Directives on Equal Pay, Equal Treatment, and equality in Social Security. Because of this the British government has made a number of changes to the way our Social Security system discriminated against women in the past. No-one is quite sure how far this covers schemes which are 'contracted out' of SERPS (as explained later in this chapter). But to be on the safe side the government has said that these schemes must begin to build up widowers' pensions from 1988 onwards, and that the retirement annuities bought with money from 'Personal Pensions' must be the same value for men and women of the same age, and must assume that everyone is married.

Most recently, a Directive was passed in 1986 on 'Occupational Social Security'. This Directive has been turned into British law under the Social Security Act 1989. It says that benefits must be equalised in schemes except that:

- retirement ages can be different
- widows', widowers' and survivors' benefits can be different
- money purchase benefits can be different
- 'optional' benefits can be different.

It does not come into force until the end of 1992, but it is worth checking through your scheme rules now to see what changes need to be made.

Two points to think about particularly are:

- When a man takes *voluntary* early retirement, his benefits need not be the same as those of a woman of the same age. But if the early retirement is *compulsory*, then benefits must be the same. This is often going to mean a change in scheme rules.
- If your scheme is 'integrated' with the State scheme (see page 22) it may have a 'bridging' pension for men retiring early and not drawing a full State pension. *Some* of these will become unlawful after 1992 – if your scheme is affected, there will have to be changes.

The new law only affects *future* benefits, but if you succeed in getting improvements, you could look for them to be backdated.

Retirement Ages

The most important result of all this activity has been to change the age at which women are made to retire from their jobs. The Sex Discrimination Act 1986 says that employers must not dismiss women on grounds of age, where a man in similar circumstances would not have been dismissed. It came into force on 7 November 1987.

A woman can now take a case to an industrial tribunal for unfair dismissal, if she is made to retire before the age of 65, unless there is a lower compulsory retirement age in that job for both sexes.

Because the situation is currently such a mess, there are likely to be further changes in the law in future years. Meanwhile, unions need to see how far they can exploit the current uncertainty, and improve the situation for their members of both sexes. The full implications of this are covered in Chapter 15, on retirement ages.

Contracting Out of SERPS

The next section looks at the rules for contracting out of the State Earnings Related Pension Scheme. These contracting out rules are minimum requirements; but there is also a maximum, laid down by the Inland Revenue (the tax people), who want to stop people getting too much tax relief. The rest of this chapter looks at both these sets of rules, for each type of contracting out in turn. The rules for adding contributions yourself, called Additional Voluntary Contributions or AVCs, to build up a bigger pension, are covered in Chapter 23.

Contracting Out with a Guaranteed Benefit

When SERPS started in 1978, the aim was to give better pensions to the workers who had nothing except the State basic pension to fall back on when they retired. These made up half the workforce. But the other half, about 10.5 million people, were already members of employers' pension schemes, some of them providing good pensions. There would have been an outcry if the government had simply closed them down, and it was considered too expensive, and too difficult, to take them over. So instead, they went into 'partnership' with them. They said that a scheme could 'contract out' provided it met a series of conditions. The central one was that it would provide at least as much pension as the person would have had out of SERPS. The pension had to be based on your earnings, and the scheme rules were allowed to use either the earnings in the last few years of your working life, or the average earnings throughout that time revalued, as SERPS itself does. In return for this, the employer and employee both paid a lower rate of National Insurance contribution.

Most employer-run pension schemes are contracted out, and have been since 1978. This means that when you reach retirement, the DSS works out what you would have had if you had always been in SERPS. Then the pension the State will pay for any years you actually have been in SERPS is taken away. What's left is the Guaranteed Minimum Pension (the GMP). This is the minimum the employer's scheme has to pay, whatever its other rules lay down. There has to be a special clause in the rule-book saying that it will do so.

> Margaret has a working life of 22 years after 1978. She's been in a contracted-out scheme for 17 of those years. The DSS works out her total SERPS entitlement as £44 a week, and tells the scheme that it must pay 17/22nds of this, which comes to £34. Even if the scheme was going to pay less, they now have to make it up to the full amount.

Contracted-out schemes have to make other commitments as well. There have been alterations to these in the 1986 Act, so these details are of the new arrangements rather than the old ones.

The scheme must provide a widow's pension, of at least half the member's GMP, if the widow would be entitled to State widow's pension. This is called the WGMP. Schemes are allowed to get away with providing a good pension for the member, but only the minimum for the widow. They can also use up part of the lump sum that most schemes give as a death benefit, to buy an annuity for the widow (she has no choice in the matter).

For anyone dying after April 1989, schemes also have to provide widowers' pensions, of half the members' GMPs, where the widower is over the age of 45 or has dependent children. But this only covers pension that has built up since that date, so the first widowers' benefits are very small.

Mary dies in 1990, when her husband Joe is 55. He still does not get any State widower's pension, but he gets half the GMP Mary has built up in the last two years. Since it is building up at the rate of 1/80th a year, and Mary's band earnings are £160 a week, he gets 2/160ths of that, which comes to all of £2 a week.

Until the year 2000, however, if you were in SERPS rather than in the employer's scheme, the widow inherits the full SERPS pension, as explained on page 15. To ensure that she does not lose out because her husband has belonged to the employer's scheme, the State takes responsibility for the rest. It adds the other half of the Additional Pension to the basic pension book. Even if the scheme is actually giving a better pension than the State would, it makes no odds. The State still adds its half.

Because the State doesn't give a widower's pension, though, this will not operate in the same way when a woman member dies. The scheme will have to pay out a benefit for her husband if he qualifies, but there will be nothing added on from the State.

The same principle applies when a member dies in retirement. The scheme must provide only half a male member's pension to the widow, and the State adds on half the SERPS pension, ignoring what the scheme is actually providing. The State assumes that the employer's scheme is not providing a widower's pension, and so pays all the pension automatically. Where there is a widower's GMP due, because the member was in service after April 1988, they'll assume that only a benefit at that minimum level is being paid, and make up the rest.

Other Rules for Contracting Out

- There has to be a rule about 'solvency'. This means that schemes have to have enough money in them at all times to pay at least for the members' GMPs. The Occupational Pensions Board (OPB), the government body set up to monitor occupational pension schemes, keeps an eye on this. If a scheme goes bust (which hardly ever happens) the GMP must have priority over other debts except the pensions already being paid. If a scheme cannot meet its obligations, the government picks up the bill, but only for the GMP.
- Inflation is also covered. When someone retires from a contracted-out scheme, the scheme's duty was, until April 1988, only to carry on paying the pension at the same rate as when s/he retired. The State took on the obligation to make up all the increases. For GMP built up after April 1988, the scheme must increase it by 3% a year once it is in payment, but the State still picks up the bill for inflation above that level.
- There are tough obligations to people who leave the scheme. These are explained in Chapter 19.

In return for making these commitments, the employer, and the member, pay less towards the National Insurance Fund. This money is then available to go into the scheme instead. The employer pays 3.8% less NI on the slice of earnings between the Lower and Upper Earnings Limits (explained on page 8), and the employee 2% less on that same slice. This is called the 'rebate' or 'abatement'.

To start the process of contracting out, a company must give notice to all the members, and consult the recognised trade unions. It need not accept their views; consulting means just that. Nor does the law lay down a procedure for consultation, or the level in the union at which it must happen. So it can mean just telling one or two shop stewards what's happening. The notice period is usually three months, but if the employer has written permission from the recognised trade unions, it can be reduced to only a month. If the employer is simply applying for a new certificate because he is setting up a new scheme to replace an old one without making changes to members' benefits, then the requirements to give notice do not apply. The same procedure has to be followed if a scheme that is already contracted out wants to contract back in.

The next step is to get the approval of the OPB, the government-appointed, semi-independent board. It does have some trade union representatives on it, though their numbers have been whittled away over the years. There are also employer representatives, and experts from the pensions industry.

Once a scheme has its 'contracting-out certificate' from the OPB, it has to report every three years on whether it is still solvent. In between, it must report if any changes in the scheme, or the fortunes of the company, mean that there is doubt about its solvency. It also has to get approval if it wants to make any major changes that affect contracting out. It's possible for the OPB to cancel a certificate if the conditions aren't being complied with, and they do this with a small number of cases each year. The main reason for cancellations is that employers are not paying the contributions they should; the OPB gives them a certain amount of leeway, and then cancels if the record becomes too bad.

If a company goes into liquidation, and there is not enough cash in the scheme to cover the benefits – perhaps because the company has not paid in either its own or the members' contributions for a while – the Secretary of State can 'deem' that they have been paid. This means that the members will at least be paid full SERPS benefits and, again, it happens with a trickle of cases each year.

Long-term sickness is not affected at all by contracting out. The company scheme has no duty to pay any pension to people who retire early because of ill health; it can treat them as if they have left the company. If they are ill enough to be given a basic invalidity pension by the State, the earnings-related element built up before April 1991 is added to this as well.

There is nothing to say that a scheme has to contract out. It is a question of what is best for any particular scheme. Many companies, including some big ones like GEC, found it suited them better to contract in and leave their scheme on top of the State scheme.

The Tax Rules for Pension Schemes

The Inland Revenue also takes an interest in how much pension a scheme is providing; but what it cares about is the top limit, the most that is given. This is because putting your money in a pension scheme has big tax advantages, compared to putting it anywhere else. The money that you put in as contributions is deducted from your earnings before income tax is calculated:

Jill earns £200 a week, and pays a 5% contribution to her scheme, which comes to £10 a week. So this is deducted before the tax calculation is done, and she then pays the same amount as she would if she were earning only £190 a week.

The income that goes into the fund, from investments or capital gains, is not taxed. Other sorts of investment will have income tax, corporation tax, or capital gains tax, taken off them. For instance, if you put your money into the building society, they pay a 'composite' rate of tax on the interest it earns, and the money you get at the end is what's left after that tax has been paid (though this is changing).

When the money comes out at the other end, it's treated as earned income, whereas money from other sorts of investment used to be taxed at a different rate, as unearned income – and might be again, under a future government. The lump sums you get at retirement are completely tax free, and though there's now a top limit on how much you can have, at £90,000 it's still high enough to provide a very sizeable tax advantage. Employer contributions are not counted as part of the employee's taxable income, unlike other perks such as private medical insurance and company cars.

It's estimated that pension schemes save about £5 billion a year in tax. The higher paid you are, the more useful a pension scheme is to you in cutting your tax bill. So it's not surprising that the Inland Revenue takes an interest. Unfortunately, though the people they are really interested in are the highly paid, several of their rules have an impact also on the ordinary person.

The pension schemes to which most workers belong keep their benefits well within these top limits. So there's plenty of room for negotiation.

The details of the tax rules will be covered in Chapters 9–20, where the different benefits are covered. This is a summary of the major points:

- The maximum figure that can be counted as permissible earnings is £64,200 a year. This figure will be increased in future, in line with the rise in the Retail Prices Index. If an employer wants to provide a pension on earnings above that, he can do so, but it must be with a scheme that does not receive tax relief, or else directly out of the company's profits;

- The pension must not be more than two-thirds of your total earnings in the last year before you retire. This is on top of the State pension; if you are contracted in, it's on top of both the basic and the earnings-related elements. There are some special rules about calculating the final pay for very senior people, but these are not covered here;

- The death benefit must not be more than four times your earnings, plus a return of contributions with interest;

- The pension for a widow, widower, or adult dependant must not be more than two-thirds of the member's pension taking account of years s/he could have worked to retirement. There can also be a children's pension. The total must not come to more than the member's own pension would have been;

- Although the scheme must have a fixed retirement age, it is allowed to give a full 2/3rds pension at any age between 50 and 75;

- The employee can contribute to pensions each year a maximum of 15% of his or her earnings,. This includes both the main scheme, and any additional contributions s/he wants to make. There's no limit on how much the employer can put in;

- Part of your pension can be turned into a lump sum, or the scheme can give one automatically. This can be up to 1.5 times your final earnings, or it can be 2.25 times the pension, if that is more;

- Pension increases after retirement are allowed, up to the increase in the cost of living.

These rules are laid down, and policed, by a separate section of the Inland Revenue called the Superannuation Funds Office (the SFO). Local tax offices have nothing to do with the running of pension schemes, and know very little about them. The scheme manager needs to keep in touch with the SFO and, if he breaks the rules, they can take the tax relief away from the scheme. This hardly ever happens, because the threat is enough to keep most scheme managers in line. If you ask for something to be done that would bring the scheme managers into conflict with the Inland Revenue, they will simply refuse to do it.

Contracting Out without an Earnings Guarantee

Under the original rules laid down in the 1975 Social Security Act, contracting out was only possible with a pension scheme which is defined in terms of benefits. The government claim, though, that these rules are putting off many employers from contracting out, because they would be afraid of the commitment they were taking on. So they have now made it possible for people to contract out schemes where only the contribution is defined. The benefits will be whatever is earned on the investment, and there's no guarantee.

This new type of scheme is called a contracted-out money purchase scheme (a COMP). They were allowed to start in April 1988. The main take-up has been for industry-wide or multi-employer schemes, or for small employers. In a few cases, employers have set up a 'lower tier' COMP scheme for younger people, or for the groups that they exclude from their main scheme, such as part timers.

The minimum amount that can go into a COMP scheme will be the equivalent of the contracting-out rebate, 5.8% jointly between employer and employee (split 2% to employee, 3.8% to employer). The employer can, if s/he likes, pay it all, or collect the employees' 2% from them and pay it over. The member pays the contracted-out rate of NI contribution to the State.

For the first five years of the scheme, from 1988 to 1993, there is also an 'incentive' payment of 2% of the employee's earnings, from the National Insurance fund. But this will only go to people who were not in jobs covered by contracted-out schemes before 1 January 1986.

The government has laid down rules about the pattern of benefits, though not their size. These are called your 'protected rights'. The minimum contribution must go towards a pension paid at State pension age, and a spouse's pension, increasing by 3% a year once it's being paid. The annuities payable at retirement date must be 'unisex and unistatus'. This means they must be the same for men and women of the same age, and must assume that beneficiaries are married at the time of retirement. So if the scheme is running on this minimum basis, there will be no scope for retiring early, or for any lump sum death benefit. Someone – either employee or employer – has to put extra in, in order for there to be extra coming out.

When someone comes to retire, the DSS will do the arithmetic on their SERPS pension as if they have been in a guaranteed benefit contracted-out scheme. Then they will say, 'For this many years, this person was in a COMP, so we will deduct that proportion of the Additional Pension, and assume they are getting the same amount from their COMP scheme.' They will not check to see whether or not you are getting that amount.

So, looking back to our example on page 33, Margaret was in an employer's contracted-out scheme for 17 out of 22 years. That is all the DSS, in looking at the position at retirement, is concerned about; it makes no odds whether it was an earnings-linked or contribution-linked scheme. It still deducts 17/22nds of her Additional Pension. If she's in a COMP, she might get more, or she might get less. It would be pure chance if she ended up with the same amount.

There are special limits on the way schemes like this can invest their funds. This is because the government knows they are risky, and wants to keep the risk down. So buying shares in the employing company or any other company associated with it, putting more than a certain amount in any one investment, and investment in higher risk items like futures, options, and commodities, are all restricted. It's laid down how much must be in UK shares, how much overseas, how much in property, and so on. These limits are on the investment of the funds of the whole scheme, not just the contracted-out part.

These schemes are supervised by the Occupational Pensions Board, who have to give them a certificate and can take one away at any time.

Unions need to be wary of this sort of scheme, which has all the problems of money purchase schemes explained in Chapter 3. At the minimum level, younger people may do better than under SERPS, but they may not; older people almost certainly won't. It's only worth looking at a COMP where the employer is promising a good deal more than the minimum.

Taxation of COMPS

The Inland Revenue has said that COMP schemes have two options about the rules they follow. One possibility is to keep to the same limits as for earnings-linked schemes, explained above. This means the employee can pay in 15% of earnings at most, with no limit on what the employer pays, and the scheme must not give more than two-thirds of earnings as a pension, and keep to the other limits on benefits also.

The alternative is to follow roughly the same rules as pension schemes for self-employed people, and the new Personal Pensions explained in Chapter 6, do. There will be a contribution limit of 17.5% of earnings, jointly for employer and employee. Up to 15% of earnings may come from the employee. Within this total, 5% of earnings may be used to provide a death benefit. There would then be no limit on total retirement benefits. The lump sum will be restricted to a quarter of the fund held for each member at retirement. There is a top limit on permissible earnings of £64,200.

5

What Do We Want the Employer to Do?

Why Do We Want an Employer's Pension Scheme Anyway?

A man who reaches 65 can expect to live, on average, another 13 years; a woman another 21 years after she reaches 60. That's a long time to live on the State pension. But there are also quite a lot of men and women who do not live until they retire – nearly a third of men; about 12% of women.

It's all very well to say jokingly that you do not want to be worth more dead than alive. The wages your employer is paying are supporting not just you, but also your family. So there is a responsibility to provide for them if anything happens to you, the worker.

'But I'd Prefer to Have the Money in my Pay Packet'

A lot of people would. They are hard pressed to find enough for everything they want to do, and they would rather not think about tomorrow anyway. It's up to you whether you take that line as an individual, but if a pension scheme is on offer, you are giving the employer something for nothing by saying this. The employer is willing to put in an extra contribution – which might be another 5% or 8% of wages, or even more. You are telling him to keep it! You would not do that with ordinary wages.

A good pension scheme can be a good investment, and good insurance. People sometimes think that they would get a better return on their investment by putting it elsewhere, for instance into a building society, or buying shares. But almost certainly they would not.

Pension schemes have big advantages over other savings schemes, because of the way they are treated for tax purposes. If you put money into the building society, it comes out of your wages after tax has been taken off. If you put it into the pension scheme, it's taken out first, and then tax is only deducted from what's left. On top of this, pension funds do not pay income tax, corporation tax, or capital gains tax on their income from investments. So even if they are not very clever about where they put their money, they tend to have an edge on other forms of saving.

The lump sum you have from an employer's scheme when you retire is tax free. There are limits on this, but they are too high to worry us very much – the most you can get from one of these schemes is £96,300, which most of us could live on quite comfortably.

There's also the life assurance; that is, the money that the pension scheme gives both as a lump sum and as a spouse's or dependant's pension, on your death. The better schemes cover you also if you are too ill to work, with a disability benefit. If you have to buy these at your own expense (as you often will have to, if you go outside your employer's scheme and buy a personal pension), these could cost as much as the total contribution you are making to the employer's scheme. And as you get older, or in worse health, these costs would usually go up if you were making your own provision. With the employer's scheme you are sharing the risks with all the other members, and so the price for each of you is the same.

Employers' pension schemes are not perfect – far from it. There are many which do not give a good pension, and are bad value for money. Most of them are not designed to cope with bad bouts of inflation, as we had in the 1970s, and most of them give a poor deal to early leavers.

But because of the way it works, and the special tax privileges it has, a good employer-provided pension scheme is an efficient way of saving for your retirement, and of insuring yourself and your family against the risk of death or long-term illness.

Why do Employers Run Pension Schemes?

It may seem a mystery why the employer should bother. A good pension scheme is quite expensive – why does he not simply make the workers rely on the State, or buy their own 'Personal Pensions' under the new system? But having a good pension scheme is useful to him also – it's a management tool. Here is a quote from a students' textbook about pensions:

> An adequate pension scheme will assist the employer in his recruit-ment and retention of labour and enable him to dispense with the services of his employees in an orderly and humane manner as they age and contribute less to the profitability of the business. In addi-tion, regular retirements mean easily visible openings for promotion. [from *Pension Schemes; design and administration*, CII Tuition Service, 1976]

As that suggests, now that pension schemes are fairly widespread, it is important for an employer to provide one if he wants to show himself as a good employer, and if he is competing for labour with other companies who have pension schemes. This applies particularly with white collar staff, but increasingly also with manual workers. On top of this, many employers have found the pension scheme very convenient as a way of easing people out, through early retirements, rather than making redundancies. Time and again, shop stewards trying to resist job losses have been told by their members, 'Don't stand in our way', if a good deal is offered on the pension scheme. In 1987–8, for instance, there were over 400 early retirements at the company's request from the Ford scheme – far more than there were people leaving for any other reason.

The National Association of Pension Funds, in a discussion document for its members published in November 1987, said this about early retirement provisions:

> [Pension schemes are] a key weapon for managing early retirement and redundancy requirements. Employees can be encouraged to retire early by offering them enhanced early retirement pensions. The costs can often be substantially met from the occupational pension scheme. Where the employees affected are not members of an employer scheme, all redundancy costs will have to come directly out of company funds.

What Sort of Scheme?

The sort of scheme that most employees are in at the moment is called a final earnings scheme, and was explained on pages 21–2. It's the one that unions as a whole support because it gives you some certainty. It is an inflation-proofed investment if you stay in the scheme to retirement age – or in the public sector, even if you leave. It's not such a good deal for early leavers in the private sector, but even there it has improved. Chapter 19 explains the rules on early leavers, and how to get the best deal.

The pension you get in one of these schemes is based on your earnings when you retire, or when you leave the scheme, not on your earnings when you put them in to the scheme. Think back to what you were earning 10 or 20 years ago. It would not buy very much today. In 1970, when average earnings were round about £25 a week, you would have laughed at anyone who said that average earnings were now over £200 a week. But you wouldn't be laughing if you had to live on a pension calculated on the basis of your 1970 earnings. In a final earnings scheme the employer usually agrees to meet the 'balance of the cost', which means that at least some of the risk is thrown on to him/her. This is right, because that's the business s/he is in. Employers are far better equipped to cope with the risk than is the individual pensioner at retirement date.

There are other types of scheme worth looking at though.

Revalued Average Earnings

In many cases, in real terms – that is, the amount that the money will buy – your earnings actually go down in the last 10 or 15 years before retirement. This can happen, for instance, to manual workers, especially in heavy industry, where they can't keep up the piecework rates, or they go off shifts. SERPS uses this revalued earnings formula to take account of these problems, and it has considerable advantages. The disadvantages, though, are that:

- It's difficult for an ordinary person to work out;
- It's difficult for the company to work out;

- People on incremental scales, as many staff are, expect to get their best earnings in real terms shortly before they retire. For them, this type of scheme doesn't give as good a pension as a final earnings scheme would.

These disadvantages have been putting many people off revalued earnings schemes, but a few have been introduced recently. Mecca Leisure, for instance, have a clever one where all the contributions are put in terms of 'voucher pounds' which increase in line with inflation until the date you retire. They publicised it by means of cartoon strips and videos, and do not seem to have had much problem getting people to understand it. Schemes like this can give better treatment to those who leave early. So if you are offered a revalued average earnings scheme, think carefully about it.

Money Purchase Schemes

These are the opposite, in many ways, of the final earnings scheme.

The employer's liability is for a fixed level of contribution. The risk of having to live with a bad pension is thrown on to the member.

From 1978 to 1987 investment returns were very good, and the results in money purchase schemes also looked good. When you're in a final earnings scheme, you don't see the results of this – the employer or the Inland Revenue may pocket any surplus (for an explanation of the rules on this, see page 246). But there is always a risk of things going wrong, or simply stagnating. In October 1987 stock exchange prices dropped by 25% in three weeks. Your pension would have too, so that a person retiring just after the crash could have had less money for as long as they lived.

If an employer is prepared to put a reasonable amount of money into it, a money purchase scheme with a good insurance company or other provider can be quite acceptable. It's also perhaps worthwhile with very small employers, or schemes that cover several employers in one industry, or where the future is not secure, if you can't get anything better. When a money purchase scheme is a COMP (explained on pages 37–9) it can be worse than SERPS for an older worker.

They can also be worthwhile as schemes into which you put additional contributions on top of your main pension. These are known as AVC schemes, and are explained in more detail in Chapter 23. The risks are still there, but they are only the same as they would be with any other place you could be putting the same money as ordinary savings, and the tax position is much better, as explained in Chapter 23.

'Hybrid' Schemes

These are often described as having a 'money purchase underpin'. The employer agrees to pay pension on a final earnings basis, but says that if the amount of investment income earned on the member's own contributions, plus a proportion of the employer's payments, do better, so there is extra money in the fund, then the extra will be added to the pension. A few employers have brought these in recently. They give a better deal to early leavers than a simple final earnings scheme, but this means they also cost more money, so employers tend to be rather wary of them.

Flat Rate Schemes

There are only a few schemes like this still actively operating, but many companies have flat rate schemes still lurking from the past. Even those who now have a good pension scheme may well have a very small deferred pension from this sort of scheme. You cannot usually get it out before retirement, but you might be able to negotiate to get it increased, to take some account of inflation. This is covered in more detail on pages 93–4.

Lump Sum Only Schemes

If your employer won't provide a full pension scheme, or if you're trapped in a bad scheme and can't get rid of it, it might be more use to you paid as a single cash sum when you retire. Getting a very small pension reduces the amount of Income Support (what used to be called Supplementary Benefit) that you can get.

The Inland Revenue allows you to take a tax-free cash sum on retirement of not more than 1.5 times your final year's earnings, provided you have 40 years' service or more or 20 years if you joined before 17 March 1987.

If you have fewer years than this, the maximum is lower. You can have 3/80ths of your final earnings, for each year you are in the scheme. That figure is rather arbitrary, but it's intended to fit in both with the way that scheme rules are drawn up, and with the Inland Revenue's top limits.

Lump sum schemes can be very simple, and people like to have a lump sum in their hands when they retire. They can be useful where there are a lot of part-timers, who could not earn enough to get a pension worth having.

But in any scheme you can get the lump sum arrangement – either by reducing the pension or automatically (this is explained in Chapter 14). The disadvantage of having only a lump sum is that, because of the Inland Revenue restrictions, you are not allowed to have a very good scheme based on that principle. For a better overall package, you need some of the benefit at least as pension.

Harmonisation of Schemes

According to the NAPF survey, 57% of all schemes are open to both staff and manual workers. But about a third of them also provide extra benefits for 'senior executives'. Many others restrict membership, for instance, to:

- Staff but not manual workers;
- Monthly paid staff only;

- Monthly paid staff, senior foremen, hourly paid staff who have been with the company a certain length of time;
- Staff, and those manual workers who have been granted 'staff status' at the company's discretion.

Or there may be two or more schemes in the company, covering different groups, with the members, and the company, paying different amounts. The manual workers' scheme will usually be the lower standard.

In general, we should aim for harmonisation, so that everyone in the company is covered by either the same pension scheme, or identical ones.

There may be additional costs, over and above those of having more people in the pension scheme, if a staff scheme is opened up to manual workers. When the actuary works it out, s/he may decide that the company will have to pay more per manual worker into the scheme than it does for staff, because:

- There is a larger proportion of women among manual workers than among the staff. As women retire earlier and live longer, it is more expensive to provide for them;
- The manual workers are, on average, older than the staff. It is more expensive to provide a pension for an older person, because there is less time ahead for the contributions to build up interest.

Other factors, though, partly balance this by reducing the cost per manual worker. They tend to have a shorter life expectancy. That is, they have more accidents, and more chance of contracting chronic illnesses before they retire, and after they retire they die sooner.

If you are told that it is going to cost a lot more to have manual workers in the scheme, try to find out why. The employer may be adding in other costs that should really be separate, or the scheme hasn't been adequately financed in the past and s/he's taking the opportunity to put it right.

In one way, though, there is almost bound to be an extra cost for the first few years. When a scheme starts, or is opened up to a new group of people, the ones who volunteer to join will usually be the older ones. But if new recruits are encouraged to join, this problem does not last long. Much of the employers' costs will anyway be met by the saving on NI, if the scheme is contracted out.

You could also be faced with an opposite position, with management trying to introduce a new lower tier scheme, perhaps a COMP on a money-purchase basis, and encouraging manual workers, or lower grade clerical staff, to join that, while perhaps excluding them from the better final earnings scheme. This idea should be opposed on principle; at the very least, if there are two schemes available, everyone should have the free choice of which to go into. If that is agreed, the unions will then need to work hard to persuade as many of the members as possible to take up the higher-tier scheme, even if the cost is higher.

Possible Arguments and Responses

One problem with harmonisation, or with achieving the right to enter the staff scheme where there has been no scheme before, is that the level of members' contributions will almost invariably go up, since staff tend to pay a higher amount into their scheme. The average contribution to a works scheme was 3.5% of earnings in 1988, and to a staff scheme it was 4.2%. But the real cost of an increase is often very small, by the time you have taken tax relief and the reduction in National Insurance contributions into account. It is worth working out a few examples, so that you can make a definite statement when the employer asks, 'Are you sure your members want it?'

A manual union making a claim for harmonisation with the staff would be sensible to discuss it with the staff unions, and get their agreement first. There may be difficulties if the staff feel that the manual unions are eroding their differentials. The manual unions might be able to point to other areas – use of the canteen, or holiday entitlements – where differentials have gone without damaging the staff. At least there should be agreement between the unions that the staff will not actively oppose the works claim.

The issues on admission to the pension scheme, or harmonisation of existing schemes, are the same as the arguments for staff status in other areas, like sick pay and holidays. A quick summary of these arguments is:

- Everyone is important to the company. It can't get along without its manual workers, any more than it can without its managers;
- Differentials in terms and conditions are outdated, and against union policy. The differentials should be in terms of money, not anything else;
- An atmosphere of 'them and us' is bad for the employer and bad for industrial relations.

The employer's response will be based on the extra cost, because s/he will often be putting a lot more into the staff scheme than into the works one. S/he may also say that:

- Better pensions are a traditional fringe benefit for staff which s/he does not wish to disturb. If there have been discussions between staff and manual unions on this, and harmonisation is a joint policy, this argument will be much weaker;
- S/he does not think manual workers value pension schemes as staff do. Point out that, if this were true, you would not have raised the issue at all.

The best you may be able to get from the company is a commitment to 'move towards' harmonisation between staff and works conditions, perhaps with a definite timetable attached. If so, you will need to make sure that the commitment isn't lost sight of in future negotiations.

As explained on page 108, you should claim credits for past service when manual workers are admitted to the staff scheme.

6

The New Personal Pensions

The new Personal Pensions (PP) system started in July 1988. There are no guarantees in Personal Pensions. What you get depends on how well you pick your PP scheme, how good its investment policy is, and how the stock market and interest rates are doing at the time you retire. PPs are 'money purchase' pensions. What these are, and how the benefits build up, was explained on pages 26–7.

The Background
Before going into the details, it's useful to look at the background and see how the system came about, and what were the government's real reasons for the changes it has made.

The history goes back to the 1970s, when inflation was high and the value of pensions, especially those being preserved for people who'd already left their employers, was being savagely cut. There were a lot of complaints about this, but the pensions industry tended to regard it all as a furore got up by the press, and reacted badly to the criticism. Members got their exact legal rights, they said. It was only their expectations which were not met.

This left the door wide open for a 'think tank' linked with the far right to enter the fray. The Centre for Policy Studies was originally set up by Sir Keith Joseph. Just before the 1983 General Election it published a paper called 'Personal and Portable Pensions for All'. This suggested breaking up occupational pension schemes, and giving individuals their own pots of gold which they could carry with them from job to job. They had a great deal of press publicity, and after the General Election Norman Fowler set up a major conference on the issue of early leavers.

The TUC, CBI, and National Association of Pension Funds all succeeded in making themselves look negative and reactionary, and the positive, forward-looking proposals seemed to be coming from the CPS. To quote from their paper,

> The absolutely prime advantage of PPs is for an individual to have a greater sense of involvement with what we believe to be his personal savings. It becomes clear to him that pensions really are 'funded' but can be honoured only if a future generation creates the profits to pay for pensions; the consequences of this understanding would have a profound effect on many aspects of the UK economy, and would lead to a better national understanding of economic affairs.

48

The government then set up an inquiry in November 1983 in. provision for retirement. It was asked to cover the whole question of the State pension system, and whether we could afford what we already had in place.

Before it had reported, though, the government issued a Consultative Document in July 1984, pursuing the idea of what had now become 'Personal Pensions'. Most experts, including the government's own Occupational Pensions Board, were hostile. PPs, they said, were going to create great problems of administration and supervision. The risk of low returns and poverty in old age made them unsuitable for the average employee; and they would make the occupational pensions system very unstable.

The government largely ignored this, and published a Green Paper – usually the first step on the road to legislation – in June 1985. It suggested that in the long term SERPS should be abolished and Personal Pensions made compulsory for everyone. The Green Paper described Personal Pensions as a person's 'own investment for retirement not a promissory note to be presented to a future generation' and suggested that it would help economic growth because 'the increase in private investment and savings which will arise in the short term should lead to a build up of assets from which the economy should benefit in the future.'

There was a stormy response, including an angry declaration from one of the members of the government's own inquiry that their report – which has never been published – did not bear out the conclusions Mr Fowler had reached. More seriously for the government's plans, the financial institutions made it clear that they did not see much benefit to themselves in taking on large numbers of badly paid marginal workers whose contributions would be too small to give any profit.

As a result, when the White Paper was finally published in December 1985, the pension proposals had been considerably altered. SERPS was now to be cut back, rather than abolished altogether. Occupational pension schemes were to be made voluntary rather than conditions of employment. Anyone would be able to take out a Personal Pension, contracted out of the State scheme, for themselves. This is the system that was brought in under the Social Security Act 1986.

How Personal Pensions Work

There are two sorts of Personal Pension; the Appropriate Personal Pension (APP) which is contracted out of SERPS, and the ordinary PP which sits on top of it. You cannot have more than one APP at once, but you can add one or more separate PPs to an APP. So since July 1988 employees have been able to choose between their employer's scheme (if one is available), membership of SERPS, or 'doing their own thing', by contracting out on their own, with an APP. It is also possible to leave the employer's scheme, but stay in SERPS and take out a Personal Pension without the contracted-out element. And as an extra complication, anyone who is in an employer's scheme that is contracted *in* (explained on page 36) can have a special APP that just replaces SERPS.

If you contract out in this way, then when you come to retire, the State will deduct a proportion of SERPS entitlement to take account of the time spent in an APP scheme. They will simply assume that you are getting that much, and will take no notice of the amount that is actually being paid to you.

On page 33 there was an example of how the DSS decides what Guaranteed Minimum Pension has to be paid to a person who's been in a contracted-out scheme that gives a guarantee. Using the same example, this is how it would work if Margaret was in a Personal Pension:

> Margaret has a working life of 22 years after 1978. She's been in a contracted-out APP scheme for 17 of those years. The DSS works out her total SERPS entitlement as £44 a week, and tells her that they assume her APP is paying at least 17/22nds of this, which comes to £34. The DSS then pays the balance, £10. Even if the APP pays less, Margaret will not get anything extra from the DSS.

People who take out APPs will pay the full rate of National Insurance contribution, and the DSS will pass on the rebate (explained on page 8), after the end of the tax year, to the providers. This 'clearing house' arrangement will only work if the employers send the DSS the right money, and the right information, and if this is then being passed on correctly. There will be a good many mistakes and delays. The person who will suffer from these is the APP-holder, since until the money actually reaches the scheme, no interest can start building up on it.

For people who have not already been contracted out in their employer's scheme for two years or more when they start the PP, the government will add an extra 2% of earnings to their minimum contribution, up until 1993. The government is describing this as an 'incentive'. This is simply a bribe to persuade people to go out of the State scheme and into a private one. This 2% is being found from within the National Insurance Fund. That is, National Insurance contributions paid by everyone are being used to finance the benefits of those who choose to leave the State scheme. About 1.5 billion a year is going out in this way.

Neither the rebate nor this 'incentive', however, can overlap with periods when a contracting out rebate has already been paid. Married women and widows paying the reduced rate contribution will not be eligible for an APP, and therefore not for the 2% incentive either, as they have no SERPS entitlement to contract out of.

The minimum contribution must be spent only on pension, which can only be paid at State pension date, and a spouse's pension of half the member's own. If there is no spouse, the value of the pension can be paid to another dependant or to the estate, as a lump sum. This package is called the Protected Rights. As with a COMP scheme, explained on page 38, these must be unisex and unistatus, and increase by 3% a year once in payment. It will not be possible to turn the APP into cash, unless it is tiny (less than £104 a year).

The idea is that these Protected Rights replace what the individual is giving up from the State or employer. Because the National Insurance Rebate is flat rate, while the cost of buying benefits in a money purchase scheme rises with age, there is a 'break even point' above which it is no longer remotely sensible to stay in a contracted-out APP. This will depend on the overall investment returns on your money, and on your age in 1988. But according to the government's own figures, the points at which APPs for that year are likely to produce less than the GMP for that year are as shown in this table:

First age at which the projected pension from the invested rebate is less than the corresponding GMP:

Man	Personal pension rate of return		
Age at April 1988	3%	3.5%	4%
16	41	46	49
20	43	46	50
30	45	47	50
40	45	45	47

Woman	Personal pension rate of return		
Age at April 1988	3%	3.5%	4%
16	31	36	37
20	35	36	40
30	35	40	40
40	43	43	45

At ages about five years below that, you should be very cautious about staying in an APP. This also applies to COMP schemes, which were explained on pages 37–9.

A scheme providing Appropriate Personal Pensions must be approved by the Occupational Pensions Board and send reports to it every so often.

Each person will be allowed to have only one APP at a time, and cannot change more than once a year. They can, however, add other PP schemes, so long as they do not go above the Inland Revenue contribution limits (explained below). If they want to buy other benefits, such as life assurance or a policy allowing retirement at an age earlier than the State pensionable age, it will cost extra. For an older person, the cost of providing just these benefits could be as much as their contribution to the employer's scheme would have been. When a person takes out an APP, the firm selling it to him or her will arrange to send in all the details to the DSS in order to claim the rebate and the incentive. The employer need not be told; all they need to know is that the person is not a member of the company's own scheme any more.

Contributions above the minimum will have to be paid separately. Very few employers are willing to make things easy by deducting the money from your pay packet, so you have to send it directly to the provider, once a month or once a year.

Based on one insurance company's quotation, it's estimated that for a man aged 50, earning £200 a week, the cost of providing a death benefit of twice his annual earnings and a widow's pension of £70 a week would be round about £12 a week.

Employers will be allowed to continue to cover people for death benefit if they want. This is because the one part of a pension scheme that can remain compulsory is the death benefit, so long as they do not ask members for any contributions. They would also be able to run a scheme covering people for long-term disability, of the type called a Permanent Health Insurance scheme (explained in Chapter 16), since these do not count as pensions.

Tax Rules for PPs

The Inland Revenue's rules on the maximum allowed for Personal Pensions are different from those for earnings-based pensions. There will be a maximum figure for contributions, and for the size of the tax free lump sum, but not for the pension itself; the more you put in, the more you get out.

The maximum contribution is 17.5% of earnings for anyone aged 35 or less, 20% for those aged between 36 and 45, 25% for those aged between 46 and 50, 30% for those aged between 51 and 55, 35% for those aged between 56 and 60, and 40% for anyone over 60. This is on top of the National Insurance Rebate and incentive contributed by the DSS.

The protected rights annuity can only be taken at State pensionable age. But policies covering the rest of the pension can be arranged to allow retirement at any age after 50. Life assurance premiums of up to 5% of earnings, within the total premium, will be allowed tax relief. The maximum lump sum at retirement will be a quarter of the fund available, with a cash limit of £96,300 altogether.

There will be tax relief 'at source', as there is with mortgage interest payments, at the basic rate. You'll pay the contributions out of your taxed income, and the people from whom you are buying the pension will then claim the tax back from the Inland Revenue.

Transfers

Transfers are allowed between the different types of scheme. But when someone dies before retirement, part of the transferred fund must be used to provide an annuity. The DSS are imposing restrictions on the transfer of 'protected rights'. Transfer values are calculated in the same way as for employer-based schemes, following the rules in the Institute of Actuaries' Guidance notes (explained on page 167). People who move from an employer's scheme into a PP don't have the right to transfer pension accrued before April 1988 into a PP scheme, so long as they remain with that employer, but the scheme rules can allow it. When a GMP is put into a PP scheme, it becomes a 'protected right'. So the person would then lose the earnings-linked guarantee for the years already done in the past, as well as for future years.

On the other hand, if a scheme contracted out on a final earnings basis allows someone to transfer in protected rights from an APP or a COMP scheme, the employer will have to create a final earnings GMP for them. This may make employers reluctant to allow this sort of transfer in but unions should press for it to be available. Schemes have no legal duty to let someone back in, once they have left.

Investment of PPs

PP schemes are all money purchase, but can be invested in different things. They can be based on insurance policies and annuity contracts; unit trusts; friendly societies; or deposits with banks and building societies. Some have a 'with profits' or 'unit linked' element. That means that the pension will be based on the bonuses added by the insurance company, or the growth of the units which are invested in stocks and shares. Others are based on fixed interest rates, or linked to something like the mortgage rate, as in many AVC schemes today. The annuities at retirement will all come from insurance companies, because this is a specialist business for which there are special controls. Individuals can arrange for their PP to be invested in exactly the stocks and shares they want, but the cost of running a scheme like this is high, so it is really only open to the very rich.

Selling PPs

There are no limits on how much the various organisations can charge for running PPs. The government is leaving it to 'market forces'. The rules of the Securities and Investment Board, the new City body which is supposed to 'regulate' the way investments are sold, say that the buyer must be told what the charges are 'where these are identifiable'. But if they are simply buried in the overall cost, you need not be told.

If you ask, you'll be told the commission and expenses. The scheme must also estimate paid up pensions or transfer values over a five year period. This must include the provider's own assumptions about expenses and other non-investment factors.

These new financial rules also forbid providers to advise customers to buy any investment unless they have reasonable grounds for believing it is suitable for them. They must bear in mind the customer's own financial and personal situation, and the nature of the investment. This is called the 'best advice' principle. As explained on pages 26–7, older people do much worse out of money purchase schemes than younger ones, and get a better deal out of SERPS. If you are middle aged or older, you are most unlikely to do better out of an Appropriate Personal Pension than out of SERPS. So this principle of 'best advice' ought to mean that these people are told by the sales reps not to buy an APP, but to stay in SERPS.

The rules also restrict advertising of PPs and 'cold calling', which means phoning you or coming to see you without your having requested the sales representative to do so. How firmly they are enforced depends on how well the City does the job of policing itself. There are a lot of loopholes still.

7

The Response to Personal Pensions

The unions are very much opposed to Personal Pensions. To quote Peter Jacques, the head of the TUC department dealing with the subject:

> These personal pensions will have no relationship to the member's place of work, income, years of service, or final earnings. They simply depend on the net investment income generated by the respective contributions and like all such money purchase schemes, they provide workers with no real certainty about their future pension income ... They undermine the collective ethos of occupational pension schemes and instead of pooling the risks which are shared by all, personal pensions isolate individuals in a way which throws risks on those least able to bear them.

Many members, though, have been attracted to them. They see them as a way of paying less, and can be seduced by the promises made by a sales representative – giving figures which are really only an expression of hope. The next section looks at the way they will be sold.

How PPs are Sold

The people selling the PPs are usually doing it on commission. There is not very much commission, though, from selling the rock bottom Appropriate Personal Pension. It's restricted to 4% of each premium, and it is only paid when the premium reaches the insurance company – after the end of the tax year, when the DSS sends it. But commission on the rest will be the same as for other policies and can be rolled up in one sum paid when the policy is first sold. More than half – sometimes as much as three-quarters – of your first year's premium payments will be swallowed up in commission payments.

This means that selling the APP on its own is only worthwhile if the providers can sell a lot of them, or if they use it as a 'loss leader' to attract people as customers and then sell them other products. Over the first 18 months of PPs, over 4 million were sold, largely at the minimum level, by these two methods.

In future, selling APPs to ordinary individuals will only be worthwhile if the sales reps can save themselves trouble and expense by getting the employers to do much of the work, by arranging 'bulk purchase' by their workforces. The sales operation here would be in two stages. The first step would be to talk to the gullible personnel officer or plant manager, and convince them that it would be a good

55

thing to allow access to the employees, perhaps through arranging a meeting in the canteen or even giving out their home addresses. Then as the second stage the rep would sell the scheme directly to the workers. Unions should resist this sort of sales operation strongly, unless the employer is prepared to underwrite the benefits of the scheme. Companies should be asked to send out directives from head office, telling local management not to allow sales representatives on the premises.

The sales reps will be keenest on selling a complete PP package, based on contributions and benefits up to the Inland Revenue limits, to higher earners, or to those who they think are going to be earning big money in the future. This could be people in advertising, computers, specialist technical areas, and middle management and upwards. They will be suggesting that their customers persuade their employer to contribute also.

Advice to Scheme Members about Personal Pensions

Stewards have to be cautious about giving advice on 'investment matters' because it is a criminal offence under the Financial Services Act to do this without being authorised. It is still possible, though, to shout about the virtues of your occupational scheme, since this does not count as an 'investment'. You're also entitled to talk about the difference between occupational schemes in general and PPs in general, and to explain the difference between, for instance, deposit and unit linked schemes. Where you must start being careful, though, is if you are asked about the merits of a particular PP scheme, or requested for help in choosing between PP schemes. The idea of the new law is that specific advice on different policies will only be given by 'independent intermediaries' who are in a position to look across the whole market.

To ensure that they are able to give full advice, the employer, or the pension scheme if it is a separate corporate body, can become authorised under the Act. Or they can make an arrangement with an independent intermediary to give advice and help to the employees. Or, if they form a tie-up with a particular scheme, they can become 'company representatives' and be trained up to talk about that scheme.

Try to get the employer to agree that anyone thinking of taking out a PP will be offered a definite appointment with someone knowledgeable, in work time, to talk over the issues and check that they understand what they are doing. There will always be a 14-day 'cooling off period' whenever anyone has signed up for a PP, so this could be used for that purpose. If after this they do leave the company scheme, they should be asked to sign a form saying that they understand what benefits they are losing.

On top of these management procedures, the unions could give people 'checklists' of questions to ask sales representatives, to help them compare the PP with the employer's scheme. The TUC's list has the following questions:

- What commission or agency charges are payable to the PP scheme?
- What are the administrative and redemption charges?
- What are the penalties for a break in employment?
- What provision is made for dependants' benefits?
- What are the rights to ill-health early retirement?
- What are the final pension figures in the plan, discounted for inflation? What are the investment assumptions behind this figure? How does it compare with investment experience over the last 20–30 years?
- What level of pension is guaranteed by the plan?
- What consultation rights are there for PP holders?

The answer to the last question will usually be 'none'. Whereas in an employer's scheme there is some scope for influencing the benefits through negotiation, there will be none with the insurance company or unit trust. You will buy the policy, and then the only new contact you will have with the provider will be when they are pestering you to buy something else.

Union representatives are sometimes approached by insurance sales reps offering substantial 'incentives' (in plain language, bribes) if you let them on the premises or recommend their particular policies. *Don't do it.* You'll probably be breaking the law, and you could be sued for negligence by a member to whom you gave the wrong advice. And you'll discredit yourself with the members as well. The harder these policies are sold, the more likely they are to be a bad deal, because so much of your money will have gone on the sales commission.

Now that We Have Personal Pensions

There are a number of points of policy to think about, with the new situation. Most employers have committed themselves to defending their schemes, and not encouraging PPs. This section goes through the issues you and they must think about, to make that effective.

Voluntary Membership
As explained on page 29, since April 1988 all schemes, except those that only provide death benefit at the employer's expense, have had to be voluntary. Since the majority of schemes before this were compulsory, employers and scheme managers have not in the past had to work hard at 'selling' the scheme, or persuading people of its merits.

From the trade union point of view, compulsory pension arrangements had great advantages. It meant that the cost and the benefits were spread right across the company, and young people still at the stage of believing that they will never die or grow old, could be brought in the scheme 'in their own interests' even if they didn't want to join. It also reduced the chance of management picking and choosing those who they wanted to give better benefits to, and saving money by leaving out those not considered to be 'career' workers.

So now we no longer have compulsory membership, we need to think about creating a situation as close to it as possible, on the voluntary basis. Much depends, therefore, on the way the scheme is put over to the potential members. It needs to be done positively, with the assumption that 'you really ought to join', rather than 'you might join if you feel like it.' Points to think about, and discuss with management, are:

- When your booklet was last updated;
- Whether it's understandable by the average person, who is not a pensions expert;
- When, and how, the information about the scheme is presented to new joiners. Is it merely handed out by a supervisor, or are the benefits explained properly by someone who knows what they are talking about?
- How members are kept up-to-date with the way the value of their scheme is building. Does the company issue annual benefit statements; does it put reports about the scheme in the company newspaper; does it give the pensions management the chance to see the members face to face and be seen by them? Companies often put a great deal of effort into the way they present the company's own reports, and little or nothing into those on the pension scheme – though it may have more money in it than the company itself does. If they are telling you that they value the scheme, and want people to stay in it, suggest that they should put in enough resources to allow it to be presented properly. Chapter 24 covers the information that must be given, by law, to all members about their pension schemes.

Procedures for Joining
Each person should have to give some answer about whether they are joining or not. The application form should be altered so that the person who decides not to join has to sign a section saying, 'I understand what I am giving up by not joining.' This means that no-one can claim that they believed they were in the pension scheme when in fact they were not, and those who might stay out of the scheme simply because it's too much bother to join, will have to take some action whatever they do.

Rejoiners
The next point is the policy when someone who's been in a PP scheme wants to return to the fold. PP schemes become steadily

worse value as you get older, and your contributions have less and less time to build up interest and dividends. Final earnings schemes, however, are good value for the older person. Any honest adviser should be telling the person over 40 to get back into the company scheme, especially if they have any sort of health problem. If that person comes knocking on the employer's door, both management and unions are tending to say, 'once you've chosen to come out, you're out.' But do you want to be seen to be that hard hearted? You are putting someone in an impossible position, if they are being told on the one hand that a PP scheme is not in their best interests, but on the other hand that they can't go anywhere else.

You're also being inconsistent, if a new recruit of the same age would be allowed to join the scheme. This would be a particular problem in industries where people are quite often made redundant and re-employed; how can you give better terms to the person who's been out of the company for a few years, than to the person who's always been there?

It may be better to say that people can rejoin at any time, but as if they were new entrants, without any credit for past service, and without being allowed to transfer their PP into the scheme.

Employer Contributions to PPs

If someone is not using up their full tax relief with their own contributions to a PP scheme, the employer can also add contributions on their behalf. But no-one has the right to insist that they do so.

The union view would be that if the company has a decent pension scheme, that is where their contribution should go, because then it can be used for everyone's benefit. So no contributions should be made to PP schemes, and that rule should be the same for all grades, from the lowest to the highest. In practice, we know that there will be contributions made by the employer to senior managers' PP schemes, but we certainly should not allow management to give out extra cash, in the form of contributions, to those whose faces fit.

The argument to use with employers here is that the complications, and the costs, jump sharply as soon as they agree to pay anything towards the member's PP. If they pay more, the employee can obviously get more from the PP scheme, but the administrative and financial burdens go up. Someone has to arrange for the money to get to the commercial provider – it can't go through the DSS, like the basic contribution – and they will have to keep the Inland Revenue informed. People might have policies with 20 different insurance companies. Keeping track of them is not an impossible task, but it's a headache.

Personal Pension costs could easily become much less controllable than those in an earnings-related scheme.

To see why, think about the next marketing executive the company recruits. The company is keen to employ this person, but s/he will

only agree to come if the company will pay an extra 5% into the PP
scheme s/he already has. If the company agrees, in a short time it'll
have the rest of the marketing team demanding the same treatment.
If the company resists, those people threaten to leave. So it pays up,
and realises that it has ended up contributing to ten people's PPs in
order to recruit one person.

Coverage of Those who Leave

There are differences of opinion among union representatives about
whether schemes should continue to cover for death benefit, and
perhaps also disability benefit, employees who have left the scheme
in order to take out a Personal Pension. On the one hand, continuing
blanket coverage does mean that we know everyone is protected
against disaster, even if they are silly enough not to take out any insurance for themselves. On the other, it means that PPs could be more
attractive, since they know that the employer will still be paying for
some of the expensive parts of the package.

Generally, unions want to see the widest possible coverage for
death and disability benefit. So even if the scheme has a waiting
period or age limit, we want to see the death benefits starting at the
moment a person starts a job with that firm. In that case, if you are
giving a benefit to those who have only just joined, you can hardly
take it away later. One answer is to provide a minimal level of benefit
to everyone, but then give a much bigger amount to those who stay
within the pension scheme. That means that no-one will be destitute,
but only those who stay within the employer's scheme will be properly covered for death or disability.

If you do this, or if you say that if someone is out of the scheme
they are out of benefit altogether, it is important to make sure that
people are clear about the rights they are signing away if they go into
a PP scheme. Everyone ought to sign a form, saying either 'I agree to
join the pension scheme', or 'I have decided not to join the pension
scheme, and I understand that by doing so I am giving up my rights
to death benefits, widow/er's and dependants' benefits, and early
retirement'.

Some schemes, such as Lucas Industries, write to the members who
are planning to opt out at their home addresses, asking for the
spouse's signature on the form as well. They are morally quite justified in doing this, since it would be the family who would suffer, but
they cannot legally require the member to show any correspondence
about the scheme to his or her spouse.

Pension Mortgages

Another marketing ploy to sell PPs is the offer of pension mortgages –
explained on page 176 – as an attraction.

Once paying for a PP linked to a mortgage, it will be more difficult
for the individual to leave and move into an employer's scheme, even

when the balance of advantage has clearly moved that way. But employers' schemes can also arrange to provide pension mortgages, in conjunction with a bank or an insurance company, so they ought to be able to offer the member equal terms, and remove the attraction of PPs.

Other Changes to Press for

Taking the opportunity of the upheaval caused by Personal Pensions, unions should also be asking employers to rethink the package as a whole, and bring in improvements, some of them quite low cost, to make the scheme more attractive. The sort of changes to suggest are:

- Relaxing age and service requirements, to bring people in from day one, and reduce the incentive to a young person to take out a PP scheme (these requirements are considered in detail on pages 69–76).
- Giving widowers' pensions for service before 1988 (these are covered on pages 151–2).
- Looking at the retirement age rules within the scheme. This probably needs to be done anyway, because of the Sex Discrimination Act 1986, as explained on page 31.
- Reducing members' contributions or making the scheme non-contributory.

This will be a matter for discussion both between the unions and the employers, and on the trustee board. The trustees do not usually have the power to change the scheme rules, but they can have a strong influence, and they should aim to use it when they can, and protect the scheme against the threat of Personal Pensions.

Part II

8

Negotiating Improvements in Employers' Schemes

Introduction

The last few chapters have looked at the changes that have been made in pensions over the last few years, and at the implications for union demands. The next group of chapters is designed to help you look at all the other elements in your pension scheme, and decide what changes you want.

Each chapter in this part of the book covers one area of the pension scheme, so that you can use it easily. But remember that the scheme is a package. It's not much good getting an excellent pension for the individual, if the person who does not live to retirement leaves a miserable amount for his or her dependants.

Chapter 25 gives some idea about how a claim is built up, and the things to think about when setting your priorities.

First of all, though, this chapter gives a list of the basic words used in scheme booklets, and what they mean. This won't cover all the different bits of jargon that you will find, but it should explain the main ones. It is arranged in the order that most booklets are arranged in. As this is not very logical, the chapters themselves are in a different order, and the references will show you where to find them.

1. Eligibility (covered in Chapter 9). This means who can join the pension scheme. It covers how old you have to be, how long you must have been with the employer, which grades or groups of employees are allowed in.

2. Normal Retirement Age (NRA) or Normal Retirement Date (NRD), covered in Chapter 15. This means the age at which the scheme assumes you are going to retire. It need not be the same as the State retirement age, though it often is.

3. Pensionable earnings (or pay, or salary) covered in Chapter 12. This is the amount of your earnings that count in calculating your pension. Sometimes it will be all your earnings, sometimes only a part. For instance, shift premiums might not count. Sometimes it will be your earnings minus an amount that equals the State basic pension, or more.

Other names for this are 'benefit' earnings; 'scheme' earnings; 'reckonable' earnings; 'superannuable' earnings, or 'contribution earnings'. In each case, it could be 'pay' or 'salary' instead of earnings.

Some money purchase schemes will not have a definition of pensionable earnings, because they don't need one.

4. Final pensionable earnings/pay/salary, covered in Chapter 12. This means the amount of earnings that are used to calculate the pension when you come to retire, or when you die. It is often an average of the earnings figures over a number of years, but it can be earnings in just one year. Only a final earnings scheme needs this.

5. Pensionable service, covered in Chapter 12. This means the length of employment that is counted towards your pension. It could be all the complete years you've been paying into the scheme, or the years and the months. There might be some time before you were contributing that counts as pensionable service. This section will also tell you the maximum number of years you can build up in the scheme. The word 'service' is not one that trade unionists like, but as it is almost universally used in pension schemes we are sticking to it.

6. Contributions, covered in Chapter 10. This will tell you how much you have to pay to the scheme, and whether it is a fixed amount each week, or varies when your earnings vary. Sometimes the booklet also tells you how much the employer is paying; if not, there are other ways of finding out.

7. Accrual rate, covered in Chapter 11. This means the rate at which your pension builds up, for each year you are in the scheme. It might be a fraction, such as 1/60th, or a percentage, such as 1.66%. In a final earnings scheme you are building up, say, 1/60th of your final pensionable earnings for each year of pensionable service.

In an average earnings scheme you would be building up 1/60th, or some other fraction, of your average pensionable earnings, averaged over your whole working life, for each year in the scheme. It might be a career average scheme, which means your actual money earnings are averaged. Or it could be a revalued average scheme, like the State scheme, where your earnings are uprated to take account of inflation.

A final earnings or an average earnings scheme can also be integrated to take account of the money available from the State. This was explained under 'Integration' on pages 22–3, and this chapter goes into the pros and cons of it.

8. Past Service Entitlement, covered in Chapter 13. This means any extra benefit you are entitled to because you were in an old scheme, or because you were given credits for years before the scheme started, or because your scheme was merged in a takeover and you carried over some entitlement.

9. Commutation, covered in Chapter 14. This means turning your pension into a lump sum when you retire

10. Early retirement, covered in Chapters 15 and 16. This means retiring at any age below someone's normal retirement age (see page 120). This can be because of ill health (also called incapacity or disability) or because of redundancy (also called 'in the interests of company efficiency') or it may be voluntary, also called 'at the member's own request'.

11. Late retirement, covered in Chapter 15. This means retiring at any age after the normal retirement date.

12. Death benefit, covered in Chapter 17. This can mean either all of the benefits payable on death, or it can mean only the lump sum, which can also be called Life Assurance.

13. Widow's/widower's/spouse's pension, covered in Chapter 17. This means what it says. Occasionally it is called an annuity. There are two sorts of pension: where the member dies in service, while still working for the company, and in the case of:

14. Death after retirement, covered in Chapter 17, and the rules tend to be different for each.

15. Escalation, covered in Chapter 18. This means the amount by which the pension is increased each year once it starts. Some schemes have a fixed percentage written into the rules. Others say that the pension is 'reviewed'.

16. Temporary Absence, covered in Chapter 20. This means what happens when you are off sick, or away having a baby, or even 'doing work of national importance', as far as your pension is concerned. It should explain whether you have to continue to pay contributions, or can pay them when you come back, or have the company make them up, and what happens to the benefits if you die while you're away.

17. Leaving Service, covered in Chapter 9. This will explain your rights and the choices you have when leaving the company, except if you retire early.

18. Alterations, amendments, and termination, covered in Chapters 21 and 22. These clauses will say what your rights are if the scheme is wound up or changed, and probably also that the company reserves the right to wind it up or change it.

19. Miscellaneous clauses, covered in Chapter 20. Many booklets also have a section near the end of extra points. They may include:

- Life assurance continuation. This means that the insurance company will give you favourable terms if you leave the employer before the age of 60, and want to take out life assurance privately.
- Assignment. This will be a warning that you must not 'assign' your benefits, which means giving away your legal right to them.
- Evidence of health. This will explain when and if you need a medical examination before coming into the scheme.

20. Additional Voluntary Contributions, covered in Chapter 23. These are extra payments you can make to build up your pension faster. The rules on these, and union policy on them, is explained on pages 194-5.

21. Trustees, covered in Chapter 26. As explained on pages 223-6, these are the people in charge of your scheme, and who supervise the benefits that have to be paid. Sometimes the booklet will name them, but others contain just a general statement about them. Getting members appointed as trustees is important to the unions, and the question is covered in detail in Chapter 26, along with negotiating rights in general.

If your scheme booklet doesn't have all these sections, don't be too surprised, but put 'proper communication' down on your list of negotiating items. Far too many employers are secretive about their pension schemes. You now have legal rights to the proper information, as explained in Chapter 24.

How these Chapters are Arranged
This part of the book is simply about employers' schemes, not about the new Personal Pensions, since there's no question of negotiating with them. It concentrates on the final earnings type of scheme, but also touches on the other main sort, the money purchase scheme. Each chapter covers:

- What you must have, for instance under any rules about contracting out;
- The most you can have under the Inland Revenue rules;
- What schemes tend to provide, and what improvements you can expect to get;
- The arguments to use in negotiating, and the sort of objections the employers may raise.

In Chapter 25 there is also an idea of the costs, but although this will be helpful, don't use it as more than a very rough rule of thumb. There's an explanation of how pension schemes are funded, and how the costs are calculated, in Chapter 27. This should help you to understand how it is that the costs in different schemes can vary so much. So the figures in this chapter are only guidelines.

All the cost figures are given in terms of a percentage of the pensionable payroll. This is how the employer will usually express them. If you want to know how much any particular item might cost your employer, you need to know the total payroll cost for last year, so that you can convert the figures into cash. You can get this out of the actuary's valuation (explained in Chapter 27). If it's a year or so out of date, uprate it to take account of pay rises you have had since.

Sometimes the employer gives the union side of the negotiating committee access to the detailed figures, or the chance to consult the experts who are doing the costing for the other side. This is useful, and you should always ask for it.

Note: in a number of places, there are figures from the NAPF surveys. See Chapter 25 for an explanation of these.

9

Eligibility and Membership Conditions

As explained on page 29, all schemes now have to be voluntary. But they do not have to let everyone in, and there are big variations between schemes as to who they let in, at what age, and how long they have been with the company.

In general, the unions will be trying to bring the widest possible group of people into the scheme, while the employer is trying to keep down the numbers allowed in. Your argument is that, if the employer believes the scheme is a good one and worth paying for, then it is worthwhile for everyone, not just a select group.

If you have a limited scheme, the employer is using the profits being made by the whole workforce to pay for better benefits, and therefore a higher level of deferred pay, for a particular group. So there are first and second class citizens, and some people with high overheads – and therefore high employment costs – and other, 'marginal' workers with lower employment costs. It's in the interests of both groups to even up the costs, so that one is not undercutting the other.

The employer's objection, whether he admits it or not, is usually going to be the cost. The scheme may be cheaper per head if it takes in a larger group, but there will be a larger bill.

Each person allowed into the scheme is paying perhaps 5% of his/her earnings into the pension fund. On top of this the employer is paying perhaps 10%. So if the scheme at the moment has 50 people earning £200 a week in it, the employer is paying 10% of 50 x 200, which is £1,000. If another 10 people earning the same amount join, the cost might drop to 9.5% of each person's earnings. So the employer will then be paying 9.5% of 60 x 100, which is £1,140.

Whatever the employer is paying, it will come out of the profits of the business, which are created by the whole workforce. If the scheme only allows in a narrow group of people, a particular group is being subsidised by the rest.

The Legal Rules

The rules about equal access to pension schemes were covered on pages 29–32. These only deal with giving the same access to men and women. Other than this, a company can limit its pension scheme to any category of employee that it wants. Or:

- There can be a special scheme for one person, or a very small group of people;
- Management can select particular people.

There are some restrictions on company directors and partners, but they need not concern us.

If there is a pension scheme you could join, you have a legal right to the basic details about it, as explained on pages 198–9.

There are very few restrictions on how wide the offer of membership can go. Schemes can let in everyone, from the age of 16 and the day they are taken on, until they reach the company's compulsory retirement age.

Different Points to Consider

The rest of this chapter is divided into:

1. Earnings qualifications
2. Upper age limit
3. Lower age limit
4. Waiting periods
5. Anniversary dates
6. Part-timers

For each item, we've looked at what schemes tend to provide, and what improvements you can achieve, and then at the arguments you can use, and what the employer will say. The general principle behind all the different arguments is that the scheme should cover as many people in the company as possible.

1. Earnings Qualifications

Typical Arrangements and Possible Improvements

Some schemes only allow in people with earnings at or above a certain level.

Restrictions like this should be opposed on principle, as they are really a way of picking and choosing whom the company wants to belong.

Possible Arguments and Responses

Intentionally or not, these provisions discriminate against women, since they are usually the lower paid. This will probably make them unlawful when the 1989 Social Security Act comes into force at the end of 1992.

People on lower pay put as much into the organisation as anyone else, so why should they be excluded from the benefits? It is going to be bad for industrial relations on other matters, if the groups who are kept out feel resentful of the fact, as they have every right to. It also puts the pension scheme in a bad light, if it looks like a tax fiddle for the higher paid.

The employer may say:

- That the scheme is not worth it for the lower paid, especially if it is integrated (see pages 22 and 90–3). In that case he should redesign the scheme, to make it worthwhile for everyone; or
- That he cannot afford to bring everyone in – so you will need to start arguing about how much he can afford to give everyone a fair deal (see page 69 for some of the arguments to use on the question of costs).

The unions' argument, that the only differential should be on wages, not conditions, applies here as it does on questions of staff/works differentials, covered in Chapter 5.

2. Upper Age Limit

Typical Arrangements and Possible Improvements

Pension schemes very often exclude anyone with five years or less to go to retirement – over 60 for men, over 55 for women. A contracted-out scheme is allowed to exclude them, even though they will be in the same 'category of employment' as anyone else. The reason for this is cost. The older you are, the more expensive it is to provide either pension or life assurance.

There is no reason for the employer to be allowed to get away with this. We should work on the principle that if someone is fit for work, s/he is fit for the pension scheme.

Older entrants ought at least to have life assurance coverage. If you are negotiating a new scheme, or one to take the place of an existing one, it is important that current employees of all ages are allowed in, even if there is to be an exclusion for later entrants over a certain age.

After the Social Security Act 1989 comes into force, the upper age limit will have to be the same for men and women.

Possible Arguments and Responses

The arguments you can use are:

- If the employer is claiming to provide a benefit for all his workers, he should not be allowed to exclude a few people just because it is inconvenient or expensive to offer them that benefit;
- The older worker is going to need the life assurance most, and find it the most difficult to get any coverage elsewhere;
- Very few people close to retirement age are ever taken on in new jobs, so the total cost will be very small, even if the cost for any one person is quite high. If the employer has taken someone on who is close to retirement, it's for a good reason, like a particular skill. So the employer ought not to exploit him or her.

3. Lower Age Limit
Typical Arrangements and Possible Improvements
Pension schemes are allowed to let in anyone from the age of 16. In the public sector, age 16 entry is usual.

In the private sector, the most common entry age is probably 21, and schemes have ages ranging from 18 to 25. Some employers are talking of increasing it still further, and only letting in people in their 30s and 40s to the final earnings scheme, while having a lower quality 'COMP' scheme (explained on pages 37–9) for younger people. This should be opposed on principle. It could be acceptable to have the COMP scheme as an optional alternative to the main one, so long as the choices are going to be properly explained to employees.

Ideally, entry age should be 16, but since there tends to be a high turnover of young people in jobs, and they are not at all interested in pensions generally, age 20 may be more realistic. But you should seek life assurance coverage for anyone who's too young to join the full scheme, with the employer paying for it. This should include people like YTS trainees and apprentices, even if the pension scheme does not.

The younger the entry age, the more important it is for the leaving service provisions (see pages 163–9) to be properly worked out.

Possible Arguments and Responses
Arguments for reducing the entry age are:

- Young people may well have dependants; if not a spouse and children, then possibly a parent who would have to pay off the HP on the motorbike if anything happened to their son or daughter;
- The earlier you make the offer, the less likely they are to take out a Personal Pension in the meantime. Once they are in a Personal Pension scheme, the power of inertia will work to keep them there. The employer should use the power of inertia in the opposite direction, by getting them into the pension scheme so that it will be a bother to come out;
- One needs to be in a scheme from an early age to get full benefit from it, because so few people do stay 40 years with one employer. A woman needs to be in the scheme from the age of 20 in order to get a full two-thirds pension. So too does a man, now that so many employers have effectively reduced the age at which men are expected to retire;
- In a contracted out scheme the cost of benefits for young people is likely to be little more than the NI Rebate, and indeed could easily be less.

Arguments the employer might use are:

- The young aren't interested, and won't thank you for offering them the scheme, if it would mean they had to pay extra contributions;

- They will leave quickly and there will be an administrative problem in sorting out a lot of small pensions. These may not give value for money when people come to collect them, because of inflation;
- The scheme has a maximum number of years for which you are allowed to build up pension. If you work for the employer for longer than the maximum, you don't get any further pension. But there's often no need to have a maximum, and it can be arranged so that those with longer service can retire earlier without losing, as explained in Chapter 15.

If you have to fall back simply on asking for life assurance for those too young to join, the only argument the employer really has is administrative problems. Cost hardly enters into it, as the extra premium for insuring the life of someone under 20 is tiny.

If the employer says that a large proportion of young people leave very quickly, ask for evidence of this, from research into personnel department records. If it is correct, then outside the pension scheme negotiations, you ought to be looking at the reasons for this. Are they using the youngsters as cheap labour, and getting rid of them as soon as they have to pay a full wage? This is not going to be a problem that you can solve within the pension scheme.

It's possible that the employer will say that the insurance company that is running the scheme is imposing restrictions. But you can easily negotiate better terms with it, or you can change insurance company. It's a competitive market, with a lot of people looking for the business. Most often, what will have happened is that the insurers have produced their standard 'package', and the employer has accepted it without question. They'd be happy to adjust the terms if asked, especially if it means more people coming in to the scheme and therefore more premiums.

4. Waiting Periods
Typical Arrangements and Possible Improvements
How long should you have to work for a company before they bring you into the pension scheme? There are any number of variations; Ford UK for instance makes you wait for six months, while Volvo UK makes you wait a year. The Local Government scheme now allows anyone to join immediately, though manual workers used to have to wait a year.

Any scheme should provide life assurance from the day you join the company. If there really is a problem of a lot of people staying for a very short time, or perhaps of seasonal workers, then a waiting period for the pension is acceptable. But it shouldn't be longer than one year, and once people are in, their pension benefit should be backdated. There certainly shouldn't be different waiting periods for different groups of employees.

Possible Arguments and Responses
There's a straightforward financial argument you can use here, in opposition to that of the employer. If, by letting people in to the scheme sooner, he cuts down on the turnover of employees, it will pay for itself. Suggest that he works out the cost of recruiting and training a new person, and therefore what he will save if he can cut staff turnover down by a few percentage points.

If the employer insists that there is a serious problem of people leaving very shortly after they come to the company, it ought to be looked at separately.

If he's not recruiting for the moment anyway, then making the concession now is not going to cost him anything until his fortunes change.

It is especially unfair to people who have had a pension scheme in their previous employment, to force them to have a gap in their entitlement. It could mean that they will feel obliged to take out a Personal Pension just to fill in that gap, against their own long-term interests.

5. Anniversary Dates
Typical Arrangements and Possible Improvements
Many schemes, particularly smaller ones, let new people in on only one date in a year. This is usually the same date on which new rules come into force, contribution rates change, and so on. This is called the 'anniversary date', and is often 6 April, to coincide with the beginning of the tax year. It can, though, be any other date.

This will be the date at which premiums to the insurance company are fixed, which is why new entrants will be allowed in then. But most insurance companies will now accept monthly entry. If it really is necessary to put on this limit, the life assurance coverage should be immediate, and once the member is in the scheme, their benefits should be backdated.

At worst, entry dates should be twice a year, and you should not accept both a long waiting period and a rigid entry date.

Possible Arguments and Responses
The argument here is that the employer is penny pinching; saving a fairly small amount, but inconveniencing a few people quite a lot. These 'small print' clauses can also devalue the scheme in ordinary members' eyes. If someone joins the company shortly after the anniversary date, and then finds that instead of waiting a year to join the pension scheme, s/he must wait nearly two years, s/he won't think much of it. So the money the employer is putting into the scheme to prove how enlightened he is will be wasted. And once again, it will tempt people to take out a Personal Pension simply to fill in the gap, and bringing them back into the company scheme will be more difficult.

6. Part Timers

Typical Arrangements and Possible Improvements

Many schemes let in only 'permanent full time staff', so that in total, only about half a million out of the 4.4 million part timers are covered. This discrimination may already be illegal under European law, and from the end of 1992 it will be illegal under the Social Security Act 1989 as well.

What 'full time' actually means in the pension scheme varies a good deal from company to company, or even within one company, at different plants. Some schemes define 'part time' as anyone working below 30 hours a week – which is really a misuse of the term. Others define it as 25, 20, or 16 hours a week. The more rigorous the company is at keeping part timers out, the more clear it is that they are regarding them as 'second class', cheap labour.

There is a problem, though, with an integrated scheme (explained on pages 90–2) where the benefit for a low paid person can be extremely small. A reasonable compromise is that anyone whom the company defines as part time is covered for life assurance, however low their earnings, automatically. Anyone should also have the option to join, but with a clear explanation being given of what benefits they would have from the scheme. If the scheme is integrated, then any deduction for the State benefit should be pro rata, that is, if they are working half the normal hours, only half the State pension deduction should be made.

The British Steel Scheme has a deduction of once times the Lower Earnings Limit, but guarantees that final pensionable pay will not be less than 75% of all gross pay. So in no case is a deduction going to be more than 25% of pay.

Turner and Newall, in both their Staff and Works schemes, give a guarantee that pension will be the greater of either:

- 1/60th of pensionable pay less the deduction of three-quarters of the Lower Earnings Limit; or
- 1/80th of pensionable pay with no deduction.

The definition of 'part time' and 'full time', being used in the pension scheme may not be the same as for in other conditions of service. It may also not have kept up to date with modern working conditions. So it will need looking at anyway.

In many of the traditional industries, like heavy engineering, there's a long standing resistance to part time work, and therefore reluctance both to acknowledge it exists, and to make any concessions that might imply accepting it as a permanent feature. So, for instance, shop stewards may say, if asked how part timers are treated in the pension scheme, 'It's not a problem. They don't exist in our workplace.' Going rather deeper, one then discovers that the canteen workers, the cleaners, and many clerical staff are part time. But they are invisible to the production workers until they start thinking about it.

The second reaction is 'But we're against part time work.' This is a hypocritical attitude in many cases, coming from male production workers who are accustomed to doing long hours of overtime and to going out to evening meetings, and whose lifestyle is only made possible by the fact that their wives or girlfriends do paid jobs for half the working day or less, and unpaid work at home the rest of the time. It also goes against general trade union policy today of recruiting part time workers, and against the facts of life. The number of part timers has increased enormously in the last few years. Full time workers are doing themselves no service by pretending this is not the case, and therefore allowing the employers to get away with offering lower deferred pay to this group. There is nothing wrong with part time work in itself, if it is decently paid and has good conditions.

Possible Arguments and Responses

What you will have to counter with the employer is the assumption that part timers are working only for 'pin money' and are not concerned with fringe benefits like pensions. If this was ever so, it certainly is not true for many people today. People work part time because they need the money, and because their other commitments prevent them from working full time. They may be:

- married with children;
- looking after an elderly or disabled parent;
- single parents;
- wanting financial independence from their husbands.

None of these factors means that they will take the job less seriously. They will simply be unable to work full time. But their income will nonetheless be vital to keep up the family's standard of living.

Employers take on part timers because it is convenient to do so. It means they can use machinery more intensively, but part timers are a form of cheap labour. In the past, unions have largely colluded with this; the employers need to be told that this is no longer on.

10

Contributions

What You Must Have

There is no minimum level of contributions that you or the employer must pay to the pension scheme. If you are contracted out, you save 2%, and the employer 3.8% (after April 1988) on National Insurance contributions. It is assumed that this joint 5.8% goes towards the contracted out scheme. But in an earnings related scheme it may be less, and for a good scheme it can often be more. (In a COMP scheme, as explained on page 39, it has to be at least 5.8%, plus the incentive if that is payable.)

What the Inland Revenue Allows

The limits on how much can be contributed vary according to the arrangements under which the Inland Revenue are approving the scheme (explained in Chapter 4). But for a revalued average or final-earnings scheme, approved under the Practice Notes, they say that:

- The employer must contribute something to the scheme, under normal circumstances – that is, except when on contribution holiday because there is a surplus on the scheme (explained on pages 247–8). He must not set it up and then charge employees the whole cost.
- The employee's contribution in total (including any Additional Voluntary Contributions) must not be more than 15% of total earnings.
- With a scheme approved under the new COMP rules (explained on pages 37–9) the employee's upper limit remains at 15% of earnings, but the total joint contribution is 17.5% of earnings. This is on top of the National Insurance Rebate.
- An employee can have a refund of contributions if s/he has been a member of the scheme for less than two years (it was five years before April 1988). S/he repays any contracted out National Insurance Rebate, and then pays 20% tax. This will not include the value of any part of the employer's contribution.
- Under the Finance Act 1986 (explained on page 246) the employer can have a refund of contributions also, if there is a surplus on the scheme, but pays 40% tax on any money refunded. Although this is called a 'refund' it is not really one, because it includes the member's contributions as well as the employer's.

Members' and Employers' Contributions

There are two sets of contributions to consider – yours, and the employer's. So this section is divided into two parts, covering each in turn.

It is unwise to get into a negotiation solely about contributions. The discussion should be first and foremost about benefits. If you get drawn into an argument about the precise 0.5% extra contribution, before you have told the employer exactly what benefits you want, you may find the arithmetic being manipulated against you. There is a lot of guesswork in calculating what pensions will cost, and the employer is more likely than you to be able to arrange the guesswork to suit himself.

Members' Contributions

Typical Arrangements and Possible Improvements

People in most contracted out schemes are paying between 3% and 5% of their pensionable earnings (never look at the contribution rate by itself; always look at the pensionable earnings, explained on page 96, as well).

This average figure has stayed pretty much the same in the last few years, as the NAPF survey shows:

Table 10.1 Comparative levels of employees' contributions

Overall Average Contribution Rate	Staff Schemes	Works Schemes	Combined Schemes	All Schemes
	%	%	%	%
1988	4.71	3.50	4.50	n/a
1987	4.38	3.76	4.52	4.38
1986	4.71	3.79	4.48	4.48
1985	4.63	3.63	4.53	4.45
1984	4.52	3.60	4.55	4.41
1983	4.56	3.50	4.47	4.38
1982	4.51	3.52	4.44	4.33

Some schemes have much higher contribution rates – especially in the public sector. The police, for instance, pay 11% and the fire brigade 10.75%. This is because they have specially early retirement dates because of the stress of their jobs. The government has pushed up the amount the members pay in the last few years, in effect penalising them for those arduous jobs.

For most people, a rough rule of thumb is that if you are contracted out and are paying more than 5%, or contracted in and paying more than 3%, you should need convincing that the scheme is good value. You will also want to know what the employer is paying. But see Chapter 12 for a discussion on what should be counted as pensionable pay.

Increases in Contributions

If the employer wants to increase the members' contributions – or even make the scheme contributory where it was not before – there are several points to watch:

- It should only happen where there is a clear increase in benefits, negotiated with the unions;
- The employer should be putting in more of an increase than he is asking the members to do; and
- Before you agree an increase in contributions, make sure your members will accept it. It is easy to get carried away in negotiating, especially when it gets very detailed. Take soundings of how the members feel before wasting a lot of time getting the small print right.

Legally, if the employer suddenly starts deducting extra contributions from your pay packet, especially if they are to pay for extra benefits, then unless you protest very quickly you can be deemed to have accepted them. This puts you in a weak position if the employer wishes to go over the union's head. There haven't been many court cases on this, though, and the legal system in this country means that one cannot know precisely what the law is until the judges have made rulings on it.

Sometimes employers insist on increasing the contributions and say that the scheme will be discontinued for anyone who refuses to pay. This would then mean they lost their life assurance benefits, as well as having their pensions frozen at that year's earnings levels (with the increases laid down by law, and explained on pages 165–6). They would lose the benefit of the scheme in future. You can argue of course about bad industrial relations and a breach of good faith. But unless you are in a position to achieve effective industrial action, it will be better to give in, and to negotiate to ensure that benefits are not frozen, while a two-tier system is allowed to remain.

Possible Arguments and Responses

If the employer is trying to impose too high a contribution rate on the members, you will need to argue that:

- People will not feel that the scheme is value for money, and therefore the 'public relations' advantage to the employer is much reduced;
- This will mean that it is very difficult to persuade new employees to join, or to get people to stay once they have joined, and this will weaken the scheme overall and the benefits the employer aims to get from the scheme (see page 42);
- The scheme will look bad in comparison with other employers in the area, and in the country as a whole. Put together the NAPF figures to present at your negotiations, and also try to collect details of other pension schemes run by large employers

in the neighbourhood, or in the industry. Try your local Trades Council, or your union's head office, for details of other schemes.

The employer's response might be:

- That the members will value the scheme more, the more they pay for it. Your reply would be that what's important is the value for money they feel they are getting;
- Or (especially if you are negotiating a new or much improved scheme) that he can only just afford what he is offering to pay anyway, and any more would 'break the camel's back'. It may be worth reminding him that he is getting corporation tax relief on the contributions, so it is not costing nearly as much as it first appears. Beyond this, you simply need to bargain about how much he really can afford, in the same way as you would on wages (see page 41 for some of the lines of argument here).

If he wants to increase the contribution, he may say that he can't afford to introduce the improvements suggested without a much bigger amount coming from the members. You would need to weigh up your views on this, and decide whether the improvements are value for money in themselves.

Non-Contributory Schemes

These are schemes where the employee makes no direct contribution. The employer pays it all. But really, the money is still coming from the employee – where else can it come from? If it were not going into the pension scheme, it would be available to spend on other things, perhaps on wages. So you are still paying. As an unusually frank pensions manager once said, 'It makes no difference to me whether I take the contribution out of your pay packet before you get it, or after. I still get the money.'

There are several disadvantages in a non-contributory scheme, and they come down to the question of control. If your scheme is non-contributory:

- You will find it more difficult to get negotiating rights;
- You'll be in a weaker position to get member trustees; and
- The employer will often resist changes strongly.

The argument that pensions are deferred pay is still as strong as ever. But the ordinary member will not be so interested in something s/he feels s/he is not paying for. So it will be more difficult to prevent the employer simply riding roughshod over your arguments. Here is part of a letter from a company, with a very poor non-contributory pension scheme, after being approached by the union seeking improvements:

We have considered the various proposals made in your letter ... and in view of some of these feel it is necessary again to bring to your attention that the scheme is non-contributory.

It is the company's belief that in view of the above the scheme ... is very fair and ... makes overall markedly superior provisions to those of the new State scheme without any demands on the employee's income...

In view of the scheme being non-contributory and being an invested fund with an insurance company rather than separate investments by the trustees etc, the company do not propose to depart from their present policy regarding appointment of trustees.

The exception, where a non-contributory basis is useful, is where a low-level 'ride on top' scheme has been agreed, giving just a death benefit and a lump sum on retirement. This may be all the members want, or you may accept that it is all the employer can afford at the moment. This sort of scheme is very cheap, costing between 2% and 4% of pensionable payroll for most companies, so splitting the contribution will produce a very small amount. It may not be worth the members' while to pay for it, and get enmeshed in complications on refunds and transfers. It is therefore simplest for all concerned – including the company, because the administrative costs of collecting a small contribution are high – for the scheme to be non-contributory for the member. But make it clear that this does not alter in any way the principle that the pension is deferred pay.

Occasionally, a company will offer the alternatives of either pension scheme improvements, or making the scheme non-contributory. This can also happen when there are negotiations over a contribution holiday (see Chapter 27). It can look very tempting – but think carefully before you accept it, as it's not offered simply out of the goodness of the employer's heart.

The Employer's Contribution

The rules of most pension schemes lay down what contribution the employee should make, as a fixed percentage of earnings. But for the employer, there's not usually a fixed amount laid down. Instead, there is a commitment to pay the 'balance' – whatever the actuary calculates is left over, after the member has paid up and the investment income is taken into account. A typical wording in a trust deed would be:

The company shall decide with the advice of the actuary the amount of contributions payable by the company to the plan as are necessary in each year when other income and receipts of the plan are taken into account, to provide the benefits payable under the plan in respect of the members thereof.

Sometimes there is a minimum percentage laid down in the rules, or perhaps in a letter of understanding between the company and the unions, but more often it is left entirely flexible.

What the Employer is Paying

scheme booklets will state somewhere what your contri-
fewer say exactly what the company is paying. Often,
very general phrase like this, from English China Clays staff
scheme. The Group pays the balance of the cost of pensions and the
entire cost of life assurance benefit.' Other booklets are more specific.
Kimberly Clark for instance says:

> The Company currently contributes to the scheme at the rate of 8%
> of eligible earnings. It is the Company's responsibility to ensure
> that the scheme always has enough money to meet all its liabilities.

Under the Social Security Act 1985 (covered more fully on pages
198–203) members now have to be told the basic details of their
scheme when they join, and at any other time if they ask. One of these
details is 'how members' and employers' contributions are calculated'.
This has not been tested out in court yet, but probably the sort of
general statement given above, or something saying that the employer
pays whatever the actuary says they must, would be sufficient.

There are several other places, though, where you can now look to
see what that contribution is. These are:

- The scheme's annual report. From 1989 onwards, all schemes
  must provide an annual report and accounts, as explained on
  pages 198–203. The accounts have to include figures for the last
  year's contributions, broken down into the ordinary one and
  any special payments. The actuarial statement will also need to
  say if the employer is taking a 'contribution holiday';
- The actuarial valuation. Any valuation that has been done with
  an 'effective date' after November 1987 has to be available to the
  unions. This will not always say exactly what the contribution is
  – it may only give a recommended figure, or it may tie it up in a
  way that is difficult to understand – but it usually will;
- The company's own accounts. These now have to give a figure
  for pension contributions along with that for pay, but it doesn't
  have to be broken down between different schemes. You should
  be able to find out from here, though, some figures for the
  employer's contribution to schemes where you have no representation – such as the 'top-hat' scheme for senior executives.

Possible Improvements

It is now a great deal easier to find out what employers are paying and
most of them, therefore, do not bother to try and hide it. What you
should aim for, though, is a clear statement in the scheme booklet,
like that in the Kimberly Clark one. Arguments to use for this are:

- Many members will have no idea what the employer is paying
  in, and may well not appreciate that he pays in anything at all.
  The member will value the scheme far more if s/he knows that
  the employer is putting something in too. S/he will also think

better of the employer for putting this money in. All this means s/he is less likely to leave the scheme and go into a Personal Pension, where only his/her own money would go towards the pension.

- Now that in general you are not allowed to have refunds of contributions, the member will understand the reason for this much better, and resent it less, if s/he appreciates how much the employer is also leaving in.
- It is the member's deferred pay, and s/he has a right to know.

The employer may argue, if you are talking about starting a new scheme or greatly improving an old one, that he doesn't know what his contribution will be. Technically, this is true, but there should be a fair estimate available from the specialist advisers. If they are not giving one, they should be sacked and new advisers obtained.

If the employer really has not got an idea, that's bad management. A pension scheme is a long-term commitment, like building an office block, and no manager who was any good at his job would dream of going in for this investment without figures that were as accurate as possible.

How Much Should the Employer Pay?

The NAPF survey (Table 10.2) showed that in contributory schemes the average employer's contribution is now about 2.3 times the average employee's contribution.

Table 10.2 Comparative levels of employers' contributions where scheme is contributory

Average Contribution Rate For	Staff Schemes	Works Schemes	Combined Schemes	All Schemes
	%	%	%	%
1988	9.20	6.40	8.60	n/a
1987	9.22	4.93	7.83	8.00
1986	10.63	6.23	9.24	9.36
1985	11.50	7.31	10.24	10.31
1984	11.95	7.26	10.48	10.62
1983	12.18	7.12	10.67	10.76
1982	12.90	7.33	10.65	11.04

Note: For 1988 the figures cover only contributory schemes, as the NAPF altered the questions in their survey.

As you can see from the table, employers tend to pay far more into staff schemes than into works schemes. There are many schemes where the benefits are reasonable, but the employer's contribution, compared to the employee's, is low. In the Kimberly Clark example above, for instance, the employee is paying 5% against the employer's 8%.

Other employers, however, contribute very large amounts. For a long time, before it was taken over by Hanson Trust, Imperial Group was paying four times as much as the members.

During the last few years, when pension schemes have been doing well, the employer's contribution has often fallen year by year. At Ford, for example, it went down from 1.77 times the member's contribution in 1983, to 1.27 times in 1988.

A Rule of Thumb

Rounding up the figures in the NAPF survey, one can take a ratio of 2.5 times the member's contribution as a reasonable rule of thumb. Points to watch out for are:

- If the employer's contribution is less than 2.5 times the member's, then it should come up to at least that level before there is any discussion of increased payments from the members;
- Any contribution that is being made to pay for past service should be treated separately from this, and met wholly by the company. It is a bill they should pick up, because they owe it to those members from the past;
- If you get to the stage of talking about increased contributions from the members, the employer's extra contribution should be in the same ratio as above. So if an extra 1% is asked for from the members, the employer should be paying an extra 2.5%.

Possible Arguments and Responses

It's best to admit from the start that there is no magic about the 2.5 times ratio. It could just as easily be 2 times or 3 times. It is simply a rule of thumb based on the average ratio among good employers.

Based on this, the argument will be:

- That the employer will not want to fall behind comparable employers. If you can find others in the district or the industry who are paying more than 2.5 times as much, so much the better;
- That the employer is better able to afford the contributions, and in any case they are the members' deferred wages. Take care with this argument, though. You do not want to be led down the road of a direct trade-off between pensions and wages.

The employer's main response will be that s/he cannot afford to put more into the pension scheme. As with wage negotiations, it will be for you to convince her/him that s/he must find more. S/he is also likely to come up with such statements as:

- Her/his precise contribution at any one time is irrelevant, as s/he carries the risk of making up the balance if anything goes wrong. You can say that you value this 'fallback' role, but you are sure that both s/he and you wish it never to be used. The best safeguard of this is a proper contribution rate throughout the lifetime of the scheme. To say that her/his annual contribution doesn't matter because of this 'fallback' is rather like saying that the shareholders should not be interested in the annual accounts because they can always wind up the company. This is not an idea many directors would support.

Should There be a Fixed Employer's Contribution?

Over the last few years, employers have been reducing their contributions when the scheme is doing well, or even cutting them out altogether. As a result, there is often a demand that the amount the employer pays should be fixed, in the same way as it is for the member. This demand is understandable, but there are two problems with it:

- If your scheme is based on earnings, there does need to be a guarantee that enough will go in to pay for the benefits. No-one knows exactly what those benefits will be, because no-one knows whether average earnings will be £40,000 or £400,000 in 20 years' time. The actuary makes calculations, but usually gets them wrong, as explained on pages 239–41. If there were no-one to call on for extra cash when necessary, the benefits would have to be cut instead. It's true that over the last few years there's been no need of this, because pension schemes have had more money than they needed, but back in the 1970s there were years when the experience was the opposite, and we could easily go back to that. If there were bad years, we would certainly want the employer to bail the scheme out;
- Having a fixed employer's contribution, and benefits that depend on that, leads you inevitably to the idea of a money purchase scheme, explained on pages 26–7, where the risk of the funds doing badly is thrown on to the retired member, who is not well equipped to cope with it.

A rather better idea – if you can achieve it – is to get a statement from the employer that says something like 'Normally the Company expects to pay at least xx% into the scheme, in comparison to the member's x%. However, the Company has a commitment to pay as much into the scheme as is needed to meet the costs of the benefits, and will follow the advice of the actuary on this.'

As explained in Chapter 22, however, if the costs of the scheme become too heavy, in the company's view, there can never be anything legally to stop them simply winding up the scheme and starting again, or doing without.

11

Accrual Rate

This is the rate at which the pension builds up, for each year you are in the scheme. There is no minimum rate now, even if you are contracted out of the State scheme. But a scheme contracted out on a benefits basis (see page 33) must agree to pay the GMP in every case, even if the benefits provided under the scheme's own formula would be less.

What the Inland Revenue Allows
The Inland Revenue will allow you to have a pension from the employer of up to two-thirds of your final 'remuneration'. They are not worried whether this is contracted in or out, so you can have this on top of the full additional pension from the State, if you want and if someone will pay for it.

The Revenue assumes that people will stay with a company for 40 years, so they will accept a 1/60th scheme without question. They will also accept a scheme with a higher accrual rate if:

- It is not based on full earnings (for instance, because the State pension is deducted from it); and/or
- The maximum service allowed is less than 40 years.

An employer can give a two-thirds pension after 20 years. This is not usually on offer to manual workers – but it is for senior management, especially if they change employers late in their working life.

In calculating that two-thirds limit, pension earned with a previous employer, and frozen or transferred, has to be taken into account.

Most of this chapter deals with final earnings and revalued average earnings schemes, but the last section covers the other types of schemes. The chapter is divided into:
1. contracted-out schemes
2. contracted-in schemes
3. integration
4. other types of scheme
5. past service
Schemes which give a lump sum only are dealt with in Chapter 14.

1. Contracted-out Schemes

According to the 1988 NAPF survey, staff generally did much better than works members on their accrual rates, as you can see from their Table 11.1.

Table 11.1 Fraction of eligible earnings accrued as pension per year of pensionable service (the figures in brackets represent the percentages by membership).

Rate of Acrual	Private		Public		All final pay schemes	
	%	%	%	%	%	%
1/45th	2	(1)	2	(*)	2	(1)
1/50th	6	(4)	9	(*)	6	(2)
Other fractions more generous than 1/60th	10	(12)	1	(7)	9	(11)
1/60th	61	(62)	21	(7)	57	(42)
1/80th + 3/80th lump sum	4	(8)	61	(80)	9	(33)
1/80th	6	(3)	4	(2)	6	(3)
1/100th	3	(3)	-	(-)	3	(2)
Other fractions less generous than 1/60th	8	(7)	2	(4)	8	(6)

* not available

Many manual workers are in schemes which only give about the same amount as SERPS. Often people would in fact be better off in SERPS, because they would not have any problems about frozen pensions there.

The new English China Clays scheme has a lower tier with 1/120ths for each year of pensionable service, and is contracted out.

On the other hand, some schemes give a much better rate. For the final earnings element of its hybrid scheme (explained on page 43) Rank Xerox gives 2% a year for 33 years, for instance. Ford now gives 1/55th to both hourly paid workers and staff.

The commonest accrual rates are 1/60th and 1/80th, but it is perfectly possible to have any other.

As a broad generalisation, you can say that the average manual worker's scheme is either 1/80th non-integrated, or 1/60th integrated. A staff scheme, or a harmonised one covering both groups, is more likely to give a full 1/60th.

If the accrual rate is low, improving that will be the first priority. If the accrual rate is 1/60th, then concentrate on the integration factor. If it's worse than this, for instance 1/80th integrated, you'll need to try to improve both at once.

Once you have reached 1/60th, it probably isn't worth trying to build it up further until all the other elements in the scheme are up to the level you want. However, if you are looking for an earlier retirement age, you might well want a better accrual rate as part of the package, so that people can earn as much pension as before, but in a shorter time.

Improving the accrual rate is expensive, because it will improve everything else, like the early retirement pension and the widow's pension. At Tioxide, moving from 1/80th to 1/60th cost about 3% of payroll.

You can calculate roughly how much it will cost by working out how much bigger a typical person's pension will be:

- An 80ths scheme will give a half-pension after 40 years – £100 for a person on £200 a week.
- A 60ths scheme will give a two-thirds pension after 40 years – £133 for a person on £200 a week.
- The second pension is a third better than the first, so it will add an extra third to the cost of the scheme.

However, this rule of thumb does not work entirely for schemes which are just around the minimum level of contracting out. Because of the need to provide guarantees on the GMP, it may cost very little to improve the accrual rate, because the GMP will be payable in so many cases anyway.

Phasing

If you can't get your accrual rate improved all at once, you might consider a phased scheme. The disadvantages of this are:

- It makes it difficult for the ordinary member to work out his/her pension, as s/he must grapple with a lot of different sums;
- If someone retires at just the wrong time – for instance, at the end of March when the next phase of the improvement comes in April – s/he will be resentful about the agreement.

On the other hand, it could be better to make a start on the process of phasing in an improvement now, rather than waiting until the company decides it can do it all in one go.

A claim for an improved accrual rate is often the major item in a claim for staff level benefits. There are many schemes where the only important difference between staff and manual workers is that the staff have a higher accrual rate. If so, the company may well want you also to pay the staff contribution.

Possible Arguments and Responses

For an average manual workers' scheme, which could be a 1/80th scheme that you are trying to improve to 1/60th, the sort of argument to use is:

- The final pension for those with less than 40 years' service (the majority of people) will not be enough to live on;
- The employer has 'sold' the scheme as being better than the State scheme. In fact, because of the different way in which the GMP is worked out, it won't be for many people, so the employer will end up paying the GMP rather than the scheme

benefits. The member has perhaps paid more into the scheme than s/he would have into the State, and be no better off. This is certainly true in many schemes giving 1/80th of basic earnings, and is becoming more obvious now that SERPS has been running for a few years. Though the cutbacks in SERPS in the long term will make it much less likely to happen, for the next ten years at least it will carry on creating resentment among those who lose out in this way.

Remember that the accrual rate is the central issue of the pension scheme, but remember also that you must link it with the pensionable earnings definition. Any improvement you get will overlap on to a lot of other things. So the negotiations on this are extremely important.

However the employer ties his/her response up, the basic objection will be cost. It is expensive to change the accrual rate, and you may as well show you are aware of this. Try to get him/her to provide an actual figure, as the rule of thumb about cost, given above, will not apply if there are special contributions for particular items going into the fund. Then you are in a straightforward negotiating position – how much can you get from him/her, and is this single large item your top priority?

2. Contracted-in Schemes

Typical Arrangements and Possible Improvements
In theory, you can have just as high an accrual rate on a contracted in final earnings based scheme as on a contracted–out one, and the State additional pension too. There are many 'top hat' schemes which do just that. But they cost a lot of money, and it is not very realistic to aim for this. The majority of contracted in schemes are either 'riding on top' with a low accrual rate, or integrated.

Integration is covered in the next section, on pages 90–3. This one deals with 'ride on top' schemes.

These are intended to top up the State pension, and so the company's intention will be that you look at the two pensions together to give your target pension. Provided the 'target' is of a good standard, there's nothing wrong with that.

The booklet for Preston Farmers says 'Pension at normal retirement age ... will be 1/120th of final pensionable salary up to upper earnings limit ... for each year of service in the scheme after September 1977. The ceiling ... will be increased in accordance with changes to the State pension scheme of which the ceiling is at present fixed.'

Some schemes give a low accrual rate up to the upper earnings limit, and then a higher one above it.

Unicorn Industries had until April 1988 a 'higher benefit' scheme giving '1/90th of your final pensionable earnings up to the upper earnings limit, plus 1/60th of your final pensionable earnings above the upper earnings limit.'

The argument here is that the State scheme does not cover earnings above the upper earnings limit, so this must be compensated for by a higher company pension scheme. For many schemes of this sort, the contribution is the same on all earnings. This means that the lower paid are in effect subsidising the higher paid, which should be opposed.

In a contracted in scheme, it's a matter of judgement how far you want to improve the accrual rate. You're doing reasonably well if you get it better than the level at which schemes contract out (say, 1/100th of all earnings). You may do better to look at other areas of the scheme where the State does particularly badly, such as widows' pensions or early retirements.

However, with the reduction in SERPS over the long term, a scheme which aims at a 'target pension' adding the two together needs to change the level of employer's pension that it provides, if it is not to fall behind 'target'. If the employer has not suggested discussions on this issue, the union should take the initiative.

The cost problems are the same as for a contracted out scheme, except that there is no need to provide the same guarantees. Read section 1 of this chapter.

Possible Arguments and Responses
The arguments in section 1 also apply here. The negotiation will be about money, as it is with a contracted out scheme. There are further points you can throw in:

- The employer has put a large proportion of the pension fund into an inflation-proof investment – the State additional scheme. S/he is therefore not taking the same risks as those in contracted out schemes, and therefore is in a better position to give you an improved pension. There will usually have been a leaflet or announcement when the employer originally per-suaded you that contracting in was the best course. If you can find it (or get him/her to provide you with another copy) it may well give you some useful quotes.
- It was no-one's intention that you should lose by contracting in. The pension provided from two sources was supposed to be as good as that which other employers were providing from only one. So if there is any danger of your falling behind because of the reduction in SERPS, the employer ought to be willing to catch up, and improve the scheme.

3. Integration

What this was, and the different methods of achieving it, was explained on pages 22–3, so turn back to those if you have forgotten the basic points. As explained there, there are two methods of integration:

- with pensionable earnings, or
- with the pension itself.

The first method means that an amount is deducted from your earnings before the pension is calculated, to 'take account of the State pension', and the second, that an amount is deducted from your pension after it is calculated, for the same reason.

Integration is a common feature of pension schemes. According to the last NAPF survey, 52% of schemes included it. It applies to both contracted-in and contracted-out schemes, but they raise different issues, so this section deals with contracted-out schemes first.

The reason employers give for integration is that the State is already providing a pension on that part of your income, which you are paying for out of your NI contributions, so there is no need for them to make further provision. The unions, however, generally dislike it.

The Disadvantages of Integration

It gives a lower pension than you would otherwise have had. But it does also mean lower contributions. Abolishing integration will almost certainly mean an increase either in the percentage taken, or in the amount of earnings on which contributions are calculated.

But integration is particularly hard on the lower paid, because they have a bigger slice of their earnings deducted. If the company has a lot of lower paid people in it, then one of the biggest improvements you could make would be to abolish integration. If the majority are high paid, then it might be better to concentrate on improving the accrual rate. The cross-over point can be calculated fairly simply. In a scheme where one times the LEL is deducted before calculating the pension, someone earning less than 4 times the LEL will be better off in a 1/80th scheme without integration, than in a 1/60th with integration. If only 0.75 of the LEL is deducted, the cross-over point is 3 times LEL; if one and a half times the LEL is deducted, it is 6 times LEL.

Some lawyers think that after the end of 1992 integration will be against the law anyway, because it discriminates indirectly against women. Until there's a court case, though, we cannot be certain of that.

It tends to be the white collar unions who are keenest on abolishing integration, because they are anxious to have nothing to do with the State scheme, but in fact it will often be the lower-paid manual worker who gains most.

If you can't get the integration factor abolished in your scheme, or if you think people will not like a sudden jump in their contributions, you could take a first step by freezing the deduction at its current money value, and then as time goes on it can be cut down and finally abolished altogether. That way, no one will pay more in a sudden jump, but the effects of integration will be very much reduced. WGI Group, for instance, froze their deduction at £910 in 1978, saying that when the fund was sufficiently healthy, they would abolish it altogether.

The Two Types of Integration

How do the two main types of integration compare? This depends on the exact arithmetic of any particular scheme. Usually, for a person with 40 years' service, they will give an identical result. But for the shorter service person, integrating with the earnings gives the worse deal, as the example on pages 22–3 shows.

So if you can't get the 'earnings-type' integration abolished altogether, it may be worth trying to get it changed to 'pension-type'. Check the arithmetic for your own scheme first, though, using the example on pages 22–3 as a guide, as it will depend on the exact formula in your scheme.

Often, companies want to 'trade off' introducing integration against a higher accrual rate. If you find you have to accept this:

- You could try to get the position of the low paid safeguarded, as in the Turner and Newall and BSC examples quoted on page 75.
- Try to obtain a 'no worse off' formula, so that for people in employment at the time of the changeover, the company does two benefit calculations, and gives the individual the better one.
- You might be able to get the old scheme maintained alongside the new. It will then be important to make sure that people are given proper advice, on an individual basis, on whether to transfer or stay with the old scheme. This could be from the pensions or personnel department, or from an outside adviser.

Contracted-in Schemes

Integration with a contracted-in scheme raises different issues. You are getting an additional benefit out of the State, and you are paying extra money for it, instead of putting that money into the company scheme. So it is illogical to resist integration when contracted in.

Contracted-in schemes tend to have more complicated integration formulas than contracted out ones. Because the State scheme works so very differently from a private scheme, the private one can only fit in exactly with it if you have an arrangement so complicated that most people can't work out their own pension, and probably can't even understand how the formula works.

One way to get exactness is to work on the same basis as the State does, of revalued average earnings (explained on pages 25–6). Very few schemes do this, however. Most have come to the conclusion that it is worth sacrificing the exact fit for a scheme everyone can understand, but this is a decision that should be taken in the negotiations.

Take care, with a contracted-in scheme, that the State pension deduction is not made in circumstances where in fact no State additional pension is payable. For instance, a person retiring early at the company's request, rather than due to ill-health, or a younger widow without children, or a widower, will not have any SERPS entitlement.

Possible Arguments and Responses
Many companies, particularly multinationals, are very committed to integration because they see themselves otherwise as paying twice for the same benefits – once to the State, once to the pension fund. Some of the arguments you could use are:

- Integration provides a lower pension but with the illusion of a higher one, and is misleading to many people;
- It discriminates against the lower paid, and against women, who in the past may not have had the chance to contribute for a full State pension;
- The State pension is a benefit to anyone who has made contributions, as of right. It is unfair for the company to take away, in effect, the rights the State gives.

If you are in a contracted-in scheme, again the same arguments will apply. You are unlikely to win on completely abolishing integration – but you could try to reduce the size of the deduction made. You may be able to show that the scheme is getting into administrative difficulties because of the complicated sums that have to be done. How quickly, for instance, are people who leave the company being notified of their entitlement? Then you could argue that simplification would leave everyone, including the administrator, better off. Try to get the pension manager involved in the negotiations, if you think s/he'll be on your side in this one.

Since the State additional pension will be dropping in value because of the government's cuts, you need an increased employer's pension to compensate for this. The logic of this is undeniable; if the employer refuses to make a change, then in fact your pension benefits are being cut. This is a breach of faith, though it's perfectly legal, because of the way pension scheme rules are drawn up, as explained on page 177.

4. Other Sorts of Scheme

Typical Arrangements and Possible Improvements
If your scheme is not a final earnings or revalued average earnings type, trying to get an improvement in the accrual rate as the scheme stands is very much a fallback position. First of all, you should be trying to get the whole basis of the scheme changed. If you're stuck with your scheme, and the company won't budge, a few points are worth remembering:

- In a money purchase scheme, there is no accrual rate anyway. But you might be able to get a guarantee that the pension will not be less than, say, 1/80th for each year of service with the company. This would turn it into a hybrid scheme, explained on pages 43–4.
- In a career average earnings scheme, there is an accrual rate, and improving it will improve the pension, as it does in a final earnings scheme. But it still won't be good, because inflation will eat away at it so quickly.
- In a flat rate scheme, if you can't get it improved drastically, the next best thing will be to get the sum for each year of service linked to earnings or the Retail Prices Index, so that it increases automatically. If you can't get that, you'll need to go in each year and negotiate for an increase in line with inflation.

If you've got a really small amount coming to you for each year in a flat rate scheme, it might be worth 'trading it in' for a tax-free lump sum on retirement (see pages 116–17). Even if your employer won't put a penny extra into the scheme, the cash sum will be worth a lot more at the point of retirement than a trivial pension going on for years would be. For every £1 of pension per year you give up, you should expect to get at least £9 lump sum for men, and £11 for women. The difference is because women retire earlier and live longer, so they are expected to draw their pension for longer.

> Uniroyal converted their old flat-rate pension into a lump sum on retirement, and gave £54 to a man, £66 to a women for each year's service, in return for giving up a £6 a year pension.

Possible Arguments and Responses
For a money purchase scheme, the argument will be about the adequacy of the benefit, and the risks involved, especially for the older employee with short service. Then it will come down to negotiating about cost. How much is the employer prepared to provide to underpin the scheme with a guarantee? It need not be very much – the unions at the *Daily Telegraph* were told by an actuary that they could have a perfectly adequate underpinning for 0.6% of payroll.

For the other types, career average earnings and flat rate schemes, your strongest argument is that the fund, being largely unaffected by rises in prices or earnings, will be doing very nicely out of the high interest rates that tend to go with inflation. Many of these schemes are pretty ancient, and will have been set up in very different conditions. So the members' contributions will be far more generous than are needed in current circumstances. What's happening to the surplus? Is it being used to reduce the employer's contributions (as explained on page 247), or is it subsidising benefits in other sections of the fund? Either way, that is unfair to people in that scheme.

The other strong argument is that while on wages the employer accepts that they should be increased broadly in line with the cost of living or better, on pensions he is actually reducing your expectations, in real terms, by not increasing the pension or changing the pension scheme. If he accepts that pensions are deferred pay, he must agree that this is an intolerable position.

The employer may argue that there is no guarantee that high interest rates will last for long, and so they ought not to use a 'windfall' as a reason for changing the scheme. But for the last 15 years interest rates have been at levels which are astronomically high by pre-war standards – long enough for a temporary windfall to become permanent.

What may be behind the employer's resistance to improving a scheme of this sort is a dislike of the whole idea of pensions. S/he could be hoping that, if the scheme gets steadily worse because of inflation, the members will lose interest in it and allow it to be wound up without too much of a fuss. If you suspect this is what is happening, make sure you carry on putting in claims year after year, so that the employer knows you are still interested.

In the end, if you are trapped in a really bad scheme, it may be worth allowing yourselves to be bought out – on good terms. But try all the arguments first.

12

Pensionable Earnings and Pensionable Service

1. Pensionable Earnings: What a Scheme Must Have

Pension schemes can define pensionable earnings in any way. There used to be certain standards for contracted-out schemes, called the 'requisite benefit' rules, but these were abolished in 1986.

What the Inland Revenue Allows

For someone paying tax under PAYE, the Inland Revenue permits almost all earnings, which it calls 'remuneration', to be taken into account. The one exception is income from share option schemes, which cannot be counted.

The 'fluctuating' elements must be averaged over three years. This matters particularly for people such as sales representatives, who are paid partly on commission. 'Remuneration' can sometimes include, for tax purposes, an amount added on to take account of the fact that you have a company car, or private health insurance scheme, for instance. This can be included also when the pension is calculated.

If someone has artificially low earnings in the last year before retirement – perhaps because they have been sick – the Inland Revenue allows a 'notional' figure to be used. This can be a calculation of what you would have earned if things had been normal.

There is nothing to stop a scheme using a different earnings formula for the pension and the life assurance, provided that neither benefit goes over the limits.

Typical Arrangements and Possible Improvements
Earnings, for most manual workers and some white collar workers, are made up of a number of different items:

- basic wage;
- bonus;
- overtime;
- shift premium;

and so on. There are people who do not have a basic wage at all, but are paid entirely on piecework. Some items, like bonus and over-time, may be regular and contractual, or they may be very irregular. You might get the opportunity to do overtime only in the months before Christmas, for instance in a shop. Or you might be expected to do it week after week, as many school caretakers are. In workplaces with a continuous process, it may be impossible to do the job without shift work and thus shift premium. In other places, people coming up to retirement generally go on to day work.

These complications are often not reflected in the way pension schemes are designed. The pensions experts take traditional white collar pay patterns, where basic pay makes up all or most of the pay packet, as the standard.

Common formulas include:

- Annual rate of basic pay;
- Annual rate of basic pay plus bonus and shift premium, but not overtime;
- Basic pay over the last year, plus 'fluctuating emoluments' averaged over the last three years;
- PAYE earnings over the last tax year.

The more complicated the formula, the more likely it is to be interpreted differently in different places. In the Local Government scheme, for instance, contractual overtime is included but non-contractual overtime is not. There are endless arguments about how much of the average caretaker's overtime is contractual.

Some rules of thumb which should help with designing a suitable definition for your own scheme are:

- In a final earnings scheme, the pensionable pay should be the pay that people are likely to get when they are at or near retirement, and it should include the steady elements of pay, such as regular shift work premiums, contractual overtime, and guaranteed bonus. Windfalls, and payments that are completely under the employer's control and so could disappear very quickly, should not be included. You could do a survey among some of the older employees to see what their earnings pattern really is; or you could ask the employer to go back over the payroll records for the last few years and analyse it for you.
- You can have a definition which 'irons out' the fluctuations between payments to individuals, and the different levels of overtime. This can be done by fixing a multiple of basic pay – for instance, 1.25 times or 1.33 times, which is used as a notional pensionable pay figure. This can be quite effective so long as the multiple is a realistic average for people's regular earnings.
- For death benefit, on the other hand, all earnings in the last 12 months should be included.
- In a revalued average earnings scheme, or a hybrid scheme of reasonable quality, you will get most benefit from having all earnings included, since you'll get full value for contributions made at any time in your career.

- The same definition should be used for contributions and for benefits.
- If you have a complicated pay structure, with large numbers of allowances and grades, you will need to define the relevant items carefully.

Ford's definition of 'pensionable pay' is the 'Personal Rate of Pay', which they say 'includes grade rate, lead operator's allowance, tooling co-ordinator's allowance, lineworker's allowance and productivity allowance, as applicable to an individual employee.'

Make sure that people who understand the pay structure are involved in the discussions on this. The pensions manager will probably not appreciate the complications, whereas the personnel or industrial relations departments will.

Don't be afraid of going for different definitions for different groups of people. Even if you want a single scheme for staff and works, it may still be more suitable for the staff to have basic pay and the works PAYE. The NCI Group scheme, for instance, does this. It's quite straightforward for the booklet to include several definitions. Before settling on the definition you want, work out a few examples for typical people in each grade and department.

Multi plant companies may have a problem, where the wage payment system varies. You may find it impossible to reach a formula that works equally well in each plant, which would mean leaving it to local agreement within some broad guidelines. It would be wise to review the position regularly in this case, to ensure that it is being administered properly. This would be a role for local consultative committees, discussed on pages 234–6.

You also need a formula to provide a 'notional' rate where somebody has been off sick for some time. If there is a grade rate that relates fairly well to what people actually get, or an average for the workgroup, you could use that.

If you find an earnings formula that is out of the ordinary, the Inland Revenue will need convincing that it is fair.

Note: **Integration**. Many schemes also deduct something from the 'pensionable earnings' figure to take account of the State pension. This is called integration, and there are several ways in which it can be done. See Chapter 3 for a preliminary explanation. For convenience, all the different types of integration are covered in one place, in Chapter 11.

Fixing the Pensionable Earnings

In any scheme, there will be a date at which your 'pensionable earnings' are fixed for the purpose of deciding what your pension is, or your death benefit. It can be the date at which you retire or die, but often it is the end of the tax year, and is based on your P60. This has the advantage that you will know exactly what you will get, but the bigger disadvantage that the figure gets steadily out of date over the next 12 months. If for instance the earnings figure is fixed in April, anyone with a birthday in March has lost 11 months' worth of inflation.

It is best to have a certain flexibility, and for the scheme to relate the pensionable earnings figure as closely as possible to the last 12 months' earnings. If it is necessary to have a single fixed figure for the whole year (as it may be for the smaller insured scheme), then try to get it fixed at a date shortly after the annual pay settlement, and make sure it includes that. Try also to get an alternative formula of 'actual earnings over the last 12 months if higher' included for the death benefit.

If there is an improvement in the earnings formula for pensions, it could mean more money being collected in contributions as well. Make sure your examples also cover this, and take soundings among people as to how they feel about paying higher contributions, before suggesting anything to the employer.

Possible Arguments and Responses
Having decided before going into negotiations which formula is most realistic for you, your argument is that you want a scheme that is genuinely related to what you earn, and that anything else is misleading. If you have worked out some examples, use these.

The employer's argument, once again, will be cost. If you increase the amount of money which is counted as pensionable, you increase his contribution as well as your own. Try to pin him down to a figure on this. On page 84 we look at some of the arguments to use to persuade an employer to increase his contribution.

It may be said that the computer cannot cope with a change. But computer programs can be rewritten – all it takes is time and money.

On the question of the time of year when the earnings figure is fixed, again the argument is that you want a pension that is genuinely related to your earnings. Earnings, as opposed to prices, have been going up by 7% a year on average in the last few years, and that can have quite an impact on the pension.

The real reason, again, will be cost. The more expensive a change is said to be, the more inadequate the scheme must be at the moment, and therefore the greater the justification for an improvement.

2. Final Pensionable Earnings: What You Must Have

Only a final earnings or a hybrid scheme will have a definition of final pensionable earnings. Most pension schemes that were contracted out before April 1988 will be of this type.

What the Inland Revenue Allows

Whether you are contracted in or out, the Inland Revenue says in its
Practice Notes, para 6.12:

> Scheme rules may provide for 'final remuneration' [which is what
> they call final pensionable pay] to be calculated on any basis which
> falls within the following:
> (a) remuneration for any one of the 5 years preceding the normal
> retirement date. For this purpose, 'remuneration' means basic pay,
> e.g. wage or salary, for the year in question, plus the average over a
> suitable period (usually 3 or more years) ending on the last day of
> the basic pay year, of any fluctuating emoluments such as commis-
> sion or bonus ...
> (b) the average of the total emoluments for any period of 3 or more
> consecutive years ending not earlier than 10 years before the
> normal retirement date.

This means that if your 'pensionable earnings' are calculated on
basic pay, or on basic pay plus other elements that you can convince
the Inland Revenue do not fluctuate very much, you may use just the
last year's earnings to calculate the pension.

In fact, it will also allow a scheme to use the full PAYE earnings, if
the administrator can convince it that these don't fluctuate enough
to matter. But if it does believe they fluctuate, then it may insist
either that you use the PAYE earnings averaged over several years, or
that the 'fluctuating emoluments' (which would normally mean
things like bonus and overtime) must be averaged, while the basic
wage could be calculated for the most recent year.

In the 1987 Budget, the government also imposed special controls
on company directors, and on people who had been directors in the
last ten years before retirement. They now must average their earnings over three years. While this mainly affects high paid people,
some ordinary workers – for instance, in co-ops – are also company
directors, and they will be affected by this.

The effects of inflation can be coped with under another special
clause from the Inland Revenue. Practice Note 6.14 (in the same place
as above) says that:

> Whenever 'final remuneration' is that of a year other than the 12
> months ending with normal retirement date, or is an average of 3
> or more years' remuneration, each year's remuneration may be
> increased in proportion to the increase in the cost of living for the
> period from the end of the year, up to normal retirement date.
> 'Final remuneration' so increased is known as 'dynamised final
> remuneration'.

This means that, before calculating the final pensionable earnings,
you are allowed to increase each year's earnings to take account of the
increase in prices. The Inland Revenue have said that this rule has
only really been used by company directors and senior management,

but it can be very useful for manual workers whose pay falls before retirement, in real terms.

Typical Arrangements and Possible Improvements
Watch the small print. The precise method of calculation can make a substantial difference.

The simplest pension scheme will take just the last year's earnings and base the pension on them;

George Eliot has earnings of £12,000 in his last year before he retires. He has built up a full two-thirds pension, so his calculation is £12,000 x 2/3 = £8,000.

But most schemes are not that simple. More commonly, a scheme will take:

* The annual average of the last three years' earnings;
* The annual average of the best three consecutive years' earnings in the last 10 (or 13) years.

The second formula usually comes out the same as the first, unless someone has had a very bad final year's earnings. To see what effect the formulas have, let us take George's earnings again.

In his last three years at work, George earned:
1986   £8,000
1987   £10,000
1988   £12,000
The three figures averaged together give a final earnings figure of £10,000. Two-thirds of that is £6,666 – over £1,400 down on our original figure.

If George's earnings were 'dynamised' as allowed by the Inland Revenue, we might expect them to come much closer to his real final earnings figure, and so give him back some of the pension he is missing under the current formula.

Very few schemes go in for this, although many allow in their rules for it to be done, at the administrator's discretion. One that includes it in its booklet is NCI (UK) Ltd. The clause says:

it is necessary to revalue pensionable pay. In order to make allowance for inflation, pay received after the age of 55 is revalued by the Trustees using the national Index of Average Earnings ...
Final Pensionable Pay is then ascertained by taking the average of those three years' consecutive revalued pensionable pay which gives the highest result.

According to the NAPF survey, 26% of schemes go for average earnings over the best three consecutive years ending in the last ten, while the most common formula, with 28% of schemes, was the average earnings over the last 12 months. If you can't achieve dynamisation, you could try for the 'last 12 months' formula to be added as an alternative to the current one. Try also to have them calculated over the last actual year, rather than being taken back to the beginning of the tax year. The Hobourn scheme, for instance, defines final pensionable earnings as:

Whichever is the best of:
- The yearly average of the last 36 months' earnings ...
- The highest single tax year's earnings in the last five ...
- The last 12 months' earnings ...
- The yearly average of the highest three consecutive tax years' earnings in the last ten.

Allowing for the best of several alternatives can be surprisingly expensive for what looks like a small change. One company calculated that it would cost an extra 1% of payroll each year. But this shows how much you may be losing with the present formula.

It is important to make sure that the person whose earnings do fall in the last year because of illness is protected. Ask for a clause which allows a 'notional' earnings figure to be calculated in these cases. That is, a figure for what the person would have earned in that year had s/he not been ill. The Inveresk Staff Scheme, for instance, says that 'any reduction in basic salary caused by sickness will be ignored.'

A less good alternative is to say that where someone's earnings drop in the last year, or the last few years, they are allowed to continue paying contributions on the basis of their previous earnings. The Local Government scheme has a special arrangement for this, for instance for people who are redeployed to a lower grade. Though it is better than nothing, it is making the employees pay for their own misfortune.

Possible Arguments and Responses
Once you have worked out what you are going for, it will be useful to work out examples to show what difference it would make. You could ask a particular individual coming up to retirement to let you use him or her as an example, or you could use workplace average earnings to illustrate the point you are making. You might also find a recently retired person, to show how much better his/her pension could be.

Hammer away at the point that this is not a final earnings scheme, when you were told it was – that the workforce is being misled.
The employer may say:

- That wage increases will slacken off soon –- see page 99 for the answer to that;
- That it will be too complicated to work out, especially on 'dynamised final earnings'. It is not – because it is relying on figures which have to be collected anyway. It is simply a matter of adding a new detail to the computer program, or giving a new instruction to the wages clerk; or
- (The real reason), that it will cost too much. Ask the employer to

get the figures, and to give them to you. Only then can you decide whether you want to give this priority in your 'shopping list'. The more expensive the improvement turns out to be, the more you are losing at the moment.

3. Pensionable Service

What the Inland Revenue Allows

The Inland Revenue is interested in the total pension you get out at the end – the two-thirds of final earnings. So if you have a scheme that genuinely gives 1/60th of total earnings, you must have a limit of 40 years on the service which can be counted towards that pension, so that if you do 41 or 42 years you won't earn any more pension. If you have a higher accrual rate, you must have a shorter maximum period of pensionable service, as you might otherwise go above the two-thirds limit.

The Inland Revenue will let you count in odd days of service, and in some circumstances you can also credit in years you have not actually done – so long as it would not take you over the two-thirds limit.

The rest of this section is subdivided into:

1. incomplete years;
2. maximum service;
3. credited years;
4. past service.

The question of broken service is dealt with under Chapter 20 on Temporary Absence, page 171.

Incomplete Years

Typical Arrangements and Possible Improvements

Many schemes give you pension only for the number of complete years in the scheme. This means that unless you have the foresight to arrange to have your 65th birthday on the scheme's anniversary date, you could be paying in contributions for anything up to 51 weeks for no benefit.

Other schemes, though, allow you to count the months, weeks, and even days of service. The English China Clays booklet, for instance, gives a pension of:

1/60th of Final Pensionable Age for each year (and a proportion for each week) of Pensionable Service.

It is much more convenient for the scheme administrator to cope with reckoning only complete years, and in a small scheme it may be that the insurance company insist on this, as it is more convenient for them. You will be able to change this, or change the insurance company, but there will be an extra cost in doing so. Aim at least for complete months to be added in, even if you accept that extra weeks might be difficult to cope with.

You should not have to pay contributions for any service for which you are not getting credits.

Possible Arguments and Responses
The basis of your argument must be the injustice that is being done to the person who retires at the wrong time of year. Try to find an example of a specific person whom it will affect badly. For instance, someone whose birthday is in March, if the date s/he was allowed into the scheme was in April.

The employer's argument will be 'administrative problems'. The concession will cost something, but not much, because for each individual the extra pension cannot be more than one year's extra pension entitlement. He may say that the insurance company won't let the contract be changed, or that they are insisting on an extra administrative charge which is too high. Ask that the insurer states exactly what the extra cost is and why, so that you can decide whether it is worthwhile or not.

Maximum Service
Typical Arrangements and Possible Improvements
Some schemes have a 40 year maximum service rule. Others deliberately provide for a higher accrual rate (explained on pages 86–7) and a shorter service maximum. So for instance the Rank Xerox scheme has a 1/50th accrual rate, with a maximum of 33 years' service to count.

Sometimes these limits will be because of the Inland Revenue rules. More usually, it is a matter of choice not necessity; the scheme has been designed with a particular level of pension in mind as the 'correct' one.

These are limitations which affect only a few people, since there aren't many of us who can stand working for the same company for 40 years or more. Where there is no Inland Revenue limit, no other limitation should be imposed.

Possible Arguments and Responses
Here you can turn to your advantage the argument that employers always use to justify treating so-called 'early leavers' unfairly. They will tell you that 'the pension scheme is intended for those who stay and are loyal to the company, not for those who leave.'

Why then should people be penalised for being too loyal to the company?

The employer may say:

- That he sees this level of pension as 'correct'. This is illogical, because many people will get below this level as they will not have worked for the company for long enough. If it is acceptable for their level of pension not to be correct, why not those who have worked longer than the 'correct' length of time? You could also suggest that if the employer is so concerned about people obtaining too much pension because they've worked too long, he could allow people who have worked the maximum number of years to retire before they reach normal retirement age, without reducing the pension at all;

- He can't afford it. But it won't cost very much, because so few people will qualify. It might cost less than giving each of them a gold watch when they retire;

- He may simply not have thought of it, or he may have misunderstood what the Inland Revenue said. This does often happen in pension negotiations. If for some reason there's a genuine doubt about how the Inland Revenue would view a change in this rule, or any other, then the employer or his specialist advisers can write and ask for advice – but it will take a while to get an answer.

Credited Years
Typical Arrangements and Possible Improvements
There are a number of ways in which you can get credit in a pension scheme for more years than you have actually been in it. Some of these are dealt with in other sections:

- Years with the company before the scheme started, or when there was a different scheme, are covered in Chapter 13 on Past Service.

- Years credited to you because you have transferred pension rights from another scheme are covered in Chapter 19 on Early Leavers.

- 'Added years' bought by making special contributions are covered in Chapter 23 on Additional Voluntary Contributions.

Another type is where years have been credited to you because you were with the employer but not the scheme, because you were too young to be allowed in, or did not have the service qualification, but were given the full 'back service' once you joined the scheme.

The justification for this is that the employer did not have the trouble of collecting and refunding small amounts of contributions for youngsters who did not stay very long, but that people can still build up a reasonable level of pension. It is preferable to bring people fully into the scheme with a minimal qualification period, but giving them backdated credits is better than nothing.

Finally, there are years added to keep up the value of your pension, because you are working shorter hours, or your earnings have dropped in real terms because of a redeployment or downgrading. It is rare to find this, but it can be useful.

At Thorn-EMI if a member suffers a reduction in earnings, for instance by losing shift premium, s/he will be given a credit that places him/her in broadly the same position as before. This credit is cancelled if earnings subsequently return to their previous level, but the basic entitlement is not reduced.

Possible Arguments and Responses

If you cannot persuade the employer to reduce the waiting period before joining, then you can argue that backdated credits at least mean that the person who sticks it out is not penalised.

On credits where the hours of work are reduced, assuming that you have already accepted in other negotiations that this may happen, you can point out that:

- Unless a special arrangement is made, people will have been contributing towards a benefit they will not in fact receive;
- They are already making a sacrifice in terms of their day-to-day wages, and should not be asked to make a further one;
- They are possibly also sacrificing part of their death benefit by reducing their real wages, and that is as far as any limitation should go (though there are ways of getting round that problem too – see the section on'Lump sum death benefits' on pages 141–5).

The employer will be arguing, as usual, cost and complication. On cost, your arguments will be about whether s/he can really afford it or not. On complication, you can suggest that if a group like Thorn-EMI, with very large numbers of sites and different pay systems, could cope with the problem, so can the average employer. S/he may say that it is all very well for the large employer, but s/he has not got the same sophisticated records system. But after all, you could reply, now that running a company is a complicated operation, perhaps s/he ought to be keeping more careful records, so that s/he has better control of costs. (This might rebound on you though. You might not want your employer to obtain too much control over the organisation of overtime or shifts.)

Even if there seems to be no likelihood that a clause like this will have to be brought into effect, it is wise to make provision for it in the rules of the scheme.

13

Past Service

None of the Acts of Parliament covering pensions say anything about backdating entitlement. The only limit is that you cannot be contracted out retrospectively. So if your employer is introducing a contracted-out scheme, and wants to credit you with previous years, s/he has to accept the fact that from 1978 to the date you are contracted out, you'll already have a State additional pension due.

What the Inland Revenue Allows

The Inland Revenue is, as usual, keen to see that your pension does not go over the two-thirds limit overall. Normally, frozen pension, and credits from previous schemes, count towards the limit. However, the Inland Revenue has relaxed its requirements a little here. Anyone can have a preserved benefit or a credit arising from a transfer from another scheme, and then earn 1/60th for every year of future service in a new scheme even if this brings their aggregate benefit to more than two-thirds.

If a scheme that reached the Inland Revenue limits gave full past service entitlement, the longest serving employees might need to have their benefits restricted, but otherwise there is unlikely to be any effect.

The Usual Position

The granting of full past service where there was no scheme before is very rare. The larger, better schemes do tend to pick up and give credit for service in previous schemes when they introduce a new scheme or take over a new company. It also usually happens when there is a privatisation.

The questions of mergers, takeovers, and privatisation is complicated, so they are all covered together in Chapter 21. Turn to that chapter if the past service you are negotiating about was in a previous company.

This chapter is divided into:
1. Credited years when there was no previous scheme, and
2. Benefits under a discontinued scheme.

Credited Years with no Previous Scheme

Typical Arrangements and Possible Improvements

Let us assume that Megaprofits PLC are persuaded to be good employers at last, and introduce a pension scheme in 1990. With a sudden fit of social conscience, they decide to atone for past neglect and give all their 50 employees, none of whom has less than 20 years' service, 20 years' credit at the full rate in the new scheme.

Wat Tyler is 55 and has worked for Megaprofits for 20 years by 1989. When he retires in 1999, he will have 30 years' worth of pension – 10 years in the scheme, and 20 years for past service.

This is the theory, at least. In practice, it is far more usual for a new scheme either to give no credit, or to give credit at a much reduced rate.

Albright and Wilson give a pension of 1/60th for each year in the scheme since 1978, and 1/100th for each year before that.

Often, when a company is introducing a new scheme, management will say that they are taking on a big enough financial commitment at the moment, and that they would prefer to 'see how things go' before giving entitlement for past service. If you accept this, make sure you return to the question in later years.

Giving past service entitlement is expensive, because the money must be paid in at current values, not the value it would have been at if the scheme had been running a few years ago. The money will not have so long to earn interest, so that more will have to be paid in for each £ of pension it is expected to get out.

But the contribution to pay for this should come entirely from the company, because it's payment of a debt they should have dealt with long ago. They can, quite legitimately, spread the cost by 'controlled funding'. This is a sort of hire purchase system, where the employer decides the total amount s/he has to pay, and then divides the bill up over 10 or 20 years. So the burden is not as enormous as the company makes out.

Past service credits benefit most those who have been with the company longest. If the company or plant is fairly new, you may not need to give them much priority. Equally, in that case they would not cost the company much to provide. On the other hand, if you have a large group of long serving members who are going out of the door with pitiful amounts, you may feel it is very important – to the extent of younger members giving up for the moment a claim for an increase in the overall pension.

The best standard is to get full past service entitlement – 1/60th in a 1/60th scheme, for instance. Though you might wish to start with this as a negotiating point, it will often not be realistic to expect agreement on it. More possible would be a half accrual rate – 120ths in a 60ths scheme, 160ths in an 80ths scheme, and so on. Don't forget, if you are increasing the current service accrual rate at any time, to ask for the past service rate to be increased too.

Even a smaller fraction is better than nothing. If the company refuses even that, you could try a phased approach. For instance, you could say that anyone retiring in the next 10 years, with 10 years' service or more, should have credits given to make their pension up to the 10 years' level. So:

- Anyone retiring now would get 10 years' full credit;
- Next year, they would get 1 year's pension and 9 years' credit;
- The year after, they'd get 2 years' pension and 8 years' credit, and so on.

This would reduce the cost, and mean that management could see an end to their commitment.

Some companies have reduced the cost in the opposite way, by limiting the rights of the members who retire in the first few years of the scheme. This is not a good idea, as it gives least to those who need it most. It should only be accepted if you can get nothing better.

Always get the credits expressed in terms of final earnings, so that they keep up with wage increases. Without this, they will be eroded by inflation in a very short time.

Possible Arguments and Responses

The argument is that it is unfair for the company to make provision for the future, without being prepared to do something for those who have already given their lives to the company. Some points to use are:

- Younger people have time ahead of them anyway to build up a pension. Those coming up to retirement age, however, will get little or nothing out of a new pension scheme for future service only, however good it is;
- If the company is prepared to put a substantial sum of money into a pension scheme, it ought not to discriminate between its employees by giving the vast bulk of the value of it to younger people;
- The pension scheme will get off to a very bad start if people who have been promised big pensions in 40 years' time see the first people to retire under the new scheme go out with miserable pittances. They will be very cynical about the scheme, and all the goodwill the company was hoping to generate by introducing it will be dissipated;
- The company obviously agrees that there is a need for the pension scheme, and that the State scheme is not adequate, or it would not be putting in a scheme at all. Surely therefore it must acknowledge that the case for a benefit for the people nearest retirement is strongest of all, because they don't even have much from the State scheme to fall back on?

The company may say:

- 'It costs too much.' As pointed out above, it must be agreed that past service is expensive. But do they appreciate the priority you're giving this point?
- 'We've got to start somewhere – we can't do everything at once.'

But people near retirement can't wait until you've got every-thing else right, and then get around to dealing with them.

- 'They can't expect a benefit now which they haven't paid for over the years.' The company has made bigger profits over the years because it hasn't had to put any of the money into a pension fund. Isn't it time it gave some of the cash back to those who made the profits for it?

Benefits Under a Discontinued Scheme

Perhaps more usual than a scheme starting off with a completely clean slate, is for the company to decide to clear up its old schemes and put everyone into a new, better one. The general tendency in the past has been to freeze the old benefits, and you will find this sort of phrase in the booklet (taken from Clancy's Ltd):

If you were a member of the pension and life assurance plan (1973) you will receive in addition the pension that has accrued to you under the existing plan in respect of your membership up to 30 September 1977.

It's often not clear from the pension scheme booklet just what has happened to the old scheme benefits, and the only way to find out may be to ask the scheme administrator.

If the benefits are frozen, this means that your entitlement is worked out, on the day when the changeover comes, as if you were leaving the company, so that your pension is preserved for you when you retire, at the level it is then. If the freezing happened before 1978, there may well be no increases at all; if after 1978, there would need to be the legal minimum increases on GMP, explained on page 164; if after 1985, there must be the other increases on the extra pension, explained on page 165.

Even now that inflation has slowed down, a frozen pension loses its value quickly. The unions did not take this on board for some years, and meanwhile many pensions were cut drastically in real terms. If your scheme has an old frozen pension it would be worth picking up the issue now, and asking for an increase. Some companies have recently used their scheme surpluses to improve the position here. Examples are Delta, Turner and Newall, and Dowty.

Ideally, when a new scheme is started, you should see that the old ones are 'bought in' and full past service credits given in return. This will mean that each member signs a form giving up his/her rights to benefits under the old scheme, and these are paid over to the new fund to help finance the credits. If you've got a good deal, make a rec-ommendation to the members, and make sure that the company gives a clear explanation, to overcome people's understandable suspi-cion of signing anything away on the company's say-so.

If the old scheme (or one of the old schemes, since you will often be dealing with several) was much worse than the new one, then the employer will usually resist giving full credit. A reasonable fallback position is to look at how much the pension built up so far for each year is worth, on average in money terms. Then turn that into the new scheme's final earnings terms.

Mike Jupp has worked 10 years for the company, and has built up an old scheme pension of £400. Under the new scheme he would have had £1,200 for the same length of time. So you can then turn his service into credits at a third of the rate being provided in the new scheme.

This would then mean a 1/240th rate in a 1/80th scheme, for example. But this should be the point at which you settle, not where you start negotiating.

Always add in a 'no worse off' clause. Someone who retires in the next few years and whose earnings have dropped sharply might be better off under the old scheme than under the new one. So the company ought to do the two calculations at least for a few years, and pay the better.

When SKF brought in a new works scheme, instead of their old arrangement, they said, 'If you joined the plan on 6 April 1978, your pension entitlement for prior continuous service will be based on 1/3rd of such service, or the following table, whichever is the better:

Years of works service prior to 6 April 1978	Minimum pension per annum
10–19	£176
20–29	£264
30–34	£352
35 or more	£440

Where the pension scheme was voluntary, you'll find it difficult to get agreement that the people who did not volunteer should be included, and your own members may resent it if they are. But if you know that the people were not genuinely given the chance to join then you should press for everyone to be included.

This could happen if, for instance, the scheme was theoretically open to both staff and works, but at a lot of sites manual workers were heavily discouraged from joining, whereas it was taken for granted that staff would. If a particular group was specifically excluded from the old scheme – such as part-timers – then they should be brought in on the same terms as those who were in already. This should be regarded as the remedying of past injustice, and there-fore should not involve any extra cost to those members.

If the old scheme was very poor, the company may say that the credits given under a new scheme would be so small it would not be worthwhile. This might apply, for instance, if it was an old flat rate scheme, giving perhaps £10 for each year of service. In that case, the least they should do is agree to increase the frozen benefit by the amount by which prices have risen since the date the scheme was frozen, and then either increase it at a fixed rate, or keep it in line with inflation. Given current levels of interest rates, this would be easy for them to do. The money will have been accumulating interest and dividends all this time, and probably built up a nice surplus which has been used to subsidise the rest of the pension scheme.

Joanna Smith has a frozen pension in the old scheme which was discontinued 10 years ago, still worth only £100 a year. The company agrees to increase it by 150%, so that it is now worth £250 a year. It then commits itself to increase it by 5% a year, so that 5 years later, when she retires, it is worth £320.

If the old scheme pensions are invested with an insurance company, there may be problems. They may take a very long time to give information, let alone make a settlement and pay money out. So long as the policy is still with them, it still counts as business.

When a settlement is reached, the insurance company may give the new pension fund a very bad deal on the 'surrender terms', just as it does if you give up a private insurance policy before the time is up. The company may try to argue that it can't afford to give a better credit for past service because of this, but there's no reason why you should suffer because of the insurance company's commercial practices. One tactic would be to try to embarrass them by asking them along to explain themselves.

Possible Arguments and Responses
The arguments given in the previous section, on credits where no scheme existed, also apply here because it will again be the older people, with long service in the old scheme, who will suffer most if they find their benefits frozen. Some other arguments to use are:

- The destruction of people's expectations. People worked for the employer, under the old scheme, on the assumption that they were going to get a particular pension benefit out of it. Maybe they paid a particular level of contribution, maybe they accepted a particular level of wages because of this. Now, without taking any action themselves, they find that the benefits have changed (and worsened). If they had left that job, to go and better themselves, that might have been fair enough. But they stuck it out, and therefore ought to be reasonably treated.
- Where you're picking up on benefits from a scheme discontinued some years ago, you can talk about the unforeseen effects of inflation. When the scheme was first closed down, it may not have looked unreasonable to freeze it completely. But since then we have had years of very high inflation. Even 6% inflation will halve the real value of benefits in 12 years. So changes in the treatment of old scheme benefits are urgent.

The answers you will get from the company will once again really be about cost, but they may be wrapped up in other ways:

- 'It's not company policy to do this.' That is, the Board have decided it would cost too much. If you've been negotiating at local level and come up against this brick wall, try to get the opportunity to put your case directly to them (see pages 217–8 for the need for central negotiations). If possible, contact people in other plants with a similar problem, and get them to make a joint approach with you;
- 'We can't make a special case of this plant.' Make clear that, unless there are genuinely special circumstances, they are not being asked to. What is being sought is a better deal for everyone in discontinued schemes, even though that raises the cost;
- If you are picking up on something that happened a few years ago, the reaction may be that 'No-one complained at the time.' This may well be true. Unions were not as interested in pensions as they should have been and employers would often not talk to them about it anyway. It may also have been during years when inflation was not seen as much of a problem. But it's not an issue that has gone away, because the frozen pensions are continuing to lose value.

If once you can get past all these arguments and get the company to agree that it should give some credit for the benefits under the discontinued scheme, then the argument is straightforwardly about how much it can afford to give.

If it is buying out several schemes, is it giving each group the right terms? If not, those who are being badly done by should have better terms, but without worsening the position of those coming off better.

Changing the Type of Scheme

With the introduction of the new types of money purchase contracted–out schemes (explained in Chapter 4), some companies are closing down their existing final earnings based pension schemes and offering people the chance to go into a new money purchase one. Credits in the new scheme are unlikely to be offered, because there are administrative complications, but even if they are, think carefully before accepting. You'd be giving up a guarantee – even if not at a very good level – for a gamble on investment results. Try instead to arrange for the preserved pension to be inflation-proofed, at a level above the legal minimum.

In negotiating a change (resisted by the unions) to a money purchase scheme, the *Daily Telegraph* management offered that all the preserved pensions in the old scheme would be increased by 5% a year compound.

14

Lump Sums on Retirement

Most pension schemes provide a lump sum on retirement, but they can do this in three different ways:

- It can be the only benefit the scheme offers;
- It can be in addition to the pension; or
- It can be on offer to those who want to commute their pension, that is, to give up part of it in order to create the lump sum.

The minimum requirements under the Social Security Pensions Act, and the maximum for the Inland Revenue's purposes, are the same in each case. So the next sections deal with them, and then the rest of the chapter is subdivided to cover the different categories.

What You Must Have

If you are contracted out, you must not commute any of the guaranteed minimum pension, or the widow's GMP. This will also apply to the 'protected rights annuity' under a Personal Pension or a COMP. The only exception to this is if the pension is trivial, which means under £2 a week, £104 a year.

Under the 1986 Social Security Act, having more than £6,000 capital stops you claiming Income Support (the new name for Supplementary Benefit). If your capital is between £3,000 and £6,000, then it's assumed that you are getting £1 income for every £250. This would include cash from a pension scheme. For Housing Benefit the capital limit is £8,000.

Any cash you get from the pension scheme is tax free, but if you invest it, the income you receive may not be.

What the Inland Revenue Allows

It is a firm rule that you must not take more than 1.5 times your final earnings or 2.25 times your pension as a lump sum, whether it comes automatically or if you have to give up some of your pension to get it. The lump sum has to be counted in with your pension to see whether you go over their two-thirds limit.

In 1987 and again in 1989 the Inland Revenue introduced some very complicated rules for calculating the maximum lump sum for anyone with less than 40 years' service in their scheme. The most complicated parts do not affect very many people, so they are only summarised here. If you need to know more, the rules are given in Inland Revenue Memorandum No 87. See Appendix One for details of their memoranda.

Briefly, the rules are that:

- The most you can have as a lump sum, if you started with your employer after 1 June 1989, is £96,300. This is 1.5 times the £64,200 limit, explained on page 36. This limit will be inflation proofed in future, in line with earnings;
- Normally, the maximum lump sum builds up at 3/80ths for each year of service in the scheme, so that if you have 40 years, you can get 120/80ths, which comes to 1.5 times earnings.

Evelyn earns £10,000 and has been in her scheme since she was 20. So she can have a lump sum of 1.5 times £10,000, which comes to £15,000.

For anyone who has not been in the scheme that long, the maximum allowed depends on when they joined it. If it was before 17 March 1987 (the date of the Budget when the Chancellor brought in these changes) then the scheme rules can allow them to build up to the 120/80ths figure after 20 years. But for those who joined later than that, it must simply be 3/80ths per year, so that someone retiring after 20 years would only be able to get 60/80ths, or three-quarters of their earnings as a lump sum. If you joined after 1 June 1989, however, the lump sum can be 2.25 times your pension.

- If your scheme gives a pension better than 1/60ths (for instance, a 1/50th scheme like the Pan Am one for its UK staff), then it's allowed to 'uplift' the maximum lump sum, for people with less than 40 years' service, by a proportionate amount. In Pan Am's case the 50th pension is 1/6th better than a 1/60th pension would have been, so the maximum is also scaled up by 1/6th. But there is a top limit still of 1.5 times your final earnings.

These changes were overriding, that is, the law changed scheme rules whether the company did so or not.

Any other cash benefit provided by the scheme (or any other scheme with the same employer), and any 'retained benefits' from another scheme, must be counted in to this total. This includes any benefit you have built up for yourself, by paying Additional Voluntary Contributions (explained on pages 194–7).

There are two exceptions to the rules. The first is for trivial pensions. A pension of £104 a year or less can be fully commuted, regardless of the amount of lump sum payable as a result.

Secondly, if you are very seriously ill, it is possible to commute the entire pension into cash. But the Inland Revenue's Notes say that this is to be interpreted narrowly, and to apply to people:

where the expectation of life is unquestionably very short, by comparison with the average for the same age and sex ... Whether a particular individual is in this position is a matter for decision by the administrator, but the inclusion of a rule on these lines in an approved scheme is accepted on condition that it will be interpreted invariably in this sense, and that adequate medical evidence will always be obtained.

Both these exceptions are only what is allowed. Whether it actually happens in any particular scheme depends on what is in that scheme's rules.

Some schemes still operate the rules under the 'Old Code' of approval. This had a different formula for the maximum commutation. You were not allowed to convert more than a quarter of your pension into a lump sum. This formula can be more restrictive, but it still occurs in some schemes which have not bothered to change it.

The Inland Revenue also control the commutation factors – that is, what lump sum you get for each pound of pension you give up. They say that an actuary can either calculate them each time the question arises, or provide the information for the pensions manager to do so. Alternatively, the scheme can use standard rates. It won't raise any question if the standard rates are £9 for each £ given up by a man of 65, and £11 for each £ given up by a woman. But if the retirement age is different from the normal one, or if people want to retire earlier, the commutation factor should also be different.

This is because what is being given away is the cost of setting up a pension for the individual. A man retiring at 65 has an expectation of life of 13 or 14 years. But to set up a pension that will see him out will not cost £14 for every £'s worth of pension, as the money put away to start with can earn interest for all the years until it is drawn out. On a rough calculation, you need to put away about £9 or £10 (depending on how much interest rates are at any time) to cover the pension. So if you give up part of the pension, that is what you get in exchange. A woman gets a higher amount, because her life expectancy is longer so each pound of pension is worth more as a lump sum. And a person retiring earlier can expect to draw the pension for longer, so again, each pound is worth more as a lump sum.

Typical Arrangements and Possible Improvements
Schemes which Give Only a Lump Sum Benefit and No Pension
There are a number of these around, some of them very poor because they are old schemes which have never been improved, others newer and rather better. They all have their limitations, though.

The basic principle so far as the employer is concerned is that, instead of providing a pension at retirement or early retirement, the scheme gives a lump sum and then has no more responsibility. This makes it simple to administer, and it can be popular with part time workers, who might not build up a worthwhile pension on the basis of their earnings.

A typical scheme of this sort would give:

- 3/80ths of final earnings for each year of service, on retirement;
- 3/80ths of final earnings for each year of actual and prospective service (the years you could have done up to 60 or 65) for anyone who has to retire early because of ill-health bad enough to prevent him/her from doing another job; and
- a death benefit, perhaps of 1.5 times final earnings.

For the member, the disadvantage of a scheme of this sort is that, because of the Inland Revenue restrictions on how much you can take as a lump sum on retirement (1.5 times final earnings), it can be pitched only at a fairly low level. In the example above, you could improve the death benefit, but nothing else if the employer insisted on paying only lump sums.

It is possible to start with this sort of scheme, and then build a full pension scheme on top.

Pilkington's began with a scheme of this type, then added a pension of 1/80th of revalued average earnings for each year of service, and contracted out two years later.

Even if they are not willing to provide a retirement pension, the employer might agree to offer a widow's/widower's pension, and a long-term disability benefit (Permanent Health Insurance, covered in Chapter 15). This is because these elements can be insured, and then the insurance company takes over all the administration, so that the company will still not be bothered by it.

There are also some schemes that give only a flat rate lump sum, unrelated to earnings. Christian Salvesen, for instance, used to give a lump sum of £50 for each year of service. With a scheme of this type, the obvious thing is to scrap it and start again, as they have done. If you can't get the company to do this, then at least try to get the lump sum linked to actual earnings, so that however much value it has lost since it was introduced, it will not now lose any more. It may be that it will need to be at a rate which gives people little or no immediate increase in benefit, to get the employer to agree to it at all. In the example given above, for instance, you might ask for half a week's earnings for each year of service. If you can't get an earnings link, you'll need to renegotiate an increase to keep up with the cost of living every year.

A cash-only scheme ought to be non-contributory, despite the disadvantages outlined on pages 80-1. It will only cost a few per cent of payroll, and if the company is collecting very small contributions from the members it will cost a lot in administration, and also mean some very small refunds. If the company insists it must be contributory, as some do, you'll need to decide whether the attractions outweigh the annoyances.

Schemes which Have a Lump Sum and a Pension
Most of the schemes in the public services, and some of those in the nationalised industries, give an automatic lump sum together with the pension.

For each year of service in local government (and the Health Service, the Civil Service and teaching), you get a pension of 1/80th of your earnings, plus a lump sum of 3/80ths of earnings.

The Inland Revenue and the actuaries assume that 1/80th plus 3/80ths lump sum is of the same value as a 1/60th scheme. There's no particular advantage to this method as opposed to the private sector system. It's simply a pattern that has grown up. If anything, there's the disadvantage that inflation-proofing applies only to the pension, not the lump sum, and the pension is smaller than it would otherwise be, and so are the dependants' pensions.

It is possible under most public service scheme rules to turn a lump sum back into pension – but very few people ever do so.

There are also some schemes where the remains of an old lump sum scheme, on a flat rate basis, have been added to a final earnings scheme. The Cookson Group Works Plan, for instance, gives a pension plus a cash sum of £10 for each year of service. Try to get this lump sum linked to actual earnings, as explained on page 117.

Lump Sums for which you Give up Part of Your Pension
Very few schemes say in their booklets that they allow full commutation for triviality or ill-health, but in fact many do have these clauses in their rules. The trustees need to check that they are being implemented where appropriate.

What the member who commutes his/her pension gives up can vary considerably.

Pension increases, and widows', widowers' and dependants' pensions, should be based on the whole pension, not the commuted amount. If commuting affects more than the size of pension you start out with, it's poor value for money. It is possible, though, to have special commutation factors which take account of the loss on pension increases. The scheme for the trade union GMB does this, for example.

People who retire earlier than the scheme's normal retirement date should be given a larger lump sum for each pound they give up, than people who reach the full term, because what they give up is more valuable. Some companies have tried to get away with giving the same amount whatever age you are.

Ford Motor Company put in a huge programme of early retirements for people aged between 55 and 65 during the 1980s, and commuted all pensions, whatever the member's age, at the rate of £9 for each £1 given up. The pension fund profited substantially from this. In 1987 the union took it up with them, and pointed out that a fair figure would be £12 for each pound of pension for a man of 60, and £15 for a man of 55, but the company refused to make any change.

Occasionally, a scheme booklet says that you must have the employees' or trustees' consent before you can commute pension. This is paternalist, and needs opposing.

Possible Arguments and Responses

Unless the employer is using unfair commutation factors (as in the Ford example) this is not an area where the cost factor matters very much. The Inland Revenue formula has been more generous than the strict actuarial factors at some times, less so at other times, but not by very much either way. A change in the commutation rates would not usually be regarded as significant enough to alter the costing of the scheme. What other objections can employers have to commutation?

- Paternalism: 'The workers won't know what's best for them, and will go out and spend it on the Derby favourite.' Point out that you are talking about 65 year olds, not 6 year olds. If the employer thinks the workers are so stupid, why has he been employing them all these years?

- Inertia: the pension scheme administrator does not want to go through the bother of changing the rules. It's true that rule changes are a nuisance, and if this were the only rule needing change the administrator might have a point. But with recent alterations in the law, and with the other improvements you will be looking for, it won't be the only change, so he or she might as well put a batch through at once.

15

Retirement Ages, Early and Late Retirement

Since all these issues hang together, it makes sense to cover them in one chapter. However, although the Inland Revenue and DSS rules on ill-health retirement are dealt with here, the details of what to look for in your own scheme come in the next chapter, along with Permanent Health Insurance.

The question of what benefits the State gives on early or late retirement was covered on pages 11–12.

Normal Retirement Ages

What a Scheme Must Have
Any pension scheme must have a fixed 'normal retirement age' under the Inland Revenue rules. This can vary for different categories of people. If a scheme is contracted out, then whatever the scheme's normal retirement age, it must be able to guarantee that at the State retirement age of 65 for men, 60 for women, either the GMP or a pension based on the minimum contributions will be payable (though this rule is to be made more flexible shortly).

What the Inland Revenue Allows
The Inland Revenue will let a scheme have a normal retirement age of anywhere between 60 and 70 for men, 55 and 70 for women, without creating any problems. If a scheme has a lower retirement age, they will look at it specifically and may restrict the benefits.

As explained in pages 30–2, the Sex Discrimination Act 1986 says that employers cannot compel women to retire at an earlier age than men. So if everybody in the company automatically retires at age 60, women have no new rights. But if men are made to retire and then offered new short-term contracts, or are not made to retire at all, then since November 1987 the employer has been breaking the law.

The Act, however, only covers the retirement age from employment. The law on offering early retirement, and on redundancy, and on pension ages as opposed to retirement ages, was left unchanged. It's now been amended again, to even up the rules on redundancy.

It's currently almost impossible for an employer to be certain what is legal and what is not. A woman and a man working at the same job after the age of 60 will generally not be getting the same 'pay', so the employer may be breaking European law. Often the woman's pension will be building up at a different rate (as explained below, page 133) and she may not be paying contributions any more.

The various options open to employers all create legal difficulties. They'll create least problems if they set retirement age at 60 for both sexes, and amend the pension rules so that men acquire full pension rights at that age.

Some employers have thought about changing the pension scheme rules, so that women could not draw a full pension before 65. But there's a general assumption in European law that people should not be made worse off when a law is brought into effect. And many scheme trust deeds also say that rights already acquired must not be cut back. The unions would anyway oppose this change, and there would be a case for challenging such an employer in court.

The Contractual Position

Most contracts of employment specify the retirement age, and an employer cannot worsen your terms of employment without your agreement. So for existing employees, contract law means that the age at which you are compelled to retire must remain the one agreed when you start, unless you consent to the change.

This right, though, is weaker than it might seem. First, you can consent to a change simply by not protesting about it at the time. If the employer spelt it out clearly to you, and made clear that it would apply when you came to retire, then it's doubtful that an industrial tribunal would accept that you need only protest years later, when retirement was upon you. You need to object when the change is announced, not later.

Second, an employer can always alter a contract by dismissing the workers, and offering re-employment to everyone who is willing to accept the new terms. In most cases employers who do this offer a lump sum compensation payment to everyone affected, and thus 'buy out' the old terms. But if the employer wants to get tough, and enforce the changes on the workforce, then if you go to court for unfair dismissal you may well only get a basic award, which is a pretty low amount.

So if the employer tries to change the retirement age without altering the pension scheme in an acceptable way (De la Rue tried this for instance, for their hourly paid workers in 1987), the steps to take are:

- Get all those affected to write letters to the company as soon as possible, making clear that they do not consent to the change. If possible, get legal advice before drafting these letters, but if this is going to be delayed, go ahead anyway;
- Make clear to the company that you are not against the change in retirement age as such, but wish to negotiate better pension terms.

Typical Arrangements and Possible Improvements
Approximately 69% of men are in schemes with a retirement age of 65 for men, and 74% of women are in schemes with a retirement age

of 60 for women. For works schemes, the figures are 94% and 89% – so the schemes with lower retirement ages are mainly those that include white collar staff.

The goal of most unions is a retirement age of 60 for both sexes, but very few manual schemes have achieved this. Some that have got part of the way are:

ICI Staff	62 for both sexes
Albright and Wilson	62 for both sexes
Imperial Group	60 for both sexes

The reaction of some employers to the Sex Discrimination Act has in fact been the opposite – to raise the retirement age for women to 65. Bass Charrington, for instance, has done this. Others have tried to split the difference, and impose a new retirement age of 62 or 63 for both sexes.

But the 'normal' retiring age cannot be looked at on its own; you must also consider the possibilities of early retirement. British Gas, for instance, has in theory an equal retirement age of 65 for men and women. But this hides the fact that there is a 'decade of retirement' between ages 55 and 65, and people can retire as early as 55 without any reductions in their pension, in certain cases.

Lowering the retirement age is expensive. Just how much it costs in any case depends on the proportion of men to women in the payroll.

If there are already generous terms for early retirements, the actuary will have assumed in his/her calculations anyway that most people will take the offer up. So turning this into a universal benefit will not cost very much more.

If you can't achieve a reduced retirement age for everyone, it may be possible to move towards it in other ways. These are dealt with in the section on voluntary early retirement (page 125). Even if you think it unlikely that you will achieve a reduction in men's retirement age, you might want to include it in your claim each time, to show it is not forgotten.

Possible Arguments and Responses
It is union and TUC policy that men's retirement age for the State pension should be brought down to 60. But the government says that this would cost too much.

Instead, what has happened is that the employers, because of their wish to cut the workforce, have themselves been retiring people earlier. On page 42 there was a quote from the National Association of Pension Funds about the advantages of early retirements to an employer.

Only about half the men over the age of 60 are now 'economically active' – which means they are working or looking for work. Many of these 'early retired' people are quite well off, because they are white collar workers from good pension schemes with a normal retirement age earlier than the State one. Others have been given good retirement packages by the employer in order to get them to leave, since this is a much softer option than enforced redundancy. But a large group of older unemployed men are very badly off, because they have been made to go without any special treatment, or their plant or office has closed and they have been unable to get another job.

The new Sex Discrimination Act, and the European Court cases, mean that employers find it difficult to be certain what is legal and what is not in this area, as explained on pages 30–2. What ought to happen is that the government reaches agreement with all the interested groups – unions, employers, and pensioners' groups – to phase in an equal retirement age of 60 for men and women, but this seems unlikely to happen. If we want a male retirement age of 60, we cannot sit back and wait for it to come from the State. We must set out to achieve it in our employers' pension schemes.

Other arguments to use are:

- What's good enough for the bosses is good enough for you. The management with whom you are negotiating is quite likely to have a male retirement age of 60 in its 'top hat' pension scheme (that is, a scheme restricted to directors and very senior management). It would certainly be helpful to find out;
- If there have been large numbers of early retirements anyway over the years, with the management choosing who should go to suit its purposes, it is fairer and better industrial relations practice to regularise this by changing the rule for everyone;
- There might be advantages in productivity you can point to, especially if the job is heavy. Retiring people at 60 may push down costs in other areas.

What the Employer Will Say

- 'Why should I be more progressive than the State?' The justification employers use for a pension scheme is to fill the gaps left by the State, and this is one such gap – just like the death benefit, where State provision was always poor and has now been abolished altogether except for a means-tested benefit.
- 'We'll wait until the State makes us do it.'

Why? A progressive employer doesn't wait until s/he's forced by legislation to do something. If it is advantageous, he or she will do it anyway.

However, because of the State's refusal to move, one point that does need considering is how to fill in the financial gap for people who are retiring from the employment before they can have a pension from the State. This is covered in detail on pages 127–8.

Early Retirement

What You Must Have

The Social Security Pensions Act does not lay down any minimum rules for early retirement under contracted-out schemes. If you retire early because of ill-health, and are entitled to an invalidity pension, then you'll always be treated as if your scheme does not give a pension under those conditions. You'll therefore be given by the State an earnings-related addition to your invalidity benefit. If on top of that you get the benefit from your employer's scheme, the State does not want to know.

If you retire early for any other reason, the State treats you as unemployed. It can penalise people heavily for taking voluntary retirement; see page 11 for details of this.

A contracted–out scheme has to guarantee that if someone retires early, the GMP they would have been due as an early leaver will be paid when they reach State Pensionable Age. How this was worked out was explained on pages 164–5. A scheme can do this in one of three ways:

* Paying as early retirement pension only the amount over and above what was needed to pay the GMP at 60 or 65;
* Restricting the cases in which an early retirement pension is paid, so that if there is only enough in the scheme to cover the escalated GMP, or not even enough, then the person cannot get an early retirement pension at all;
* Paying the pension that the person is entitled to at the date of early retirement, and guaranteeing to increase it when s/he reaches 60 or 65.

The third method is best for the member, but the first and second have slipped into many schemes unnoticed.

The liability for widow's GMP remains the same.

The rules on this are due to change under legislation currently on its way through Parliament.

What the Inland Revenue Allows

The Inland Revenue makes a distinction between early retirement at your own or the employer's request, and early retirement due to ill health, which Practice Note 10.6 defines as:

physical or mental deterioration which is bad enough to prevent an individual from following his normal employment, or which seriously impairs his earning capacity. It does not mean simply a decline in energy or ability.

For anyone who fits into this definition, the scheme is allowed to give a pension based on his/her pensionable earnings at the date when s/he retires, and on all his/her actual and potential service. Someone retiring because of incapacity is also entitled to calculate their maximum lump sum (whether automatic or through commutation) on the basis of actual plus potential service. S/he is also entitled to continue the life assurance up to the normal retirement date.

Sheona York is 55, and has been in the pension scheme 15 years. When she has a heart attack and has to retire, she is allowed, under the Inland Revenue rules, to get a pension based on 15 years' actual service plus the five years she could have done up to her retirement date at the age of 60. So that is 20 altogether. She can also calculate her lump sum on the basis of 20 years' service.

The 1989 Budget changed the rules so that anyone retiring between the ages of 50 and 75, for any reason, with 20 or more years service, could take a full 2/3rds pension; but employers had to continue to finance their schemes on the assumption that people would still retire at the scheme's normal retirement age. From 1992 onwards, under the 1989 Social Security Act, pensions on compulsory early retirement will have to be equal between men and women. Two current court cases with the European court, Barber and Clarke, may extend this new rule further.

Any payment made under a pension scheme need not be set against payments made under a redundancy scheme, for tax and other purposes. It can, however, affect your rights to unemployment benefit or Income Support.

Retirement 'at the Member's Own Request'
Typical Arrangements and Possible Improvements
Many schemes provide only the minimum on this. They'll say that you must take a pension based on the service you have actually done, minus an amount for early payment. The justification for this is that:

- The pension will be paid for longer, so the same amount of money must be spread thinner;
- Since the pension is being paid earlier, it will have less time to build up interest. So more money will have to be used up to provide the same level of pension.

One trend has been for companies to say that there will be no reduction in the pension for people over a certain age. Swan Hunter, for instance, say that there will be no reduction for male members retiring between the ages of 60 and 65. This is, the booklet says, 'for an initial period of 5 years from the start of the Scheme' – presumably because by then management hope to have brought staffing levels down to where they want them.

Sometimes there is a clause saying that you can take early retirement on special terms if you have had a specific number of years' service.

The Local Government scheme has a retirement age of 65 for both men and women. But it allows people to retire between 60 and 65, with no reduction in their pension, if they have 25 years' service or more.

There are two ways of calculating the amounts (sometimes called 'factors') by which the pension is reduced:
The first, and the most usual these days, is the 'straight line' method in which the pension is reduced by the same percentage for

each month or year of early retirement. The no-cost level is about 0.5% a month or 6% a year, so someone retiring ten years early would have his/her pension reduced by 60%. Many schemes now use this method, but reduce by less than the full amount. De La Rue's staff scheme, for instance, reduces by 4% for each year, if the member is under 60.

The second method is to use an 'actuarial scale'. This gives the precise amount for each year by which the pension must be reduced, to give the same actuarial value.

Ofrex Group, for instance, reduces the pension to:

- for someone retiring 1 year early   91%
- for someone retiring 2 years early   82%
- for someone retiring 3 years early   73%
- for someone retiring 4 years early   67%

The result is a very heavy reduction at the top end, as you can see, and is generally worse at all ages.

Better than standard terms for early retirement are one way of moving towards shorter working lives. They allow people with long service with the company to go early without being penalised. It is expensive, however.

Many actuaries will assume that giving these terms will cost the same as giving a reduced age for normal retirement, as everyone who has the chance will take it. But this may not be quite correct. People with small pensions will not be able to afford to retire even if they want to.

Very often, employers give much worse terms for voluntary early retirement than for retirement at the employer's request, and may also say that the employer must always consent. This is not satisfactory – it allows the employer to manipulate the members' working lives. If a generous early retirement pension is affordable when it suits the employer, it should be affordable when it suits the worker as well.

The Inland Revenue's new maximum, of retirement at any age from 50 with a full pension, is going to be very difficult to achieve. A more limited claim might be:

- That men retiring between the ages of 60 and 65, and women between the ages of 55 and 60, should have no actuarial reduction made;
- That where an actuarial reduction is made, it should be at 3% or 2% at most;
- That the actuarial reduction should be calculated for the next, rather than the last, birthday.

If you are in an integrated scheme (see pages 90–2) make sure that there is no deduction to take account of the State pension until it is actually being paid. The lawyers are currently saying that this will be legal despite the Social Security Act 1989 (explained on page 32) so long as the unequal pensions start before 60 and stop at State retirement age. If this turns out to be dubious or wrong, it gives you a lever to use against integrated schemes.

The lump sum death benefit should be continued during early retirement, or at least for those going at the employer's request. If you cannot get it continued until members reach State retirement age, at least try to get it for the first two years, so that they have time to make their own arrangements.

Any early retirement option should be equally open to men and women. It's a widespread practice to offer it only to men over 60. This is legal as British law stands at present, but unfair, and should not be accepted.

There is a danger that good early retirement provisions will be misused by local management. They may pressurise people coming up to 55 or 60 to take early retirement of their own accord, rather than offer the more expensive option of special terms under a redundancy programme. Borderline cases can also be pushed unreasonably into taking early retirement 'at their own request' when they should really be taking ill-health retirement. The shop stewards' committee, or any special pensions committee you have, should monitor this point.

Filling in the State Pension Gap

Because the State does not regard 'retirement' as happening except at State retirement ages, people going early cannot receive the State pension, and so they will have a shortfall in what they expected to live on. There are two main ways in which schemes fill this gap:

- Some offer a 'levelling out' option. Ford, for instance, allows men to retire with a full pension at 62. The scheme says that the member may choose to reduce the pension that will be paid after State retirement age and increase the pension paid in the three years beforehand. But this means that the member is gambling on his own life expectancy. If he lives for a long time, the value of the cutback in pension will far outweigh the value of the extra benefit gained in those few years.
- The alternative is to offer a 'supplement', on top of the pension, to help fill in the gap in those years. This may not be allowed after 1992, but you could ask for the supplement to be paid at age 60 to anyone (man or woman) not receiving a full State pension.

Early Retirement or Reduction in Retirement Age?

Good early retirement terms are likely to cost nearly as much as a reduction in retirement age overall. They do have the advantage, though, of greater flexibility. There is no point in saying that everyone must go at 60, if it means that large numbers of people will be pushed into poverty because their pensions are not big enough. If you say people are allowed to retire at 60, those with pensions big enough to

live on will do so, but others will stay on. British Gas, for instance,
have accepted this argument and designed their scheme to allow a
'decade of retirement' between 55 and 65, so that people have an
individual choice.

Redundancy Retirement or Retirement 'at the Employer's Request'

Until the last few years, the last thing anyone thought about sorting
out in a redundancy situation was the pension. Now it is often the
first, because management know that if they offer a generous early
retirement scheme, it will be popular with the older workers and the
union will not be able to resist it. So they may be able to avoid the
need for compulsory redundancies altogether.

In the public sector, there have been long-standing arrangements
in the pension scheme for redundancy. British Gas, for instance, says
that:

> If your job becomes redundant and you have
> (a) completed 10 years' service
> (b) reached age 50 or over
> you will receive an immediate pension calculated as for normal
> retirement but subject to the minimum pension calculation as in
> ill-health [which gives some credit for prospective service].
>
> If however you have completed 10 years' service and are compul-
> sorily retired because of redundancy between the ages of 45 and 50
> you have the option to take a reduced deferred pension payable at
> age 50.

One company in the private sector that has a section on redundancy written into its scheme booklet is Albright and Wilson. This
says:

> If you are declared redundant aged 50 or over you will have the
> option to take an immediate or a deferred pension.
>
> The immediate pension will be as [for voluntary early retirement]
> except that the deduction in respect of the Lower Earnings Limit
> will not be made until you reach Normal Retirement Age.

Other companies have policies on how the pension scheme deals
with redundancies, but do not publicise them except at the sites
where the issue arises, or at times when they want to get rid of staff.
Sometimes they run a 'special offer' for a year or so at a time. Lucas
Industries, for instance, did this in 1987-8.

Many companies claim that they prefer to deal with the issue when
it comes along. This has the same drawbacks in the pension scheme
as it does on severance or redundancy pay in general. If you don't get
the broad framework set out in advance, you tend to be in a much
weaker position when redundancies turn up.

Proper redundancy provisions in a pension scheme are expensive,
and they tend to fall on the company all at one time, if for instance

there is a plant closure. But part of the point of them, as well as looking after the individual better if s/he loses a job, is to deter management from reducing staffing levels where we can.

There is, however, the opposite view that having any sort of redundancy scheme in existence gives management an easier ride. Only you can decide which view you agree with.

If you decide not to negotiate until there is a proposal for early retirement or redundancy from management, then – given the length of time that anything to do with pensions takes – you'll need to move quickly. It should happen at the same time as talking about the redundancy money, but separately.

The guidelines below are drawn up with negotiating in advance in mind. But you can also use them if you're negotiating at the time of the redundancy.

Points to Look Out For

- Anyone over 50 made redundant should be allowed to take an early retirement pension without any loss of severance or redundancy pay, and should be allowed to commute the maximum amount that the OPB and the Inland Revenue will allow (remembering that the GMP must remain as a pension).
- There should be no minimum service qualification for the early retirement option.
- The pension should be calculated on the same basis as for ill-health early retirement. That is, it should take account of actual and prospective service. If you can't get that for everyone, suggest that it should apply at the oldest ages. At least, the pension should be based on the actual years done, without any reduction for early payment.
- Life assurance should continue for everyone made redundant or taking early retirement, whatever their ages, up to State retirement age. The company will be able to arrange for coverage at a reduced price, from the insurance company they do the normal pension business with. This will have to be based on the member's earnings at the time of leaving, and you may need to agree that it lasts only for a limited time – say, two years – or that it ceases if the member gets another job.

Deferred pensions, for those too young to take the early retirement pension, must also be looked at. This is covered in Chapter 19, under 'Early Leavers'.

Under the Redundancy Payments Act, the employer is allowed to reduce the statutory redundancy payments of people within 12 months of retirement, and to offset pension payments against redundancy pay. But he does not have to do these things – so don't let him.

Advice and Information

It's important that those going know what is happening, and have proper advice about what to do. As early as possible, they should be given an estimate of:

- What their deferred pension would be;
- What their early retirement pension would be;
- How much they can commute into a lump sum;
- What refund of contributions, if any, is available;
- The amount of a transfer payment as an alternative to the deferred pension.

Full details may not be available until after they finish work, but should be passed on as soon as possible after that.

Everyone should have the chance of an interview with the pensions administrator, or an independent consultant, several weeks before they go. This should be on site, and in the company's time. It should not be a sales job for one particular option, or for any particular use of the money. If the company uses an outsider, such as an insurance broker, it will need monitoring to make sure that he or she is not suggesting the member invest the money in something that is not appropriate, but pays them high commission.

In principle, the extra cost of redundancy retirements should be met not by the pension fund, but by the company making a special payment into it. In practice, what has happened over the last few years is that companies have made use of their actuarial surpluses for this, and have argued that it is really at their cost, because they could otherwise be taking a contribution holiday. The most well-known example is that of the Mirror Group; when Robert Maxwell took over he used £70m of the pension fund to give generous early retirements to those he would otherwise have made redundant.

Possible Arguments and Responses

Management objections to redundancy rules within a pension scheme will be on grounds of cost. They may say that they don't want to make a commitment which, if there were a large number of redundancies, they would find it difficult to sustain. Once an item is written into the pension scheme, it can't be repudiated by management. It's then up to the scheme administrators to do what the rules say.

Management may say that:

- It would be unfair to treat one group of employees more favourably than any other. They may say this would be 'at the expense of the pension scheme'. But since the cost of the provisions should be met by the company not by the scheme, this argument is quite unreal.
- They want to retain their freedom of action, and if you make the cost of a future redundancy programme too great, you might find the company being liquidated completely. The weight to give this sort of argument will depend on your knowledge of the

company. Are they trigger happy types, threatening closure every ten minutes, or do they only say things when they mean them?

If you're negotiating when management have already put a package on the table, they will almost certainly have done a detailed costing already, and be balancing it against the cost of other parts of the redundancy package. It may be difficult to get them to change their minds, especially if members are clamouring to be allowed to take up the option.

If you achieve something good in this area, and especially if it is an agreement at local level:

- Let stewards in other parts of the same company know; and
- Tell the union head office.

Late Retirement

Women, as explained on pages 29–31, now have the right to work on until 65, if men in the company are also allowed to do so. But if the pension scheme still retains their retirement age as 60, anyone who does so will be treated as a late retiree. So too will any man who retires after his retirement age – but it is rare now for people to do so, unless they are very senior management.

What the Inland Revenue Allows
The Inland Revenue now says that you can take a pension of 2/3rds of your final earnings at any age up to 75. (Once you reach 75 you have to draw the pension, even if you continue working.) If your pension under the scheme rules comes to less than 2/3rds, you can go on building up extra years.

Alternatively, the scheme can freeze the pension at normal retirement age, and base it on your earnings at retirement age. They can then increase it either by an actuarial factor, or by the increase in the cost of living, whichever is the greater. The standard 'actuarial factor' accepted by the Inland Revenue without question is 7.5% a year, but others can also be arranged.

If someone dies in service after normal retirement date, s/he can have either the benefits given for death in service (explained in Chapter 17) or s/he can be treated as having retired the day before their death.

You are also allowed to 'retire' and draw your pension but carry on working, or to draw your lump sum benefit while leaving the rest of the pension in the scheme. If you do this, though, you cannot have any more as a lump sum when you do come to retire.

You don't pay National Insurance contributions any more once you reach State retirement age. So you are not technically 'contracted out' of SERPS either. Your GMP increases by just over 7% for each year that you postpone your retirement beyond State pension age, just as your basic pension does.

However the Social Security Act 1989 will mean that death benefits have to be the same for men and women of the same age. This can only be achieved if those working on after the scheme's retirement age are still covered for the death benefit at the full rate.

Typical Arrangements and Possible Improvements
If your pension continues to build up, you will probably also continue to pay contributions like anyone else. On the other hand, if the pension is frozen and increased by a percentage each year, you normally stop paying contributions.

In recent years, freezing the pension and increasing it by the standard 7.5% has given about the same result as if your earnings had increased in line with the national average. If your employer has given smaller pay increases, therefore, a late retiree could have done better from the frozen than the continuing pension. It also gives the person better value for money, since they are no longer paying contributions. But other members may resent this, especially if they would have preferred to see men's retirement age lowered rather than women allowed to work on, and it may be seen as fairer for a late retiree to continue to pay contributions like anyone else.

There are considerable problems about equal treatment of men and women under the 1989 Social Security Act. The best option is to give people the choice of methods, but to ensure that they are properly explained at the time.

People who want to take the lump sum at their normal retirement date, and carry on working, should be allowed to do so. But they should be made aware that there will be no more to come when they do retire.

16

Ill-Health Early Retirement

Typical Arrangements and Possible Improvements
The NAPF 1989 Survey showed that 35% of scheme members were given the Inland Revenue maximum allowed for retirement on health grounds. Permanent Health Insurance (explained on pages 136–40) schemes were much more common for staff than works members. There are still many hourly paid members who, however ill they are, are treated by the scheme in exactly the same way as if they were retiring early of their own free will.

There are some schemes with good benefits around. Swan Hunter, for instance, says that

> Provided that adequate medical evidence is produced, your immediate pension is based on your pensionable service to normal retirement age and final pensionable salary at the date of ill-health retirement, without reduction for early payment.

Some schemes give half, rather than full, prospective service. ICI, for instance, do this for people with ten years' service or more; for those with less service, the rules are tougher.

The public sector has a pattern of its own. The Civil Service, local government, the NHS, and teachers all give a partially increased pension for members who have completed five years' service, calculated as:

- Service between 5 and 10 years is doubled;
- Service between 10 and 13 1/3rd years is made up to 20 years;
- Service over 13 1/3rd years has 6 2/3rds years added.

In each case, the addition must not increase service to more than 40 years or beyond age 65.

Some schemes have a two tier definition of incapacity. Pilkingtons, for instance, is far more generous to those with permanent total disablement than to those with simple ill-health. However, this creates borderline cases, and gives the trustees the nasty role of sitting in judgement.

Other schemes give only what they would give in any other early retirement. The AI Welders' scheme says:

> If you are permanently unfit to work because of ill-health or serious accident you may retire early and receive an immediate pension. This will be calculated as for a normal early retirement pension but will be reduced because it is being paid early.

133

There is usually a clause in the rules saying that the pension can be 'augmented' (that is, increased) in cases of particularly bad health. If you press for an improvement in the general provision, you may be told that it's not necessary as the trustees always look sympathetically at difficult cases. If this is true, it would cost no more to put it fully into the rules.

However carefully the rules are drawn up, this is an area where the trustees will always have to exercise their judgement. They will have to decide whether a particular case does or does not fulfil the definitions.

Improving this provision is not very expensive, unless your company has a particularly bad health record. For the average company it would cost round about 0.5%. Smaller companies may be wary of it, because the potential cost of a young person struck down by a serious disease can be huge. This can be dealt with by insuring against the risk; however, the increase in AIDS-related illnesses means that the cost estimates are rising sharply at present. Insurance companies may want to exclude AIDS-related illnesses altogether, so that no benefit would be payable in these instances.

This is not acceptable. If the scheme cannot get insurance to cover these cases, then it should carry the cost itself. It is no good having a scheme which claims to protect you against serious risks, if it ducks out of paying when the actual event arises. The negotiating aim should be a pension based on all actual plus prospective service, without a service qualification. If you can't get that, the first concession would be allowing a service qualification to creep in. This would affect comparatively few people. It is mainly older people, who would often have been with the company quite a while, who need to retire early because of ill-health.

The service clause tends to be included because of the pension administrators' usual fear of being taken advantage of. But seriously ill people are in no position to shop around and choose a company that has a good pension benefit that they can collect the day after they have started.

Other points to watch are:

- The company may insist on a definition of incapacity more rigorous than the Inland Revenue's. They may, for instance, say that you can't have a pension if you are fit to do any job, regardless of whether or not there's a suitable job they can move you to. The more restrictive the wording, the fewer people will be eligible, and the less the scheme will cost.
- It is possible to arrange that someone who can only take part time employment, because of disability, can get a part pension. This can be helpful, but you do need to make sure that it is being properly administered and not abused.
- Any increases in pensions in payment should also be given to early retirees.

- The administration of ill-health pensions needs to be carefully monitored by the unions. It is not unknown for senior managers to be retired early 'due to ill-health' when the company has really decided that it doesn't want them in the job. If they don't in fact qualify, that's an abuse of the scheme, and will cost the pension fund money which could be used for other members. If the company wants to retire someone and make a special payment into the fund, then it's open to them to do so.
- At the other end of the scale, are the ordinary members who might qualify getting proper information? Are workers who have taken a lot of time off because of sickness being pressured to leave, rather than retire early? Do local management, who will be the first 'official' point of enquiry, know the conditions?
- The company may say that anyone seeking early retirement on account of ill-health must have an examination by the company doctor in addition to evidence from their GP. This is fair enough, as GPs' diagnoses do vary a good deal in quality, but the doctor doing the examination should be someone you can trust, and should be responsible to the trustees, not the company. There ought to be a clearly laid down procedure in cases of dispute. This might allow for an examination by an independent consultant, paid for by the employer.
- The life assurance should continue, at the rate it was when the member took early retirement. Someone who's had to retire sick will find it virtually impossible to get private life assurance at all, let alone at a price s/he can afford.

Possible Arguments and Responses
The general arguments here are:

- The whole idea of a pension scheme is to protect you and your dependants against the time when you cannot work. This might be because you are too old, which is a foreseeable event, or because of an unforeseeable event like death in service. Serious ill-health is a similar unforeseeable event, and ought to be treated as such within the pension scheme, by giving reasonably generous benefits.
- Equity. It is not in anyone's interest to put a premium on death. But unless you have a decent ill-health pension, the family of the person who just *doesn't* die in a car crash, but is an invalid for the rest of his/her life, will be much worse off than the family of the person who does die. They will at least have the death benefit, and probably a widow/er's pension. This is a cruel and illogical situation.
- One of the justifications for having a private pension scheme is to fill in the gaps in the State scheme. Although the State scheme does give some recognition of long-term invalidity, it's not satisfactory – and will get worse as the benefits of SERPS are reduced.

The employer's response will probably concentrate first on cost. But as pointed out above, it is not a very expensive benefit, because the numbers who have a really large number of years' credits – because they are young when they fall ill – are very small.

They'll also raise the possibility of abuse. Especially if there has been what s/he regards as bad experience with the sick pay scheme, the employer may well suggest that 'too many people will take advantage of it'. If you are ready to agree to the safeguard of a genuinely independent medical examination, this should be enough. If the company is afraid that the trustees will not do a proper job, and be a 'soft touch', it should say so, and provide evidence.

Management may also have a feeling about differentials. One of the long established traditions of British industry is that if anything drastic happens to managerial staff, they are looked after, whereas for manual workers and lower grade clerical staff, it's just too bad. There's still a habit in some companies of sacking manual workers who are off sick for long. Management may therefore not want to erode the difference in status. If you think this is behind their reluctance to improve in this area, bring it out into the open and ask them directly to justify it. The union attitude is that any differential should be in terms of pay, and not extended to conditions of employment like this.

Permanent Health Insurance

A 'group permanent health insurance' scheme is, in effect, a long-term sickness scheme. (It's nothing to do with BUPA or private hospital treatment.) It provides an income for anyone who is too ill to work, after a certain length of time, for as long as s/he is ill. Payment can continue even if that person is taken off the employing company's payroll, and even if the company goes out of business. Normally under a PHI scheme, the sick individual will be paid benefit until s/he reaches retirement age. Then s/he will be transferred to the company's pension scheme.

The 'permanent' in the title means permanent as far as the insurer is concerned. Once an insurance company has accepted a contract for a PHI scheme, it has to go on providing the benefits for as long as the employer is paying the premiums, even if it is making a massive loss on the deal. The premiums do not stay the same however, so an insurance company wanting to get rid of an employer can push them up and up. But the insurers cannot cancel the contract (the employer can), and anyone already on their books for benefit would remain so. According to a 1988 survey, 109,000 'establishments' (workplaces) were covered by PHI at that time.

What the Inland Revenue Allows

Whereas pensions have the Superannuation Funds Office to themselves, PHI is dealt with by the ordinary taxperson who handles the rest of the company's affairs. It's possible therefore to get different rulings on tax treatment in different parts of the country. But if a peculiar ruling is given, the insurance company can generally sort it out with the Inland Revenue head office.

A PHI scheme is usually non-contributory for the employee. The employer gets tax relief on the premium. The benefit paid to you can come through the employer. It's then taxed as earned income under PAYE, with National Insurance contributions deducted. Alternatively, it can come direct to you from the insurance company. In that case, you get a 'tax holiday' (you don't pay any tax on it) for the first tax year, and it is then treated as unearned income.

Typical Arrangements

PHI schemes have a standard pattern, arranged by the insurance companies. These are not regulations, but if you ask for anything different in your scheme, you are most unlikely to find an insurance company offering it.

The standard pattern is:

- After someone has been off sick for a specific period of time (3 or 6 months are the most common periods), s/he will be transferred to the PHI scheme, which will pay a proportion of earnings as long as the person is incapable of work. Some schemes define this as meaning 'any work', others as incapable of doing 'your job'. The second alternative is more expensive. It means people won't be transferred to light work, so there will be more claims.

  The proportion is often 50%, occasionally 66%. There will always be a restriction so that you do not receive more than 75% of your actual earnings before you fell sick. In calculating this, the benefit is added together with the State scheme benefit or income from any other source, such as accident insurance scheme. This is supposed to encourage people to go back to work. The insurance companies say privately that it is management they tend to have trouble with, 'malingering' more than manual workers. Some schemes take into account just the single person's State benefit, others their dependants' benefit as well.

- The benefit may increase each year by a percentage, or it may not. The cost is higher if it does. A typical rate of increase would be 3% a year.

- The scheme may pay the pension fund contributions in addition to the benefit paid out to the member, or they may be taken out of the member's benefit. Again, the premium will be higher for the first alternative.

- Most schemes provide for 'partial disability' benefit. This means that, if the person is able to do some job, but it is worse paid than his/her previous one, s/he will get a reduced benefit to make up his/her earnings to the 'target level'.

- There will be a list of exclusions. That is, no benefit will be payable if the disablement is the result of, for instance (using the sort of words they would use)
  intentional self-inflicted injury
  intemperance or drug addiction
  war, invasion, riot or civil commotion
  (most recently) AIDS.

When they first started in this country PHI schemes had much longer lists of exclusions. Since then, experience has shown that most of them are more trouble to the insurers than they are worth, and many of them have been dropped. One that is still common is pregnancy. Some schemes exclude any illness or disablement resulting from pregnancy or childbirth; others impose an extra waiting period, usually of three months. A fairly standard wording would be:

> Benefit will not be payable in the case of a female member incapacitated from pregnancy or childbirth, unless incapacity continues for a period of three months after the conclusion of the pregnancy in which case the deferred period for purposes of benefit shall be deemed to commence after the expiry of the aforementioned period.

This may be illegal after 1992 under the 1989 Social Security Act. A lot of schemes impose an eligibility period. That is, the employee has to be with the company a certain length of time before s/he qualifies. If the scheme doesn't impose it, the employer may.

Since PHI schemes are not technically part of the pension scheme, they could continue to cover everyone after the pension scheme stopped being compulsory in April 1988.

They are covered by the Sex Discrimination and Equal Pay Acts and by the 1989 Social Security Act, and therefore if they are offered to men they must also be offered to women. But because the insurance companies say that they have actuarial evidence that women have more serious illnesses than men, they do not have to charge an equal amount to men and women, and in fact they 'rate up' the premium that is paid for women workers by as much as 50%. So if the workforce in your company is largely female, the company may resist putting in a PHI scheme on the grounds of cost.

Surveys of the insurance companies which run PHI schemes are published every year by magazines like *Pensions Management* (see address list). You need to be a pretty large company to have a scheme designed for you. An average sized one would have to take a scheme off the shelf.

If the insurance company doesn't want the business, either because it doesn't like the look of your company or because it's overloaded with new work, it will tend to ask a very high premium to discourage you rather than say no. So it's always worth shopping around. For some manual jobs, though, the premium will always be high because there is a specific risk.

What You Should Look For

- A good level of benefit – two-thirds of PAYE earnings if possible. You'll have to accept the 75% limit on earnings and NI benefits, but try to make sure that only the individual's NI, not that of the family, is covered by this;
- Regular annual increases. Even if they are not very large, they will be better than nothing;
- As few exclusions as possible – in particular, no exclusion of AIDS;
- A waiting period that ties in properly with the sick pay scheme, so that someone can come off sick pay and go on to PHI without a gap. If your sick pay scheme is good enough, you'll be able to accept a 6 months' waiting period, which reduces the PHI cost a good deal;
- Coverage for everybody. If you have to accept a service qualification, it should be no more than one year, and age limits should be as wide as possible. You probably won't succeed in getting part timers covered, but it's worth a try;
- Pension rights safeguarded. The insurers should continue to pay the contributions to keep your pension up to date.

Why PHI Rather than Early Retirement?

One advantage of a PHI scheme is that it caters for the long-term sick who are eventually going to come back to work, as well as those who are not. The person who has had a bad car accident will eventually return, though s/he may be away 18 months, and so s/he could not take early retirement. But there's a need for more coverage than the ordinary sick pay scheme would give.

PHI does not 'write off' someone who does not want to feel his or her career is finished, as early retirement does.

It will generally also give a better level of benefit, except for long-serving people who become ill a few years before retirement. To safeguard them, a good early retirement clause can also be included in the pension scheme, and the person transferred to whatever is better for them. The cost of this is very small.

If a scheme is introduced, you may find that the insurance company police it more strictly than management would have done. They are likely at least to be equally tough to everyone, since they don't know the people and won't be motivated by office politics or friendship. But if you feel they are being unfair, ask for a three-way meeting between the company, stewards, and insurers. If the company makes the request, the insurers are unlikely to refuse.

All this is assuming that the company already provides decent sick pay, not just SSP at the minimum level. If it does not, then that ought to be the priority rather than PHI.

Possible Arguments and Responses
Arguments you can use are:

- 90% of sickness is over within six months. The PHI coverage is for a very small group who are unlucky enough to be ill for longer. Without this provision, they would be dependent solely on State benefit. PHI is therefore cost effective, as it will help those who need it most.
- If someone who the employer values becomes ill, the employer will be likely to make special arrangements for him/her. The person may, for instance, be kept on the payroll. A PHI scheme allows the employer to make provision for everyone in that event, without favouritism and without a heavy financial liability.
- If the staff already have a scheme, you can argue that the manual workers are just as valuable to the company as they are, and should be treated as such. There is no evidence that manual workers abuse these schemes.

Management's response may first of all be founded on ignorance. They have not have heard of the idea. Once they have researched it, they may object on various grounds:

- Cost. But these schemes are not really expensive. Ask them to obtain a few quotes, without commitment, so you all know what you are really arguing about, and can talk straightforwardly about money;
- They may say that PHI is more expensive than providing the same benefits through the pension scheme. It is more expensive than providing an early retirement pension of a comparable standard. But very few schemes do reach that standard. If the employer starts using that argument, ask him to improve the early retirement pension to that level instead, to show his good faith;
- They probably won't say it to you, but they may be worried about the implications in employment law. They won't be able to sack sick people so easily if they are still on the payroll. It may be worth bringing this out into the open, in the hope of making them feel ashamed of themselves;
- If they say they doesn't feel they can go 'out in front' of other employers, and that there are too few PHI schemes for manual workers for them to follow, find out about a few companies that do have PHI for their employees, in the same sort of industry and the same size. Try your trades council or your union's head office for information.

Finally, if you can once get them to the stage of having exploratory talks with the insurance company, they will probably do the rest for you. Insurance salespeople can be very persuasive.

17

Benefits on Death

Lump Sum Benefits on Death in Service

What You Must Have
The various Social Security Acts do not say that schemes must have any lump sum death benefits, and the State no longer even provides the meagre £30 death grant.

The 1975 Social Security Pensions Act does say, though, that a contracted out scheme must have a widows' pension and the 1986 Act brings in a widowers' pension for years after 1988. Companies are allowed to eat into the lump sum death benefit to provide these.

What the Inland Revenue Allows
The Inland Revenue allows a maximum death benefit of four times earnings. This can be full PAYE earnings, even if the pensionable earnings figure is less than this. It will also allow you to use a 'notional' figure, by updating the last full year's PAYE figure by an amount to take account of inflation. This would apply if for instance someone had been ill for a while before dying, so that their final P60 was a very low figure.

The cash sum is tax free, so long as you fulfil the conditions laid down. The main one is that the benefit is payable at the discretion of the trustees. This means that, so far as the tax people are concerned, when you die you don't own the money. The trustees do, and it's therefore not counted in your estate. Because of this, you cannot instruct them about who is to receive the benefit. The final decision must be with the trustees.

There is a general legal rule that money left unclaimed after death, if it is still outstanding when sufficient time has been left for the settlement of a person's affairs, goes to the Crown. For this reason most pension scheme trust deeds have a clause saying that the ultimate beneficiary once the trustees have taken all reasonable steps to find a relative or dependant of the dead person, is the fund itself. This means that the money is not unclaimed, and so the Crown doesn't get it. The maximum length of time a fund is allowed to hang on to the money, without deciding what to do with it, is two years.

A scheme is also allowed to refund all the member's contributions on death, with the addition of interest. The Inland Revenue does not say what it regards as the correct rate, but in general it will be much lower than actual rates of interest. This is the member's own money, and so frequently it is paid to the 'legal personal representatives' and can be taxable.

The beneficiary for a lump sum on death can be the husband or wife, a relative, or a person who was financially dependent on the member (such as a cohabitee, or an elderly parent the member was supporting) or another nominated person such as the friend s/he shared a house with.

Typical Arrangements and Possible Improvements
The NAPF survey showed that in 1986 about a third of staff schemes gave the full four years' earnings, but only 4% of works schemes; over a third of these gave between 2 and $2^1/_2$ years' earnings; and 7% of works schemes give a fixed amount of money, which will often be very small. (In the more recent surveys, they have changed the way they collect the figures, so that the information now provided on this is not much use.)

Some schemes vary the amount by length of service, and/or whether or not you have children. The National Health Service, and other public service schemes, for instance, give one year's earnings to everyone, but for those with service of more than about 25 years it can rise to a maximum of 1.5 times earnings. The GEC Plan gives twice earnings, plus an extra 1.5 times pensionable pay for each child.

A good many schemes discriminate between men and women, or between married men on the one hand, and single men and women on the other. AI Welders, for example, gives three times earnings to a woman or single man, but only twice earnings to a married man or a widower with dependent children. This is legal at present, because the Sex Discrimination Act does not cover occupational pension schemes, but not a good idea. A married woman's earnings will be just as necessary to the standard of living of the household as her husband's, and the difficulties of adjusting to the new situation just as great. It will become illegal at the beginning of 1993 when the Social Security Act 1989 (explained on page 31) comes into force.

More reasonably, some schemes have different benefits depending on whether there is a widow/er's pension payable. So Kimberley Clark gives three times earnings on the death of single people, or twice earnings for those who were married, along with a widow/er's pension. It also allows for the member to write to the trustees to say that there is a dependant who s/he would like to see treated in the same way as a widow/er and in that case the smaller death benefit and the pension would be paid.

Occasionally schemes discriminate by giving different benefits to different grades of employees who are paying the same contribution. This might be the result of an old 'red circling' – that is, special provision to ensure that a group with better conditions in one respect do not lose when the scheme is changed overall. For instance, if a scheme is changed from giving a death benefit of four times earnings to giving twice earnings plus a widow's pension, those who already had four times earnings might be allowed to retain it and have a right to the widow's pension, whereas new entrants would have to start on the new terms.

Alternatively, it may be a matter of giving management better value for money in the pension scheme, and thus the manual workers subsidising them.

A few schemes have both a death benefit, and an extra 'accidental death benefit' either for everyone or for a particular group of people. If this is included in the pension booklet, the chances are again that it is a result of an old 'red circling'. The scheme may have had a much higher life assurance rate than the Inland Revenue now allows, and so part of the benefit has been hived off into a technically separate scheme, so as not to jeopardise approval.

Rank Xerox Ltd pays a lump sum of four times salary, plus a refund of contributions plus interest. In the event of death by accident, there's a further two times salary.

A number of schemes deduct from the lump sum the cost of providing the minimum widow's pension required by the Social Security Pensions Act for a contracted-out scheme, and after 1988 they may do the same for the widower's pension (see Chapter 4, pages 31–4 for an explanation of this). So the widow is being asked to pay for her own pension. This should be opposed.

The lump sum and widow/er's pension should be looked at together. If there is a good widow/er's pension there will be less reason to seek a large lump sum as well. So a contracted-in scheme that does not provide a widow/er's pension should give a bigger lump sum than one that does.

An average level of lump sum for a contracted-out scheme is about twice earnings for a works scheme, rather more for a staff or joint scheme. This is an area where the public services fall down, with their benefit varying between 1 and 1.5 times earnings depending on length of service. If your scheme is below average, you should probably make death benefit a priority. If it meets the standard, you might well think about leaving this alone for the moment and concentrating on other things.

A very rough rule of thumb for cost is that a death benefit equal to one year's earnings will cost 0.75% of payroll or less. This does depend a lot on the ages of people covered, and on the proportion of men and women. Because of their lower mortality rate, women are cheaper to cover for death benefit than men.

The small print here is important. Check on:

- The definition of earnings. Even if the rest of the scheme is calculated on basic earnings only, or has a deduction for State pension, for the death benefit the definition should be either PAYE earnings for the last 12 months, or the last pay period's earnings multiplied up to give an annual figure. If people's earnings fluctuate at different times of the year, the first method is better, because otherwise someone dying at the 'wrong' time of year is penalised. If earnings are fairly steady, the second is a better safeguard against inflation.

- If someone has been sick for, say, four weeks or more in the final year before his/her death, a 'notional' PAYE figure should be created. If there's an easily calculated group average rate, then you can use this. Or you could use the average for the weeks the person has worked, and multiply this by 52. You could not use that, though, for a person who has not worked at all in the last year. So another alternative is PAYE earnings for the last full year worked, uprated by the increase in prices since that date.

- Interest should be added to the refund of contributions. Some of them will have been paid in when the general level of interest was much lower than it is now, so it is not reasonable to ask for anything approaching current market rates, nor would the Inland Revenue allow it. A 4% or 5% rate would be reasonable.

- Those who are excluded from the pension scheme because they are too old, or too young, or have not worked for the company long enough, should be included for the death benefit. The company is also allowed to retain blanket death benefit coverage even for those who have opted out into a Personal Pension scheme, but union views differ about whether this is a good idea or not. The question was covered on page 60. One possibility is to cover them for a much lower level of benefit than anyone else, say once times earnings when everybody else is on three or four times, so that their dependants are not penalised too much by their actions.

- Part timers ought to be covered, however few hours they work. The loss of their income, even if fairly small, is bound to create financial difficulties for the family.

If you have a fixed lump sum in your scheme, for instance £500 or £1,000, try to change it to an earnings-related one, even if at a level which gives no immediate improvement. In the long run this will mean that it keeps up with inflation. Otherwise, you will need to renegotiate the level of death benefit every year if it is to keep its value.

Death benefit is one of the simpler things in a pension scheme to change. Even in a large scheme it is usually insured, to safeguard the scheme if a busload of people went over a cliff. So improving it is just a matter of raising the premium, and this can be done very easily. If you're negotiating on a scheme, and the discussions have dragged on so that it is too late to implement most of the changes this year, you should at least be able to get the improved death benefit brought in and backdated. This would mean that the dependants of anyone who died between the anniversary date and the date you finally settle gets an increased payment from the company in due course.

Keep an eye on how the death benefit is administered. Questions to ask, via the member trustees or the pensions consultative committee, are:

- How long is it taking for benefit to be paid out?
- Is it simple for members to make their own wishes clear as to where the benefit goes? Is a form to fill in for this included in the scheme booklet?
- Is it genuinely kept confidential? Or if someone has family circumstances which are not all they seem, is s/he going to find gossip spreading after s/he fills in the nomination form?

Some schemes adopt the procedure of sending, once a year, a new nomination form to each member, and an envelope with the individual's name and the date on. If the member wants to change the nomination form, s/he fills it in, and puts it into the envelope, which is then sealed up. The pensions administrator then throws away the previous envelope, without looking at the form inside, and puts the new one in its place. Only if the member dies is the envelope unsealed.

The disadvantage of this is that when the letter has to be read, there is nothing that can be done if it has been incorrectly or unclearly filled in.

Possible Arguments and Responses
The arguments for a bigger death benefit are:

- It's cost effective. It takes only a comparatively small increase in premium to give a much better level of benefit.
- Not to have a good death benefit puts the employer in an extraordinarily bad light. People naturally feel very strongly if someone they have worked with for a long time dies, and they see the company treating his/her dependants shabbily. It may well give the company a bad name, and undo all the goodwill a progressive policy elsewhere has created.
- This is an area where the economies of scale are enormous. It is much cheaper for the company to take out or increase group life assurance than for the member to do so as an individual, certainly so far as the older person and anyone not in the best of health is concerned. It's certainly cheaper to provide it this way than through a Personal Pension scheme – so this is a good incentive for people to stay in the company scheme.

The employer's objection will chiefly be money. As always, it will be a matter of what priority you give this item in your overall claim, and how much cash is really available. It's easy to be flexible in negotiating this point, without damaging or overcomplicating the structure of the scheme as a whole.

The employers may also say:

- They don't feel people will be able to handle a large sum of money, and so this may be wasted. This is a sexist and paternalist argument. The implication is often that wives cannot cope with money. In response, you can say that the employer should ensure that proper financial advice is available to the dependant. But advice is as far as it should go. There should be no question of the employer making a judgement on that person's abilities.
- They don't see the need for a large death benefit. Funerals are expensive, but they cost hundreds rather than thousands of pounds, and you can't know that any member has large financial commitments. In response, you could point out that people frequently do have substantial debts, whether the company appreciates it or not. They will have organised their lives, one assumes, to take account of this, but unexpected death will create considerable problems. Even a young person, not yet married or with a family, may have piled up debts for consumer goods.

The employer may suggest that, as there is only a limited amount of money to go round, it would be better spent on improving the widow/er's pension. On the other hand, some employers will say the opposite, as pointed out on page 150. What your reaction to this is will depend on the size of the widow/er's pension because a balance needs to be struck between the immediate lump sum, and the longer term widow/er's pension. A benefit of three times earnings, plus a spouse's pension of half the member's prospective pension, would be a reasonable balance.

Death in Service – Spouses' and Dependants' Pensions

What You Must Have

A scheme that is contracted out under the Social Security Pensions Act must have a widow's pension, but the legal minimum is only half the member's own GMP. As from April 1988, there must also be a widower's pension of half the member's GMP, but only of the proportion that has built up since that date. In both cases, the widow/er's pension need only be paid where the member was over 45 when s/he died, or had dependent children under 16.

There's no obligation to pay a pension to any other dependant, and if an eligible legal widow/er exists, the WGMP (Widow/ers Guaranteed Minimum Pension) must be paid to him or her, even if s/he is not living with the member. Once people are divorced, though, this obligation ends.

If the scheme is contracted in, there is no obligation to pay any dependant's pension.

A COMP or PP scheme, contracted out on a money purchase basis, need only pay the widow/er a pension based on the annuity the accumulated money in the member's fund will buy. For a member who has only been a few years in the scheme, with a young spouse, that will be very small indeed.

What the Inland Revenue Allows

The Inland Revenue will allow a pension scheme to provide a benefit for widow, widower, or dependant, of not more than two-thirds of the member's pension, calculated on his/her earnings at the date of death, and his/her potential service up to retirement date.

As with the lump sum benefit, the 'earnings' definition can be different from that used for the member's own pension. This means that even if the member's own pension is integrated (see page 90–2) the widow/er's need not be.

If there is a widow/er and a dependant, or more than one dependant, then more than one pension can be paid, so long as the total does not come to more than the member's own prospective pension. Dependant is defined as:

a person who is financially dependent on the employee, or was so dependent at the time of the employee's death ... A relative who is not or was not supported by the employee is not a dependant. But a child of the employee may always be regarded as a dependant until s/he reaches the age of 18 or ceases to receive full time educational or vocational training, if later.

A scheme is allowed to reduce the pension if the dependant is younger than the member, and it can suspend it, or remove it altogether, if the person remarries.

Typical Arrangements and Possible Improvements

According to the NAPF, 89% of members are in schemes which give a widow's pension of half the member's own; 47% of schemes in the survey also provide a widower's pension if he was dependent, and 47% of all schemes now give a widower's pension automatically.

The cost of providing a full widower's pension as well as a widow's pension will depend a lot on the proportion of men to women within the scheme. In practice it will not vary a lot between a dependant's and an automatic pension, because the actuary will assume everyone will claim to be dependant. Either way, it should be small, because the chances of a woman dying in service are also small.

There are many variations in the amount and type of pension given. The meanest schemes give only the minimum required by the State, and deduct it from the lump sum.

More common, but still pretty mean, is to give only that minimum, but without deducting it from the lump sum. Some schemes which are otherwise fairly generous do this.

The reasoning here is the opposite of that used by other employers for reducing the death benefit. Here, they are saying that the widow ought to have as much control over the money she receives as possible, and therefore as little as possible ought to be tied up in pension. Neither argument is right, as discussed on page 149.

There are some schemes which give pretty well the full amount allowed by the Inland Revenue.

> Albright and Wilson give two-thirds of the member's prospective pension, and say that 'In all cases where a Widow's Pension is not payable a Dependant's pension up to the amount of the Widow's pension may be paid at the Trustees' discretion to any person whom they consider to have been substantially dependent on the member at the date of death.'

For most schemes, however, it may be more realistic to look for a half pension based on all actual plus prospective service. 'Service' should include any years when the pension scheme was in existence, but before there was a widow/er's pension, and any years for which back service entitlement has been given for the member's own pension. Any pension should be payable equally to the widow or widower, or to any other dependant where no widow/er exists.

Some schemes, rather than paying a proportion of the member's pension, pay a proportion of earnings.

> Unicorn Industries pay a quarter of earnings regardless of how long the member has been with the company. No-one loses by this, and the gainers are the shorter service, older people.

> Any improvement in the spouse's benefit is a moderately expensive item. Extending the pension at the full rate to widowers is also not expensive, especially when you take into account the fact that the scheme will now have to provide some pension for them.

Children's Pensions

Rather than provide an automatic additional children's pension, a lot of schemes say that if the widow dies while the children are dependent, so that they become orphans, then the widow's pension is carried on for their benefit. This is cheaper than paying a children's pension in every case, because only a few widows would die while their children were young.

A number of schemes, while providing a widow/er's pension which is below the Inland Revenue limit, add on to it reasonable children's pensions which bring the package as a whole up to the limit.

The Kimberly Clarke booklet says:

> If you die in service and any of your children (maximum 2) are under age 16, or older if still in full time education, a further benefit is payable to them.
>
> The amount of this benefit, known as a children's allowance, will be £100 p.a. or half of the pension, multiplied by the number (maximum 2) of qualifying children, whichever is the greater.

In this case, you could only improve on the widow/er's pension by cutting back on the children's pension. This would often in fact be a reasonable thing to do, as the children will receive the benefit of the widow having a higher pension, and it will also help the widow/er without children. It will therefore cost money to do this, because far more widow/er's pensions are payable than children's pensions.

Where there is a children's pension payable, it is fairly usual to give better treatment to children both of whose parents have died. In the Kimberly Clarke example above, for instance, the booklet goes on to say that 'If no widow/widower's pension is payable, the amount will be doubled.'

Some schemes extend the same special benefits to the children of single parents. This is sensible, since for them the death of one parent will be as drastic as the death of two parents in other situations. This is often given only for the children of male members, not of female. This discrimination is not acceptable, though it will still be legal after the Social Security Act 1989 comes into force.

Remarriage Rules

Many schemes take the pension away if the widow remarries, and occasionally also if a widower remarries. This is very common for instance in public service schemes, where the ban is also on living together without marrying.

There are mixed views among members about this. It's often justified as a way to save money: 'We don't want to give benefit to someone who doesn't need it.' But there is an insult implied in the suggestion that any woman needs a man to support her. Also, this rule has very little value in saving the scheme money, because of the high cost of enforcing it. If there is also a ban on cohabitation, it means the scheme will be relying largely on anonymous letters from neighbours, which is humiliating.

The argument that a pension should be paid for life is that it is given as of right, and has been paid for by the member's contributions on that basis.

Age Limits

Many schemes reduce the pension if the widow is more than a certain number of years younger than the member.

The Albright and Wilson booklet says:

If the Widow is more than 10 years younger than her husband the Widow's pension will be reduced by 2% for each year by which the age difference exceeds 10 years, to a maximum reduction of 50%, but the resultant pension will not be less than the Widow's Guaranteed Minimum Pension.

The argument is that, if a widow is much younger than her husband, the pension is likely to be paid for longer. But to pursue the logic fully, the pension ought to be increased if she is older than her husband, and this is never done. It is a penny pinching measure not affecting many people, since most husbands and wives are quite close in age, but very annoying for those it does affect.

Whatever limits are put on, the pension can never be reduced below the WGMP. Nor can the WGMP be paid to anyone except the widow. It is possible, and a good idea, for the rules of the scheme to include discretion for the trustees to divide the benefit where necessary. If a member has a legal widow/er, but has lived with someone else for many years, then the trustees could divide the benefit so that the legal spouse got the WGMP and the other person got the rest.

Contracted-in Schemes

In a contracted-in scheme with a low accrual rate, a spouse's pension for death in service will be rather a waste of time, as it will be very small and may only stop the spouse from getting means-tested benefits. If no spouse's pension exists, therefore, do your best to improve the lump sum death benefits instead. On the other hand, if it exists already it would be unwise to try to abolish it. So then you would have to try to make it as large as possible.

Possible Arguments and Responses

Put forward the case for a 'balancing out' between pension and lump sum. The lump sum is needed to help the widow/er meet immediate commitments, and to adjust his/her way of life, and the pension is needed for long-term living costs.

Providing a small pension only for a spouse can simply deprive the spouse of the ability to claim means-tested benefits. So since a contracted-out scheme must pay some spouse's pension, it ought to provide a good one.

The employer may suggest that the tax position is better if a widow takes a lump sum, and spends it on an annuity. While this is true, the amount you can have as an annuity varies enormously according to interest rates, so some spouses could do much worse than others, and this is not fair.

Also, if the employer's scheme gives any sort of increase in dependants' pensions, whether automatically or at their discretion, s/he will get it only on the small amount of pension not on the lump sum.

All the arguments that have been used elsewhere, about comparability with competitors' schemes, good industrial relations and so on, also apply. The employer will probably not disagree to any great extent with your arguments – just say s/he can't afford it. It may be possible to phase it in, for instance by giving a pension on accrued service only for a few years, and extending it later to prospective service. But this is not satisfactory, because it means a lot of people living on very small pensions for quite a while. The company is then saving money in a mean way, because the longer they delay bringing in the change, the more elderly pensioners will have died.

Widowers' Pensions
The most important argument for providing a proper widower's pension as well as a widow's pension is that the scheme should not discriminate between men and women. (But the employer is not breaking the law; as explained on page 31, even after the end of 1992 when the Social Security Act 1989 comes into force, widowers' and dependants' pensions will still be allowed to be unequal.) Very often, the women members of the scheme will feel pretty strongly about this. If so, you should make management aware of it. There is a tendency to assume that women don't care one way or the other about pensions, and this is partly how schemes have got away with so much discrimination in the past. The scheme administrator may be genuinely surprised to discover that women do care.

One argument the company may use is that of value for money. The actuaries' view is that the pension of a man retiring at 65, plus a widow's pension, is about equal in value to the pension of a woman retiring at 60, taking into account her longer life expectancy. This may well be so, but it's not the whole picture:

• It doesn't override the arguments about discrimination. There are many other areas where employers have to make equal provision even though it's more expensive for one sex than for the other. For example, it's often claimed that women tend to take more time off sick than men, but an employer is not allowed to provide different sick pay schemes;
• The two benefits are of very different value, so the actuary is not comparing like with like. Moving men's retirement age down to match women's is very expensive, but giving a widower's pension is very cheap;

One sometimes still hears arguments about 'The man is the breadwinner – women only work for pin money.' There are some prehistoric (male) managers around who will say this, and regrettably also some male shop stewards. It's pretty doubtful if this was ever true, but it certainly isn't any more. Most families need two incomes to survive, and the loss of either income is going to create financial problems, because the family's standard of living has been built on the expectation of that income continuing. The majority of women today do paid work for a large part of their lives, taking a break only while their children are under school age.

The surviving parent of a family is going to be in considerable difficulty looking after the children, whichever parent dies. In fact, it will be more difficult if it is the wife who dies, because of the way the State scheme works. A widow receives the State widow's pension, but a widower who was not a dependant of his wife has to rely on Income Support (which used to be called Supplementary Benefit) which is means-tested and anyway at a lower rate. Employers' schemes are intended to fill in the gaps in the State scheme.

If the company starts to argue about money, ask it to obtain a figure for the cost before going any further. It will be very low, because few women die in service. Management may have quite incorrect notions about the cost.

On children's pensions, there is usually fairly general agreement that they are a good thing. The argument is therefore straightforwardly about cost, and the priority to give them. They are not expensive.

A pension for adult dependants can be more controversial. Managements frequently jump to the conclusion that you are talking only about common law wives and husbands, and perhaps also about gay relationships. They would be covered by this, certainly, and why not? Is it any of the pension manager's business how people choose to arrange their lives? This sort of provision, though, would also give a pension to the member's elderly parent, or a sister who has kept house for a bachelor brother, or the invalid relative who has been supported by the member. Management may consider that these at least are 'deserving cases'.

You could point out that there seem to be double standards operating, as between the lump sum and the pension. The employer has no objection to the lump sum going to a widower, or any other adult dependant – indeed, employers often claim 'flexibility' as one of the main advantages. So how is the pension different? If they're honest, they'll say 'because it costs more', so that you will at least be able to strip away the less genuine arguments and start talking about money.

Death after Retirement

What You Must Have
A contracted-out scheme must provide a widow's pension of half the member's GMP, and a widower's pension of half the GMP built up since 1988, when the member dies in retirement. At present, the State pays the rest, and also picks up any increases that have been made since the member retired. In and after the year 2000, the spouses of people who die will inherit only half, rather than the full pension, so there will be much less for the State to pick up.

If the member has married after retirement and dies within six months, then even if the scheme is normally more generous it need pay only the WGMP in this case.

As the State has provided a widower's pension for death after retirement since SERPS started in 1978, it will continue to provide extra additional pension in those cases. So if the employer's scheme also gives one, the widower will be better off than a comparable widow, who gets less from the State.

What the Inland Revenue Allows
The Inland Revenue limit on pension for death in retirement follows the same pattern as for death in service – up to two-thirds the

member's pension. This can be calculated before any amount that is to be commuted is deducted, so that taking part of the member's own pension as cash need not affect the widow.

They are, however, for some reason, much more rigorous on the death benefit after retirement. They will allow:

- A 'funeral benefit' of up to £1,000; and
- A guarantee that the pension will be paid for a minimum length of time which can be up to ten years, even if the member dies in the meantime. If the guarantee is for five years or less, the balance may be taken as a lump sum. If it is for longer, it must be a continuing pension.

It is also possible to continue the lump sum death benefit. The value of this has to be included when calculating whether the member is over the total pension and lump sum limits.

The Inland Revenue allows the member to surrender some of his/her own pension to increase the size of the widow/er's pension, or to give a pension to any other dependant. However, this must not mean that the widow/er's pension will be bigger than the member's own. A scheme can also provide a pension for any other dependant, including a children's pension, without the member needing to surrender anything, but it must not bring the total package above the maximum. This surrender must be done at, or shortly after retirement, and cannot then be reversed. So if the dependant then dies before the member, the sacrifice is wasted.

Typical Arrangements and Possible Improvements

The majority of schemes have had widows' pensions for death after retirement for a very long time. Now that contracted-out schemes must do so, 96% of all schemes provide one, and about a third of these also allow for an extra pension to be paid if the member surrenders part of his/her own.

The majority of schemes pay a widow's/dependant's pension of half the member's own. Not many schemes pay a widow's pension of the maximum two-thirds. One that does is British Airways.

It's not worth putting in for a better pension than 50% unless the scheme is well above average in other areas. If you decide to go for an increase, try to get the improvement reflected in the amounts of widows' pensions already being paid.

What you can look for, though, is an extension of the benefit to widowers, and other adult dependants, in the same way as for the death in service pension, and for improvements in the small print. Look at:

- remarriage rules;
- deathbed marriages;
- provision of, or improvement of, a guarantee; and
- provision of a funeral benefit.

As pointed out earlier in this chapter, widowers' pensions are cheaper to provide than widows' pensions, as there are far fewer widowers. The majority of wives outlive their husbands. Children's pensions for death after retirement are even cheaper, as very few pensioners have dependent children.

In negotiation, bring discussion on these aspects together with a similar discussion on the death in service benefits. If you achieve a breakthrough on one, it should be conceded on the other anyway.

Don't rely on this, though. Some companies are much more generous to the widows of retired members than they are to the widows of those who die in service. This can be seen, for instance, with the treatment of death in retirement pensions on remarriage. Table 17.1 (from the NAPF 1988 survey) shows the period for which widows are paid after a member's retirement.

Table 17.1 Period of payment of widow's/widower's pension payable on death in service

Period of Payment	Private	Public	All Schemes
	%	%	%
Continues for life	80	33	75
Discontinued on remarriage	9	63	15
Discontinued if remarriage occurs before 60th birthday	4	2	4
Pension reviewed on remarriage	7	2	6

If your scheme has a remarriage rule, it ought to be dropped. Whatever justification there is for imposing it on a young widow (though it's already been argued that there is none), it really is distasteful that it should be imposed on a person over 60.

So too is the quite common rule that, where a member has married or remarried after retirement, and then dies within six months, only the WGMP, not the full pension, is paid. This is because of pension fund managers' fears of 'deathbed marriages' but there are not likely to be many of these. There are better ways of making one's fortune than by marrying an elderly occupational pensioner. It's another small penny pinching device.

On the guarantee, there are many variations, as Table 17.2 from the NAPF survey shows. The best clause is one that says that the fund undertakes to pay the pension for at least five years, and that, if the pensioner dies before that time, the balance will be paid to the spouse or any other dependant in a lump sum, with the dependant's pension starting immediately. Many schemes 'discount' the lump sum, that is, reduce it to take account of the fact that it's being paid early. This should not be accepted, though insurance companies often try to enforce it.

Table 17.2 Pension payments guaranteed for specific period

	Private	Public	All Schemes
	%	%	%
No guarantee	12	14	12
Pension guaranteed for 5 years even if over laps with dependant's pension	55	33	54
Pension guaranteed for 5 years but no overlap with dependant's pension	21	5	19
Pension guaranteed only if no dependant's pension payable	7	2	6
Some other guarantee	5	46	9

Some schemes say that the guaranteed lump sum will only apply if there is no widow/er. This considerably reduces the cost, but also the usefulness, as the majority of people who die within five years of retirement will be married.

Massey Ferguson costed the guarantee for pensioners with no surviving spouse at 0.05% of payroll, and a fuller guarantee for all pensioners at 0.25% – not a large sum in either case.

People sometimes get the impression from badly worded scheme booklets that the guarantee means that the pension is paid for only five years. This is not the case. If your scheme booklet is misleading on this, ask for it to be changed.

The funeral benefit allowed by the Inland Revenue is rarely given in practice. One example where it does exist is Inco, whose booklet says:

Disability, early, and normal pensioners are covered for a lump sum death benefit of £400. This is paid to the person you nominate.

It's not clear why this benefit is so rare, unless it is because it would be a nuisance for administrators to keep track of any pay out. Although it is only a small sum it would be worth obtaining. The Inland Revenue Practice Note which applies to it is No 12.18.

Very few schemes provide the extra life cover, because of the problems it creates for checking if you are within the Inland Revenue limits. Pan Am is one company that does, at a modest level. Other schemes, which had benefits that were always going to be below the Inland Revenue limits, could also.

Possible Arguments and Responses
If you are looking for an increase in the level of widow/ers' pensions, it will be helpful to do some research. Try to obtain figures which you can present to management on:

- The typical level of a widow/er's pension for death after retirement, for a fairly recent pensioner from your firm;
- The level of costs s/he has to face, especially housing costs. Have council rents gone up recently, for instance? and
- The proportion of widow/ers being paid from the employer's scheme who are having to claim Income Support (which was previously called Supplementary Benefit) or who are only just above the poverty line because of their pension, and are therefore only marginally better off.

If you're in a small company, with only one site, you'll probably find a number of pensioners living locally. With a large company, you'll probably have to take a sample of a couple of sites, perhaps those that run pensioners' clubs. With luck, you might be able to get a few active pensioners to find out the information for you, especially if your claim includes an improvement in pension for them. Then you can present the information to management, and ask them if they really think the level of benefit is right. Their reaction will probably be that they agree with you, but it costs too much, and so then you will need to argue about how much they can really afford. On page 43 there were some ideas for arguments you could use.

On the question of extending the pension to widowers and dependants, turn back to pages 151–2, under Death in Service, because the same arguments apply there. The question of remarriage is also dealt with in that section.

The next question is the 'deathbed marriage'. Usually, if you make sufficient fuss about this, the company will decide it's not worth defending. If they decide to stick to it, though, you could ask them to provide some facts. For instance:

- How many cases of this sort have there been in the last ten years?
- How much of the administrator's time was spent in finding out the facts, discussing the problem with the trustees, and so on?
- How much money, taking administrative time into account, did they really save?

Even if the figures show that it is not cost-effective, the employer may say that they must retain the clause 'to save the fund from the possibility of abuse'. It might be possible to compromise by having the pension reviewed, at the discretion of the trustees, rather than removed altogether.

On the guarantee period, the issue will mainly be financial, though the improvement does not cost much in itself. But you can also make the point that the guarantee provides a very visible safeguard, ensuring that people are getting value for money. People will often say they don't feel they are going to live for long in retirement anyway, and the guarantee at least means that they can know their dependants won't lose. The most generous form of guarantee gives the biggest safeguard, and the difference in cost between the least and the most generous is very small for the company.

Continuing Life Cover or Giving a Funeral Benefit

Pensioners' anxieties about the cost of their funeral are well known. The next of kin of a pensioner will often be a pensioner him/herself. If they get to hear of difficulties a good employer would probably make an ex-gratia payment anyway, to cover a debt incurred because of a funeral. In that case, why not provide it automatically? It would be less humiliating, simpler, and in the long run (taking account of the administrative time spent dealing with each case as a one-off) probably cost no more.

18

Pension Increases

What You Must Have

Under the original terms of contracting out in 1978, schemes did not have to provide increases in pensions once they started being paid. The State took on the responsibility for increasing the GMP in line with the Secretary of State's estimate of the increase in prices, and the employer's scheme only had to continue paying the pension at the same level as when it originally started.

This has now been changed, but it will take a long time before the difference is really noticeable. For GMP built up since 1988, the employer has the responsibility of increasing it by 3% each year that it is in payment. If inflation is higher than that (as it tends to be) then the State will pick up the difference.

What the Inland Revenue Allows

The Inland Revenue allows any scheme to increase pensions by any amount up to the increase in the cost of living, provided that the scheme rules allow them to do so (as most do). A scheme need not give the same increases to all categories of pensioners. Some schemes leave the widow's death in service pension out. Also, schemes need not use the same formula to increase deferred pensions (explained in Chapter 19), as they do for other pensions.

Typical Arrangements and Possible Improvements

Schemes in the public sector, both public services and nationalised industries, usually keep the pensions up in line with prices. In some cases this is because the law says they must, while in others it is a matter of decision by the trustees, but they have taken the responsibility seriously. In some of the better private sector schemes, like those in the banks and the oil industry, there is a similar aim of keeping up with inflation, though without the same sort of guarantee. Overall, private sector pension schemes have kept up with only three-quarters of the rise in prices over the last few years, and some indeed set this as their target. This means that when a loaf of bread goes up fourpence, they expect the pensioner to manage on only threepence. So they are cutting their standard of living each year, and over a 20-year period it can easily halve.

In many cases, there is a guaranteed level of increase at a low rate, often 3% or 5%, and then, if the trustees or the company feel they can afford it, it is topped up each year from the funds. The NAPF survey in Table 18.1 showed the following picture for automatic increases.

Table 18.1 Percentage of schemes providing post-retirement increases
(The figures in brackets represent the percentages by membership.)

	Private		Public		All Schemes	
	%	%	%	%	%	%
Guaranteed increases without reviews	17	(28)	70	(85)	23	(47)
Guaranteed increases plus periodic reviews	35	(40)	17	(12)	33	(34)
Sub Total	52	(68)	87	(97)	56	(81)
Pension increases not guaranteed but pensions reviewed:						
(a) on annual basis	36	(28)	11	(3)	33	(19)
(b) other frequency	9	(4)	1	(*)	8	(3)
Not increased during payment	3	(*)	1	(*)	3	(*)

* not available

Guaranteeing in advance to pay pension increases is expensive, though not as much as some pension consultants say. As a rough rule of thumb, a 3% guaranteed increase on the whole pension might add a quarter to the cost of a pension scheme.

An improvement for the pensioners ought to be the first call on the use of any surplus in the fund. The money that has built up in the fund comes from their contributions, and those made by the company while they were working there, and so they ought to get credit for it. Morally, there is an obligation to give them this before starting to think about other improvements.

There is also now a guaranteed rate of increase during deferment in the pensions for early leavers (explained in the next chapter). This is at 5%, or the increase in the Retail Prices Index if less, for any pension built up after January 1985. The Occupational Pensions Board, when it recommended a change in the law on early leavers, thought that employers would find it impossible to pay pensioners less than this – and so it ought to be.

Some employers, and some groups of trustees, say that they prefer to pay increases in the pension out of the revenue of the fund each year, rather than fund them in advance. In the short term it is cheaper, especially while the scheme is in healthy surplus. But there are problems:

• If the company is ever taken over, the new owners may feel no obligation to continue the practice;
• If the scheme surplus disappears, or there are other calls on it like an improvement in benefits for future members, the increases to pensioners may be expendable; and

- Pensioners have no bargaining power. They can't go on strike against the employer, so it is entirely goodwill they are relying on. In the USA the unions bargain for increases in payments to the company's pensioners at the same time as they do so for wage increases, but that only means that the goodwill of the unions is also involved.

You may not win on these arguments, though. The sort of company where it's unwise to rely on one-off increases is very unlikely to guarantee pension increases anyway, so you may not have a choice. But you could find a sudden change of mind by the employer, or the pension scheme administrator, if a takeover is threatened. (This happened, for instance, with Imperial Group when the Hanson Trust first came on the horizon.) Then it makes good sense to put everything that has been 'custom and practice' into rules to safeguard the scheme. If the employer does not suggest it when there is a threat, the union should do so.

A sensible target to aim at is a 5% guaranteed level, to match the increase given to deferred pensioners. If inflation is higher than that, the pensioners ought still to get the extra. If there's been a shortfall in the amounts given in the past, ask for a one-off catching-up exercise for all the pensioners. This could mean some of the oldest people getting a very substantial increase indeed.

Increases in the State basic pension should not be taken into account, even if the scheme is integrated (see page 90). But if the scheme is contracted out, it's reasonable for the fund to index-link the pension only in excess of GMP. If, however, they are giving far less than full index-linking, for instance a guaranteed rate of only 3%, this rate should be on the whole pension.

If the increases continue to be paid at the discretion of the trustees or the company, monitor the situation every year, to check:

- What increases have been paid (this will be in the scheme's annual report, explained on page 206).
- Whether different groups have had different increases. Have staff and works pensioners both got the same percentage? And what about very senior staff in 'top hat' schemes?
- Are very small increases being paid in the right way? Social Security penalises very small increases in income, but would generally ignore the same amount turned into an annual Christmas present – say £1 a week or £52 a year.

Any increase should apply to all pensioners, including widow/ers, dependants, and early retirees. The cost of making increases to pensions in payment varies very much, depending on how many pensioners there are. If there have been a great many retirements in the recent past, because the employer has been reducing staff, the cost will be much greater, but so too will the need.

Possible Arguments and Responses

As a result of inflation, people who retired a few years ago are finding their standard of living substantially reduced. Make the point that the scheme promised security in retirement. In fact, because of rising prices, there's no such security. After a few years, people have to worry about how they can cut their spending in order to survive.

Put together details of what the scheme's record on increases has been over recent years, and compare this with the actual rate of inflation. You can get details of that from Labour Research (see address list page 263). The actuarial firm Watson's produce a quarterly index of the average increases given by schemes.

Produce examples of how company pensioners are actually coping. On page 156, we suggested ways of collecting information on how widows and widowers were managing on what the company provided. You could do the same here, taking a sample of all pensioners from the oldest to the youngest.

If your procedures allow it, you could bring along one of the pensioners – perhaps a retired shop steward – to put the case to the company. Clearly s/he wouldn't be a representative, and if you have taken pension increases into the collective bargaining arena it must be existing stewards and members who decide whether anything is to be accepted or rejected. But it might mean that both sides are in touch with reality while discussing the increases.

Management will probably start by expressing sympathy, explaining how much a pension increase will cost (try to get them to put a precise figure on this) but add:

- 'We feel that with the generous level of pension on which a person retires from this firm, there is less need for increases than there might be in other schemes'; or
- 'We have kept up pretty well with the rate of inflation in the past, but there are other calls on the money in the fund.'

Even if it is true that the pension is good to start with, that doesn't make up for the fact that it falls in real value the longer the scheme goes on. It just means that people are being deluded into thinking the scheme is better than it really is. On the second point, the pensioners can hardly be blamed for either the state of the pension fund, or the other changes in benefits that the members want – so why should they be penalised?

Management may then ask how far you are willing to trade off an increase to pensioners against an increase to wages, or to other benefits. Put that way, it is unlikely that the majority of the workforce would be willing to forgo their own increases. Why should they? You may find it acceptable to postpone an improvement in the pension scheme – but make sure the pensioners get the full value of it. Don't allow management to divide workers and pensioners in this way. The workers will be pensioners one day.

If you have decided to ask for a guaranteed increase each year from the fund, the company will argue against it on the basis that 'funding' – paying for it in advance – is expensive and the money can be better used. They may also say that they are generous with agreed increases, and could not afford to be if it was insisted that they should pay into the scheme for future increases, so existing pensioners would lose out. Presumably, though, if you have decided to seek a guaranteed rate of increase it's because they have not been generous in the past, or because you do not trust their intentions in the future (or that of any possible predator taking over your company), so that is what you should tell them.

Another point is that funding in advance is good pensions practice, recommended by actuaries and many other pension experts. This is useful if they've argued about 'good practice' on other issues. The idea of guaranteeing in advance, and then funding, is that you pay for your promises when you make them, rather than offering jam tomorrow for which you make no commitment to pay. If there is an actuary, or a pensions specialist, on the employer's side of the table they will probably agree in principle, but plead necessity as a reason for not doing it.

Finally, you could make the point that the rules on surpluses under the 1986 Finance Act (explained in Chapter 27) encourage funding for increases. These rules say that the scheme rules should either guarantee increases or make express provision for reviews of pensions, if the value of increases is going to be taken into account by the actuary in carrying out the statutory valuation.

19

Early Leavers

An 'early leaver' from a pension scheme is anyone who leaves, for whatever reason, when they are too young to take a pension. So you can be an early leaver even when you have 20 or 30 years in the scheme. Most people in fact are early leavers at one time or another; very few people stay 40 years in one job, or even with one firm.

What happens to your pension then depends on several different sets of rules:

- Those laid down by the Inland Revenue;
- For contracted-out schemes, those laid down by the Social Security Pensions Act 1975, and amended in 1984;
- For all schemes, those laid down in Social Security Acts passed in 1985 and 1986.

The Inland Revenue's Rules

The Inland Revenue has always regarded pension schemes as a way of reducing your tax bill. It is right in this, especially for directors and other highly paid people. If a person leaves a job and claims back his or her contributions, therefore, the Inland Revenue claims tax back at 20%.

But this is still quite a favourable rate of tax, so it insists that the member must really have left before s/he can have the contributions back. It usually regards a break of at least one month as necessary to prove it. The IR doesn't find this easy to enforce, though, so schemes very rarely get into trouble if they try to fiddle it. But this could put the individual in jeopardy in the event of a dismissal or redundancy, because his or her employment could be counted as starting from the day s/he rejoined.

Contributions paid in before April 1975, when the 'preservation' rules first came into force, can be refunded – though the rate of inflation since then means that they will not be worth very much. If you were contracted out under the old 'graduated' scheme (explained in Chapter 2), you will have a deduction made to take account of the pension kept for you under that.

These rules apply whether your scheme is good, bad, or indifferent; even if it is an old £5 per year of service scheme of the sort that some companies still have.

Once you have a preserved pension, the Inland Revenue allows employers to increase it by the percentage increase in the Retail Prices Index. In practice very few schemes, except those in the public sector, do so.

The DSS Rules

The next important set of rules came in the Social Security Pensions Act 1975. These only affect schemes contracted out with an earnings guarantee. As amended in 1986 these rules say that if you have more than two years' contracted-out membership, your scheme must either preserve or transfer the GMP, and revalue it to take account of inflation.

If you are in a contracted-out scheme for less than two years, then the GMP can be preserved, or you can be bought back into the State scheme. This is done by the employer paying what is called a 'contributions equivalent premium' (a CEP). S/he is allowed to deduct a proportion of this from the refund of your contributions. Just how much it is depends on which years you were contracted out, because it relates to the National Insurance Rebate in each year. Broadly speaking, between a third and a half of your contributions can be used up in this way. This is called the 'certified amount'.

After this has been done, the 20% tax deduction is made. So people who are looking for a refund from their schemes will usually find that they have very little to come.

What Happens to the Preserved GMP

As explained above, schemes must preserve the GMP, or they can transfer it to another scheme or an insurance company policy. Either way, it must be revalued. Other alternatives are to pay a transfer premium to the State, if the member is moving to a contracted-in scheme, or to transfer it to a Personal Pension scheme. In the last case it need not be revalued, and what happens was explained in Chapter 6.

If it is to be revalued, there are several ways of doing this:

- The increases can be the same as the rise in national average earnings. The Secretary of State issues instructions each year, called 'Section 21' Orders, which say how much this should be. Public service schemes do this, but only a very few private sector ones follow them;
- The increases can be at a fixed rate, which was 8.5% a year compound for people who left before April 1988, and is now 7.5% a year compound for those leaving after that. If earnings increase faster than this, you get the extra from the government. If earnings increase less than this, you still get the extra, but your pension itself may then stand still once you retire, until that extra's been used up. Most pension schemes in the private sector use this method;
- The pension can increase at a lower rate, 5% a year, and the scheme pays a premium to the State which guarantees that it will make up the difference between the increases and the actual rise in the Retail Price Index before retirement age.

Whichever way has been chosen, the individual do██ ██
on the GMP element of the scheme. But it's only the ██
covered, and until recently, there were no rules saying that a██
pension had to be increased at all. Employers were reluctant ██ ██
anything voluntarily, since they considered they had no responsibility to people who had left their employment, and the unions did
not press them hard on the issue. But people bitterly resented the
freezing of their pensions, and it created bad feeling which pension
schemes still have not lived down.

The Social Security Act 1985

Finally, in 1985, the government put into effect the recommendations the Occupational Pensions Board had made three years
previously, to give a better deal to all early leavers, whether contracted In or contracted out. It is still far from perfect. The Social
Security Act 1985 said that frozen pensions had to be increased by at
least a minimum amount, and it gave people new rights to transfer
their pensions.

The new rules about increasing pensions apply to all final earnings
schemes, for people who leave after 1 January 1986. It covers only the
pension earned since 1 January 1985, but there's nothing to prevent
schemes covering earlier service, or giving the same terms to people
who left earlier. The increases under these rules are separate from the
increases in Guaranteed Minimum Pension, already explained.

The rule is that the early leaver's pension has to be increased either
in line with the Retail Prices Index, or by 5% compound, whichever is
lower, for all the years between the date of leaving and the date of
retiring. The figures are worked out over the whole of that period,
rather than year by year, and the Secretary of State will issue an
Order, each year, saying what the 'revaluation percentage' is for
people who left their scheme in each of the past years back to 1986.

So if you have several years of low inflation, and then one of high
inflation, the figures are all averaged together to give a total amount.
If, when this is done, 5% compound over the same number of years
would give a lower figure, that is used instead. This means that the
safeguards are pretty limited and if we have high inflation again, pensions can still lose their value quite quickly.

The same rules apply for spouses' and dependants' benefits where a
person dies after s/he reaches pension age. But there is nothing to say
that benefits have to be revalued if the person dies before pension
age.

Schemes which don't base their pension on final earnings have
simpler rules. They have to increase the early leavers' benefits in the
same way as if the person had remained in the scheme. In a money
purchase scheme, for instance one of the new employers' COMP
schemes explained on page 38, this means that if a percentage is
added to the account each year, or a bonus is payable, it must be paid

exactly the same way to leavers and stayers. Alternatively, the money purchase scheme can use the rules for final earnings type schemes, although very few do. New legislation, which is going through Parliament at present, will backdate the increases beyond 1985 for future early leavers, but not for those who have gone already.

Transfers

The same Act brought in a right to transfer benefits to a new scheme, or to an insurance company, for anyone who left after 1 January 1986. Employers have now to let a pension be transferred out. It can go to a new employer's scheme, an insurance company policy, or one of the new Personal Pensions. The member's right to a transfer stays open up until a year before retirement date, so you can leave the scheme and come back in 10 or 20 years' time and ask for your pension to be moved now. This means that members need do nothing in a hurry. If they are leaving and don't know what they are doing next, or if their next job or idea for self-employment is going to work out or not, they can leave the pension for the moment, and contact the pensions manager again when they are more settled. Anyone who starts investigating a transfer need not worry, either, about committing themselves too soon. They have the right to change their minds up to the date when the scheme machinery has started actually to make the transfer.

One exception to this right is if the scheme is wound up. The pension then has to be secured for you, and you cannot transfer it anywhere else.

If you are leaving the scheme but not your job, because you are going to take out a Personal Pension, the employer need not allow you to transfer any of the pension built up before April 1988. However, when you do come to leave the job you will be able to take it with you.

You never see the money in your hand; once the terms have been arranged between the various organisations, the cheque is passed straight between them.

There's no obligation on a new employer to let transfers in, though many now do. The pension you are given can be calculated in terms of extra years in the new pension scheme. This is how public sector schemes work it out. Alternatively, it could be calculated as a money amount, usually based on the minimum pension increases you would have had in the old scheme. Since these are not very generous, this is not so good a deal.

Personal Pensions

An alternative is to transfer your money into a special sort of Personal Pension scheme which just takes the transfer value and lets it build up. You can do this, as a one-off payment, even if you are going into a new company scheme and will thus be ineligible to make any extra payments.

There are also 'Section 32' transfer plans, which work in the same way. With personal pensions, these are now largely a dead letter, though if you are unfreezing an old (pre-1986) pension, then a Section 32 may be all that is available to the trustees.

The insurance companies running these schemes and the brokers who get commission from selling them will give what look like promises of huge amounts in their sales brochures. But when you look more closely, you'll usually find that:

- Very little is guaranteed; it could be only a very low percentage increase, or just the rise in the GMP, explained above, which you would have had anyway. The rest depends on how well the investments do;
- The 'projections' of performance are based on the assumption that today's very good rates of return are going to continue indefinitely, which is highly unlikely; and
- They say nothing about the rate of inflation, or the rate at which your earnings increase. To give an example of the effect this can have, if inflation were 6%, on average, then after 30 years £1,000 will be worth £174 in today's money, and you could expect your earnings to be ten times the amount they are today.

Typical Arrangements and Possible Improvements

There is only one group of schemes where the arrangements for leaving service are largely satisfactory. These are the public service schemes, which have formed what is called the 'transfer club', and do the actuarial calculations for leaving service using the same assumptions, so that pensions in identical or closely similar schemes will be valued at the same amount. There is a table from which they can work out how much a pension from one scheme is worth in another. For example, British Steel at one time had a worse pensions scheme for manual workers than for staff. So it was accepted that a pension in the manual workers' scheme was worth 75% of a pension in the staff scheme.

Also, unlike private schemes they revalue deferred pensions in line with inflation, so that pensions keep their real value.

This means that someone moving from, say, local government to the health service is able either to transfer his/her pension over to the new pension scheme, and buy in all the years s/he has already done in the old one, or to freeze his/her pension with the old employer, secure against inflation.

In the private sector, things are rather different. There is no transfer club, and although the actuaries have now drawn up partly standardised tables, there is still room for people to lose out. The new legal requirements explained above are a lot better than nothing, but still less than we should be asking for. Many employers are still reluctant to take in any transferred pensions at all, especially if they have been contracted out.

The ideal is for the pension for anyone, however long ago it was that they left, to be increased in line with the Retail Prices Index. If that is not achievable, then the whole pension, not just that which has been built up since 1985, should be increased by at least the 'revaluation percentage' explained above. Dependants' pensions should also increase by the same amount.

A further idea to pursue is that of the 'belt and braces' approach. Even if they have something better than the legal minimum, early leavers who are young are tending to lose out, with current investment returns, in a final earnings scheme compared to a money purchase scheme. As money purchase schemes have a lot of other disadvantages, explained on pages 27–8, this is no reason to change the type of scheme. Instead, you can build in a 'no worse off' clause, which says that if the investment returns on the member's share of the fund plus at least the same amount from the employer, would give a higher pension, that is what they would get. This would cost the employer more money, because at the moment schemes are making profits from young early leavers, but it is fairer all round. Another name for a scheme which does this is a 'hybrid scheme', and there were further details about these schemes on pages 43–4.

Should People Take Transfers?

The value of any transfer depends on the amount there was in the scheme to start with, and the level of increases that would be given. The higher these are, the more there will be to transfer. But if the original pension is peanuts, then taking it elsewhere will not make it any better.

In the past, actuaries used to guard the pension schemes carefully, and aimed to let as little as possible out in transfers to other schemes. The schemes that took transfers in, equally, tried to see how little pension they could give in exchange for the money. This has now been reformed, and the new rules about how the 'transfer value' is to be calculated by the actuary make the arrangements fairer. There's still room for improvement, though, especially when a lot of pensions are transferred at once, perhaps after a takeover, explained on pages 182–3.

If your employer's scheme treats early leavers badly, giving them only the minimum legal entitlement, many people – especially young ones – could be better off when they leave putting their money into a Personal Pension rather than keeping it with the employer's scheme. But in terms of collective bargaining, it will be wiser to try to negotiate a better deal from the employer rather than encouraging members to take their pensions elsewhere when they leave. Once they have left, and taken out another policy, they are on their own.

Any improvements in the employer's scheme or increases in the pension in payment will only affect those who have stayed with the scheme.

People can now transfer their pensions into one of the new Appropriate Personal Pension schemes, explained in Chapter 6. They need to be even more cautious about doing that, because it is possible to give up your rights to a GMP in this way, for service right back to 1978. Generally, the unions should be advising people to think carefully about the wisdom of giving up a guarantee for the chance of a bigger – or smaller – pension in the end.

We need further legislation before the position on transfers is sorted out. For the moment, the trade union view should be that everyone should have the right to take a transfer, whether they left before or after January 1986. Before anyone opts to do so, the pension scheme manager should provide them with a checklist of the questions to ask so that they can find out what sort of deal they are really getting, and some help with working out the advantages or disadvantages of each course of action. If the scheme manager isn't competent to do this, then he or she can make arrangements with a trustworthy independent broker to go through the issue with the members. A large amount of money can be at stake, so it is important that members are properly advised.

Possible Arguments and Responses
The argument about the rights of leavers has been going on for a long time, and follows fairly well-worn tracks. The arguments for a better deal are:

- The majority of people are 'early leavers'. Those who stay are in the minority. There are now quite a number of schemes with more frozen pensions than active members or pensioners. It is unfair that the majority should be penalised to subsidise the minority;
- People leave their jobs for all sorts of reasons, not just to 'better themselves'. They may indeed be forced to leave by the actions of the employer, in making them redundant. Why then should they lose so heavily?
- The effect of inflation is that frozen pensions, even with the improvements made by the government, decline in value over the years. It's not the intention of the pension scheme that this should happen. If there were no inflation, frozen pensions would work fairly well. Since inflation appears to be with us to stay, should not the scheme be taking account of it, and adapting the rules to match?
- Pension schemes have done very well in recent years, and built up substantial surpluses. But this has only partly come about because of good investment results. It's also because the early leavers' pensions are increasing at a much lower rate than

interest payments or share dividends, and so the scheme is making a profit from them. They have a moral claim on that profit, even though not a legal one.

The employer's response will be:

- There's only a limited amount of money to go round, and they prefer to spend it on those who stay, rather than on those who go. At times, this gets expressed in an almost feudal attitude of 'looking after those who are loyal to the company'. It reveals what pension schemes, like other fringe benefits, are about – tying people into the company so that they do not have a free choice of job.
- Or they will say that the whole thing has been solved now, by government legislation. That's already costing them money, and they don't want to spend any more than they have to. In reply, you can say that the legislation is only a half-way house, as the Occupational Pensions Board recognised when it asked companies voluntarily to do more, and that people who leave early still lose out, though much less than they did.
- They could suggest that though the government is able to inflation-proof, as private employers they can't because it's too much of a risk. If inflation took off again, they might find themselves landed with an enormous commitment. But the government is selling index-linked bonds (though pension schemes are not buying them very much), which keep up with inflation and are totally secure. A scheme can buy just the right number of bonds to cover the liabilities to the early leavers, and put them into an earmarked part of the fund that is not touched for any other reason.

Another standard response is that the other members of the scheme, 'those who do intend to stay', won't like money being spent on those who leave. This may have been true in the past, when it was chiefly long-serving white collar staff who had a pension scheme. But now that schemes have been extended to so many manual workers, who are highly conscious of the problems of redundancies and closures, it's a myth.

20

Miscellaneous Clauses

Temporary Absence

This means periods when you are away from your job – through sickness, or pregnancy, or if you're away studying, or if you've been laid off for a period, but are still being counted as an employee.

What You Must Have
Under the Social Security Pensions Act, if you are a member of a contracted-out scheme, then you are a contracted-out employee while you have a contract of service, and are in a job which is covered by the contracting-out certificate. So however long you are away, if you still have a contract with the company you need not be treated as having left the scheme.

If you are getting no money from the company for a time, it will reduce your annual earnings figure on which your GMP is calculated, and therefore the GMP you finally get.

A woman who is away on account of pregnancy, even if she has technically left work while away, can still be treated as a contracted-out employee for that gap, if she exercises her right to return to work. If she doesn't, she must be treated as having left service on the day her contract ended.

Under the Social Security Act 1989, after the end of 1992 periods of paid maternity leave must be treated as periods of full paid service in the pension scheme. Contributions, though, can only be deducted from the woman's actual pay.

Periods of paid family leave will also be covered by this, but the pension need only be calculated on the basis of what is actually paid out to the employee.

What the Inland Revenue Allows
The Inland Revenue says that, except in cases of sickness, a person may be treated as temporarily absent for up to three years for any reason, or for longer if absence is due to 'secondment to a United Kingdom Government Department, or work of national importance of a like nature', so long as there is a definite expectation of a return to work, and s/he doesn't become a member of another pension scheme.

If s/he is sick, s/he can be retained in the pension scheme indefinitely, even if not expected to return to work. If wages are being paid,

171

for instance under a sick pay scheme, the company is allowed to deduct the pension scheme contributions. But if there are no wages the company can pay both its and the member's contributions for as long as necessary.

If someone retires or dies after a period of reduced earnings, or nil earnings, resulting from sickness, the Inland Revenue allows the benefits to be calculated on the basis of the last year in which s/he had 'normal' earnings, uprated to take account of inflation since then.

Typical Arrangements and Possible Improvements
In general, schemes do not treat temporary absence, even when it is a result of sickness, very well. The wording below, taken from the Brook and Crowther scheme, is fairly typical:

> If you are absent from work through illness or injury you shall be deemed to have remained in Service as long as there is a definite expectation of your return to work but if you are absent for any other reason you will normally be deemed to have left Service after one year's such absence unless there are circumstances which in our opinion (which shall be final) justify a longer period of absence up to a maximum of three years.
>
> For the purposes of this Condition non-payment of salary during temporary absence shall not be deemed to terminate your Service but, in the case of a contributory scheme shall, if you so request and we agree, be deemed to excuse you from contributing to the Scheme until payment of your salary recommences. We may decide whether and to what extent any part of the benefits ... under the Scheme shall be reduced during periods of temporary absence and the terms on which the benefits shall be reinstated on your return to work.

It's common for schemes to allow you to retain your membership for longer if you are sick than for any other reason. Usually the company will expect you to pay contributions from any sick pay, but they do often pay your share once sick pay stops, at least for a limited period. If there is a Permanent Health Insurance scheme, explained in Chapter 15, then this will usually cover pension scheme contributions.

Death benefit is usually maintained during periods of temporary absence, at the rate at which the member was entitled when s/he first became absent. But some companies stop it after a while, or reduce the amount. In the Brook and Crowther example quoted above, for instance, the company used the clause that allowed it to cut benefits to reduce the death benefit for a member who had been sick for three years before he died, from £12,000 to £3,000.

Few companies have amended their booklets to take account specifically of maternity leave, and they have not even heard of paternity leave. Those which have, mainly where the scheme is insured and the insurance company has given the advice, usually have a standard clause saying something like this (taken from the Toyworks scheme):

> If you are a female member leaving as a result of pregnancy or confinement and exercise your right under the Employment Protection (Consolidation) Act 1978 to return to work, you will be treated as temporarily absent while you are away, but the period of absence will not rank for pension.

In some cases, then, maternity absence is treated worse than sickness absence, and death benefit is paid out only at the rate it would be for early leavers. This was the case, for instance, in the Vauxhall scheme, until the unions persuaded the company to make a change.

If the temporary absence clause in your booklet is very brief, as they often are, or non-existent, the point is almost bound to be covered in the rules at greater length, and in this case you will have to look at them to find out the position.

Layoff is hardly ever specifically mentioned in scheme booklets, although pension schemes are now quite widespread in industries which are prone to layoffs, like engineering and the motor industry. Often it is left to local procedure. One example where it is mentioned is Vauxhall, whose booklet says:

> In deciding whether service has been continuous, absence due to the following circumstances will not count as a break in service;
> (a) absence not exceeding 12 consecutive months because of sickness or accident;
> (b) layoff not exceeding 6 consecutive months because of lack of work.

Strikes and trade disputes are even more rarely mentioned. Usually, it is sorted out (so long as the negotiators remember) when the dispute is settled. But if it is not cleared up and an agreement reached, the members will have a gap in their pension entitlement. There was a long and bitter wrangle between the NUM and British Coal, for instance, over how the pensions of mineworkers should be treated after their dispute, and it ended up with the two sides going to court to resolve it. More recently, the government introduced a punitive arrangement for teachers who want to buy back their pensions after a dispute.

Points to be covered in a temporary absence clause are:

- When someone is absent through sickness, but is retained on the payroll, then s/he should be kept in the pension scheme indefinitely;
- If someone is being paid full or nearly full wages by the company, then contributions can be deducted from him/her. But if no wages are being paid, or only a small amount, then the company should make up the contributions. Ideally, this should be indefinitely in cases of sickness, pregnancy and layoffs

resulting from company decisions, and for a specific period for any other reason. The company may refuse to countenance any indefinite commitment, so you would need to decide what is a reasonable period;

- Death benefit should always be maintained when a member is accepted as temporarily absent, at the rate s/he was entitled to when s/he first went absent;
- When a member is finally taken off the payroll and treated as having left service, his/her service should be ended at the date when s/he is taken off the payroll, not at the date when s/he first became absent;
- Where it is a member's responsibility to make up the contributions on his/her return, s/he should have the option of paying by a lump sum or in instalments over a long period. (You can get tax relief on either.)

When you are negotiating an agreement which means people will be temporarily absent (for example, for study leave) check on the pension rules, and ensure that these people will not be adversely affected. In order to keep the pension booklet simple, it is probably best to give general guidelines there, and expand any special points in the specific agreement.

Reasonable treatment of temporary absence is not expensive. Just how much it will cost depends on the arrangements for sick pay, special leave, and so on. In the past there was a general assumption that most people in pension schemes were white collar, were fully covered by sick pay schemes, and would be paid by the company during any other periods of temporary absence that happen with their approval. This would have meant that cases in which people have to fall back on their provisions are rare. The reality, now that pensions have been extended to the hourly paid, is different.

Possible Arguments and Responses

The detailed arguments on this will depend on what type of absence you are talking about. The general principle, however, will be the same. People should not suffer in retirement by having a reduced pension because there have been short periods when they have not been at work, perhaps many years earlier.

This argument is much stronger where the absence has not been the employee's fault – where, for instance, it is due to sickness – or where it is sanctioned by another agreement with the employer. Study leave might be an example of this. It would contradict such an agreement if the pension scheme was then to penalise people.

For absence which the company permits, but is not paying for – an extended holiday without pay, for instance – you need to ask for better arrangements for payment of the member's own contributions. You could argue that the company, having permitted the absence, should not then make it more difficult or inconvenient for the member to fit back in than need be. Paying contributions all in a lump sum may cause hardship, especially if the person has been without pay for some time, and it is only common sense to make it smoother by allowing arrears to be paid off bit by bit.

Employers will probably reply that better arrangements for temporary absence are too expensive, both in terms of pension and in administration. Ask them to tell you what the actual cost will be, because it probably won't be much. If necessary, suggest that they work out how many cases it would have applied to in the recent past. On your side, try to find actual examples where there has been an obvious inconsistency of treatment between the industrial relations and pensions departments, and where there has been hardship because of inflexible treatment.

Life Assurance Continuation

In many booklets, especially where the scheme is insured, you will find a section that says something like this:

> Death benefit ceases on leaving, but if you leave before your 60th birthday you will normally have the option, without having to produce any evidence of good health, to take out a new and individual whole life or endowment insurance policy with the ABC insurance company to replace any death benefit cover which has ceased.

This is there to give the insurance company a bit of extra business. But it can be useful to the older, less healthy, member who would have to pay a lot more for life assurance if s/he had to have a medical examination.

However, where a member is taking early retirement because of ill-health, or is being made redundant, this clause is not enough. The company should then continue the coverage at its own expense. See pages 129 and 135 for details on this.

Many of these clauses are anyway now being dropped by the insurance companies, because they are afraid of the risk of insuring someone with AIDS. If they do insist on cutting out this clause in your scheme, ask for compensating improvements elsewhere.

Assignment

Most booklets have a clause saying something like this:

> The benefits provided by the scheme are strictly personal and must not be assigned, mortgaged, or alienated in any way.

The Inland Revenue insists on this rule, which is meant to safeguard pensioners from being pressured into signing over the cheques to the landlady. If the rule is broken, the benefits can be forfeited altogether, so that no-one gets them.

However, you can in fact borrow money against your expectations from your pension scheme – especially via a pension mortgage, which is becoming very popular now. The insurance company or the pension scheme's consultants will set this up with a building society. They get round the rules by not asking you to sign anything that says you will use your lump sum at retirement to pay off the mortgage – just pointing out that if you don't, they'll foreclose and you'll lose the house!

Evidence of Health

Some booklets have a clause saying 'Evidence of health may be required before you are permitted to join. If that is the case you will be notified.'

This is generally because of an insurance company practice called the 'free limit'. They will have said that they will insure anyone for up to, say £50,000 without a medical examination, but if the liability goes over that limit, they reserve the right to ask for one. The limit is usually pretty high, so that it won't affect most manual workers. If it is affecting a substantial number of people, ask the employer to shop around for a better insurer.

Some employers insist on all employees taking a medical examination before they can join the scheme. While one can't argue with this, the results should not be allowed to exclude anyone from the scheme. The union attitude is that 'if someone is fit for the job, they are fit for the pension scheme.' The company should also pay all the costs, and make sure that the medical examination results are retained only for use in the pension scheme.

It may be difficult to get these restrictive clauses removed and you may even find new ones being imposed, because of the insurance companies' fear of the AIDS risk. The union view here should be that if the company has adopted a particular personnel policy, it should not allow itself to be diverted because of problems over pensions. If someone is uninsurable, the company should carry the risk itself.

In schemes that are just starting up, there is often a clause saying that employees who are away sick on the day the scheme starts, or on the day they become eligible, will not be allowed into the scheme until they have completed two months' continuous employment.

As usual, this is because of cost. It's a crude way of weeding out some of the people in poor health. If the employer and the insurance company cannot be persuaded to drop this condition altogether, then at least life assurance should be provided for everyone, whether sick or not.

21

Changing or Winding Up the Scheme

What You Must Have

Increasingly these days, changes in pensions are being made by Acts of Parliament or Regulations, and these override any scheme rules. This happened for instance when the government made all pension schemes voluntary from April 1988. In other cases, the new law says either that schemes must change their own rules to match, or that they can if they wish. It is the responsibility of the pensions administrator and the scheme's solicitor to keep up with the changes in the law, and make sure that the scheme is not breaking it by mistake.

Rights to Consultation

Chapter 4 explained people's rights under the Social Security Pensions Act 1975. To summarise them, if:

- A contracted-out scheme is amended to contract in, or
- A contracted-in one is amended to contract out, or
- A contracted-out one is amended in a way that affects, or might affect, the terms of contracting out,

then the company must give three months' notice to the members, though this period can be shortened to only a month if the unions agree in writing. It must also consult the recognised trade unions, but it need not accept their views. 'Consult' means only that. The Occupational Pensions Board (OPB) then has to consent. The unions have a right to complain to the OPB if they believe they have not been properly consulted, but they have never refused a certificate for that reason.

If the scheme is being amended so that it is no longer contracted out on a guaranteed basis, or at all, then the fund must either preserve the GMPs, or buy them back into the State scheme through paying what are known as 'accrued rights premiums'. This puts you back in the State scheme as if you had never left it.

What the Inland Revenue Allows

The Inland Revenue will allow schemes to be altered, but has to give its approval. Making an alteration without its blessing may jeopardise the status of the whole scheme.

Getting final 'definitive' legal documents for the trust deed and rules is a long slow process. This is partly because of the detailed technical work that has to be done, and partly because lawyers are anyway very slow. While the documents are being prepared, the scheme will be run on 'interim' deeds and rules. This is accepted by the Inland

Revenue, and everyone else, as all right and as binding as the real thing. An additional amendment will create another interim deed or, until even that has been prepared, will be contained in the announcement of the change, which will be regarded as definitive.

What Trust Deeds Say

The way the rules of a particular scheme are changed will depend on what the original trust deed says. Deeds can say:

- That the members must be given a specific period of notice before any alteration can become effective;
- That the approval of a majority of members must be obtained (this is rare, and usually happens in older schemes which were set up originally as 'superannuation societies'); or
- That only amendments that do not prejudice the accrued rights of existing members will be permitted.

If the scheme's powers are too cumbersome and restrictive, it is possible for the Occupational Pensions Board to override the terms of the deed, but this is not often done.

When an alteration is made to any of the main benefits of the scheme, the members who are affected must be informed, in writing, and told where to get further details (for more about this, see Chapter 24).

Most schemes have a clause like this, somewhere in the booklet:

The board has every intention of maintaining the scheme, but it will be understood that future conditions cannot be foreseen; the right must therefore be reserved to amend or terminate it at any time.

This is there to protect the company. It means that you do not have the rights you would otherwise have under your contract of employment.

Typical Arrangements and Possible Improvements
Of course, we want to see that any changes are negotiated with the unions; this point is covered more fully in Chapter 25. If a scheme is changing its contracting-out status, so that formal consultation has to take place, the union should be brought in at the earliest stage, if possible before any notices have been issued to the members.

Accrued Benefits

In many schemes the rules do not allow amendments which would reduce the accrued benefits – those you have already built up through being a member of the scheme – without the specific consent of the member concerned.

It is rare for a reduction in those accrued benefits to be proposed. It might be, though, if it was being claimed that there was not enough money in the fund to pay for what had been promised. The need for individual consent gives the unions a powerful bargaining counter then. But it shouldn't be overestimated. The company still has the ultimate weapon of closing the scheme down altogether, and this freezes the accrued benefits.

Sometimes a set of alterations will be proposed, and the members asked to agree, on the basis that though it may reduce some accrued benefits for some people, the overall effect is beneficial. This should be resisted. In any changeover the aim should be that no one individual should be worse off.

It should be agreed that anyone who is potentially going to suffer will have his/her benefit calculated in the two alternative ways, and the better one paid.

The company may threaten that if people do not consent, it will discontinue the whole scheme and start again. If the proposed improvements have been discussed in detail, this is unlikely. It might well, in any case, cost them more in administrative time than the extra calculations involved. As a compromise, you could agree to limit the length of time during which the scheme had to do the alternative calculations, say to five years.

Changing the Scheme after a Takeover, a Buyout, or Privatisation

Companies can change hands in a number of ways, and so can individual plants or workplaces. They can be taken over by another company, or bought by a group formed specially for the purpose (often with the local management involved and putting in some of the money). In the last few years there have been a considerable number of changes of ownership because the government has sold off nationalised industries or parts of them. For convenience, this section refers mainly to takeovers, but other changes of ownership have the same effects, and the same points will apply.

In all these cases, there can be an effect on the pension scheme. The law does not give much protection to the pension rights of people affected by a takeover – in fact, the legal rights in this area are weaker than on many other items. The Transfer of Undertakings Regulations 1982, which were passed at the insistence of the EEC to protect employees' rights, cover everything except pension schemes.

At worst, the new employer can simply close down the old scheme (or remove a group from it) without providing for a new one, and treat employees as early leavers, with a preserved benefit.

There are two ways in which ownership of a business can change hands:

- When a business takes over another business completely; and
- When it takes over part of that business.

So ABC Ltd may buy enough shares in XYZ Ltd to give it control – this is the first type. Or it could do a deal with XYZ Ltd to buy its office equipment division as a separate entity, and that will be the second type. The big contested takeovers you read about in the newspapers, like Hanson Trust and Imperial Group, are usually takeovers of a whole business. Then the new managers may sell off complete companies within that business – as Hanson did, selling Courage off to Elders. Or they may take the company to pieces, and sell off one factory here and one there to different people.

If ownership of the whole business changes hands, then the pension scheme, as a separate fund attached to that business, goes with it. The employees can stay in the separate scheme within the new company for ever, if that's the way things work out. The contracting-out certificate needs to be varied, but only on the technicality of adding the new subsidiary's name to the list covered by the holding company on the master certificate.

Where part of the business is taken over, it's much more difficult. The employees affected have to be withdrawn from the previous scheme, and put in a different one. The old and the new companies' contracting-out certificates have to be changed, which could mean that the formal consultation under the Social Security Pensions Act has to be carried out.

In these cases, so far as the pension scheme is concerned the changeover may mean leaving one job and starting another. This can mean you have the opportunity for a refund, if you have been there for less than two years, or for taking a transfer of the value of your benefits to a Personal Pension.

The Inland Revenue recognises that it takes a while to sort out the details of old and new pension schemes, and so it will allow a 'period of grace' during which people working for the new employer are still technically covered by the old employer's scheme. This would not usually be for longer than a year, but if there are particular difficulties it will allow longer. The most common difficulty that arises is between the actuaries of the two funds, who will be unable to agree how much of the old scheme money belongs to the people involved in the takeover, and therefore how much should go over from one fund to the other.

Before the Takeover Happens

The best time to influence what happens is before the takeover documents have actually been signed and sealed, while the old and the new managements are anxious to reassure the workforce. They may make statements that 'nothing is going to change, terms and conditions will be just the same,' which can be used later. Keep copies of any announcements made or any letters sent out by management, and notes of any meetings that are held. If management are not making this sort of statement, ask them – and try to pin them down in writing – as early as possible. If you can get in as soon as something is in the wind, the sale agreement may not yet have been signed, and you may be able to influence it.

Ask the selling company specifically to include safeguards for pensions in the sale agreement. Suggest a wording along these lines:

The pension rights of the transferred employees will be maintained on the same basis or one that is no less favourable.

The assets transferred will be kept separate, and used only for the benefit of the transferred employees.

This is difficult to enforce, though it's still better than nothing. If the new company breaks the sale agreement, in theory the old one could take them to court. But all the new company has to do is hang on to the scheme for a few months and then close it, saying that it is because of 'other factors', nothing to do with the sale agreement.

In theory, you also have a right to claim constructive dismissal, if the new company worsens your terms of employment by closing down the pension scheme. But there have been no cases about this, and the law is not very clear.

So although threatening legal action, and the publicity that goes with it, may be a useful weapon, the chances of actually succeeding in court are small. It's usually better to rely on the force of the commitments made, and the need for the new employer to establish good relations with the new workers.

Member Trustees

The member trustees of a scheme have a crucial role, and may need to go to court. The trustees for the Courage pension fund, for instance, won a legal victory over their new owners Elders, and over Hanson Trust, in 1987 when they had been taken over. They went to court, and established that the surplus should remain with the Courage fund, rather than be used by Hanson Trust to offset the sale price.

It's clear in trust law that trustees have to act in the interests of all their members. Until terms are finally settled and people have left the scheme altogether, they are still members. The trustees must also not favour one section over another, which means that they should not help existing members gain better benefits at the expense of those leaving.

If the takeover is really a rescue, and it was clear that your company (or your part of the company) was going to close down if it wasn't bought, or if the receiver had actually been brought in, and sold your plant off, you're in a weak position. But if yours was a profitable plant bought as an investment by an expanding company, you could be in quite a strong position. What you should try to get will be the same in each case.

Try to avoid being rushed into agreeing a change before a deadline. You might be told 'you have to agree to this because you cannot stay in your previous company's scheme beyond a certain date.' This, though, is a matter for negotiation. It is quite usual for employees of a company that has been sold to continue in membership of that company's pension scheme for some time after the deal has been completed. This gives the purchaser time to complete the transfer calculations, draw up the legal deeds, and do other administrative chores. If the period originally allowed for this was not enough, the Inland Revenue is not going to object to a reasonable extension.

Maintaining the Package

The aim is to maintain the same package of benefits in the new company as in the old, or even improve on it. This means that any new scheme should be arranged so that it is no worse, not only as a package as a whole, but also for each individual. So for instance if the new scheme provides a better spouse's pension, but a worse death benefit, the person who leaves no spouse will lose, so his/her rights must be safeguarded.

Don't allow your pension rights to be bought out by a cash sum, however attractive it may be. Pension rights are different from cash, and one cannot replace the other in that way.

Try to insist that any benefits you get are based on the service you have done with both companies, and your final salary at the date of retiring or leaving, not on how far the money in the old fund will go. It's not your fault if the old scheme was not properly financed. It was for the new employer to find that out, and adjust the purchase price to take account of it. If that didn't happen, that's his/her bad luck, and you shouldn't be penalised. But if the new employer has made a mistake, it may cost him/her a lot to give in to you, so you could have quite a fight on your hands.

Your old company could have been acquired with the deliberate aim of 'pension stripping', that is, closing down the fund and taking out the surplus for the employer's use. This should be resisted – how to do it is covered in more detail in the next section.

If the new employer has been expanding recently, it is likely to have a fairly rigid policy on how to treat new subsidiaries, with the aim of cutting cost. In that case, you want to argue for that policy to be changed, because this is more likely to succeed than arguing for being a special case. Try to get in touch with any other recent acquisition (the company's Annual Report, or Labour Research – whose address is listed on page 265 – will tell you about them) and form a common front. Try also to get in touch with stewards in the new parent company, and ask them to make clear that they don't want to profit at the expense of the new acquisitions.

What is the company doing for the pensions of the management people it has brought in? The chances are that it is giving them better terms – possibly even very generous ones, if there are people it wants to be sure will stay. So assuming the new employer has bought your company not just because of the management skills, but because of the workers' skills as well, surely they ought to treat the workers no worse.

Possible Ways of Safeguarding Benefits

Facsimile Scheme

This means setting up a scheme identical in all ways to the previous one. This is a useful approach where the previous scheme was of a good standard, and there is no scheme in the new company, or only one that is very much worse or for which that group of workers is ineligible. Some good employers will make the setting up of a scheme like this part of the conditions of sale – Pilkingtons and Cadbury Schweppes have done this, for instance. So too have some of the nationalised industries when they have sold parts off – though they have allowed new recruits to be given benefits on worse terms, as explained below.

This means that no-one loses benefit, at least at the time of transfer, though you might find later that the old company makes improvements that are not carried over by the new employer. Go through the small print of any new 'facsimile' scheme that is produced, and check that it really is identical.

Special Terms in the New Company Scheme

Another possibility is to bring the new group of employees into an existing scheme, but with special terms. This is often referred to as 'red circling' and works best where the new scheme is generally better than the old, but has one or two features which are worse. For example:

> Old Scheme A is a 1/80th scheme with the minimum widow's benefit allowed for contracting out, but a death benefit of four times earnings. New Scheme B, on the other hand, is a much better 1/60th scheme, with a good spouse's pension, but only twice earnings for the death benefit. So Scheme A members should be offered membership of scheme B, with their level of death benefit protected for them as individuals.

The special terms would disappear when the old scheme members left or retired, and so the employer would be able to see an end to any financial commitment.

Creating a Completely New Scheme

If the two schemes are very different, or if the new employer is anxious to wipe the slate clean, s/he may decide to create an entirely new scheme and discontinue the old one. This has been done particularly in the case of very large mergers, and it often takes a few years to come about.

The company will generally have fairly clear ideas about why it is bringing everyone into a new scheme. It's a fairly laborious task, so it is not doing it for fun. Its reasons might include:

- The administrative costs of running a lot of small schemes are high;

- The board doesn't feel that local management is making a very good job of running the individual companies' schemes, and it wants to bring them all under the control of one professional pensions department;
- They want to establish a stronger 'corporate identity' and make you feel you are working for Universal Grand Magnificent Ltd, not its subsidiary Small Miserable Ltd;
- One old scheme has a surplus, while another has a deficit, and they want to use the money in one scheme to prop up the other.

The new scheme should be negotiated, rather than imposed, and in the discussions the unions should aim to ensure that the best features of each scheme are incorporated in the new one. If there was something especially good in one particular old scheme, this may not be possible, but at least that group should have their benefits protected by 'red circling'.

If there is more money in one scheme than in the others, then the members of that scheme have a moral right (though not a legal one) to benefit from it. They could do so by having specially improved conditions, or by having extra increases to their pensions and those of people who have left. It would be fairest, perhaps, if those people were given a 'money purchase underpin' (explained on page 44) to their pensions, based on the funds in the scheme at the time of the changeover. This would ensure that the surplus was used specifically for them and for no-one else.

The Old Scheme Pension
It often happens that the old scheme pension is frozen, at the value it was when the changeover took place, and only given the increases laid down by law. This is not acceptable. Instead, it should be paid at retirement date on the basis of earnings at that date. For example:

The old pension in company X was based on 1/100th of earnings. The new one, starting in April 1988, is based on 1/80ths.

Joan Smith started with the company in 1978, and retires in 1998. Her pension at retirement date should all be calculated on her final earnings of (say) £10,000 a year. So she would get 10/80ths, plus 10/100ths, of £10,000 as her pension.

Privatisations
Over the last few years, large numbers of union members have moved from the public to the private sector. Whole industries, like British Telecom and British Gas, have been sold off; so also have parts of other industries, like the transport hotels that British Rail used to run, which went to a variety of private firms.

Most of the members had previously been promised index linked pensions – that is, that the pension once they retired or left would go up in line with the Retail Prices Index, and so keep its real value. As pointed out on page 161, this is very rare in the private sector, and disliked by many private employers (and also by the Tory government).

In some cases, such as the Civil Service and local government, this is actually written into the scheme by law, under the 1971 Pensions Increase Act. In others, the scheme trustees have made a practice of following the Act, although not obliged to do so.

Because of continued opposition from scheme trustees, scheme members, and their trade unions, the government has usually not been able to make changes that affect existing scheme members. It has now developed a fairly standard policy. This is to close the current scheme to new entrants, and put them into one without indexing, and sometimes with other differences as well. This policy makes it difficult to organise resistance within the workforce, since their benefits are unaffected, and the average member is not interested enough to take a strong line on the rights of new people not yet working there.

Below are two examples of privatisations, which illustrate the different way things have worked.

Royal Ordnance Factories
The ROF workers were members of the Civil Service scheme. When the plans were laid to privatise them, the government set up two schemes, with rules and a trust deed. The Crown scheme, for existing employees, took on 15,100 members. The terms of the scheme are almost identical to the principal Civil Service scheme, except that it is contributory; a non-pensionable supplement was added to pay to cover this. There is a 'ceiling' on the index-linking commitment, which applies so long as it does not push the employer's costs above 12%. The 1984 scheme, for new entrants, is less good and does not have a guarantee of index linking.

Most of the Royal Ordnance Factories have now been bought by British Aerospace. There has been no announcement as yet of any change to the pension plans. The Leeds factory was bought by Vickers, who have made the ROF members a special section, with their rights preserved, within the Vickers scheme.

National Bus Company
The government has been selling off the bus industry, in bits, under the 1985 Transport Act. So far, 78 subsidiaries have been sold.

National Bus had two pension schemes, one for white collar and one for manual workers. They were funded schemes, less good than most public sector ones, and with some financial problems. Many employees have 'criss-crossing' pension rights with London Transport or other nationalised transport industries such as British Rail.

While the original 1982 Transport Act was going through Parliament, the unions tried to persuade the Secretary of State to order any buyer to establish a pension scheme not less favourable than the existing one. The government refused, saying that the initiative must lie with the company, and the Secretary of State must not take away its freedom of choice. They did however accept that the Secretary of State must take into account representations made by the scheme trustees.

In 1985, the unions pressed for a consortium or federation of private operators running a single scheme, at least for existing members, handing over administrative responsibility to one of their number. They had some support from pension scheme management, but no help from the government. Instead, the Department of Transport asked private insurance companies to quote for providing deferred annuities. It was anxious to see the scheme broken up as soon as possible, even though there was no buyer in sight and it was expected to take up to three years to dismember NBC. The scheme trustees (both management and member representatives) did not consider that the insurance company's package was equivalent to the current benefits.

The arguments over this hinged on index linking. The existing schemes linked benefits to national average earnings, while the new proposal was for a link to the Retail Prices Index plus 1.5%. The trustees also were given a legal opinion that:

> it would be irresponsible for the trustees to rush into a hasty and irrevocable decision on a matter of this importance.

After a last ditch attempt in the Lords to alter the Bill's provisions on pensions a national strike of bus workers on the issue took place in October 1985 – one of the very few such national actions over pensions, especially among manual workers. The government took no notice. But because the scheme itself was financially sound, the trustees were able at a later stage to increase the guarantee to 2.25% above the RPI.

As each local bus company was sold off, a new scheme was negotiated with the new employers. A fairly typical one, from West Yorkshire Road Car Company (based in Harrogate) gives 1/80th of earnings above the LEL per year of service, plus a 3/80ths lump sum. There is a 3% guaranteed increase, with a commitment to review pensions above that level.

Lessons for Others
There are several lessons to be learnt from these examples, for future privatisations:

- The unions should make their voice heard as early as possible, and as forcefully, while there are potential buyers still thinking about it;
- They should check what the trust deed says (especially any 'no-detriment' clauses, explained on pages 181–2), and try to ally with the trustees;

• When the new scheme is set up, they should be in there from the beginning, and aim to have member trustees appointed and properly trained. This can in fact give them more influence over the scheme than they could ever have had over the old public sector one.

Information to the Members

When a scheme has been revamped – for whatever reason – members often have a series of choices to take. They can stay in the old scheme; move over to the new one; or drop out altogether and take out a Personal Pension. They will often be very confused about what to do, and will need straightforward advice from the company and from the unions.

Ask the company to supply you with a series of typical examples for both men and women members, showing the effects of the old and new benefit structures. These ought to compare the potential future service pension on the old and new bases, and show how the change compares with any change in contributions. Along with this there should be a statement showing the effect of other changes, such as widows' pension rights or ill-health retirement, being brought in at the same time. Include some examples covering married women paying the reduced rate contribution, if there are members in this position.

You'll also want to tell people what the employer's record is on pension increases, and what the future policy is, to help them judge what to do.

Ask the company to hold a question and answer session at the plants affected, and also a 'surgery' to which people can take their individual queries in confidence. There should also be individual statements showing each member's options.

If the unions have negotiated the terms, and are reasonably satisfied, a joint recommendation from the company and the unions on the course of action can be useful. Sometimes this is presented at a delegate conference from all the sites affected. This gives a chance to discuss future improvements and arrangements for member participation. If there's been any uncertainty or suspicion about the company's proposals it could be helpful for some independent expert – like an actuary – to give a report to the conference about the new scheme.

If people are being given options, an important point is to make sure that an answer is received from everyone. The option form should be designed so that even if employees want to make no change, they still have to say so. Ask the company to issue a benefit statement to everyone who joins the new scheme, showing what their past service rights are compared to what they were in the old scheme. Often when this is done, owing to some odd personal circumstances it's found that some people will not get quite the benefits intended, or their details have been wrongly transferred to the new scheme. The unions need to keep a watching brief while the change-over is happening, and help the members as necessary to keep things right.

22

Closing Down Schemes

There are two ways in which a pension scheme can be closed down. One is when the employer remains in business. This could happen because s/he has decided s/he does not want to give members pensions any more; or there could be a different – and hopefully better – scheme starting up. The other is when the company is wound up altogether, perhaps because of bankruptcy.

When the Employer Stays in Business

What You Must Have

If a contracted-out scheme is being wound up altogether, the employer must inform the members, by giving them a notice of intention, and consult the recognised trade unions. The notice of intention will usually run for three months, but this can be shortened, with the OPB's permission, to a month. When the time given on the notice runs out, the scheme surrenders its contracting-out certificate and the members go back to paying contributions at the contracted-in rate. The company then either pays an accrued rights premium over to the State, which puts you back into SERPS, or buys you rights with another scheme, such as one run by an insurance company.

Companies can shortcut the duty to inform and consult by simply stopping paying their contributions to the contracted-out scheme. In that case, sooner or later the OPB has to cancel the certificate, and this takes effect immediately.

When a scheme is being wound up, details of the amount of benefit due, and who will be responsible for paying it, must go to every beneficiary, and every member who has an entitlement. If there's a shortfall because there's not enough money to go round, they must be told what it is.

What the Inland Revenue Allows

A scheme which is discontinued – which is the word the Inland Revenue always uses – can be either frozen or wound up. If it is frozen, the Practice Notes say,

> All contributions cease, but the assets of the scheme continue to be held by or on behalf of the administrator, and are applied to provide benefits according to the rules when existing members retire, or die, or withdraw from service.

In a winding up, how the benefits are dealt with, and the order of priority if there is not enough money to go round, will be covered by the rules of the scheme (explained below).

Employees in employment cannot usually have their contributions returned while they remain in service. The employer can, though, which seems very unfair. The Inland Revenue's reasoning is based, as usual, on the view that pension schemes are a tax fiddle for the higher paid. They believe that company directors who can decide whether or not to run a pension scheme will keep opening new ones and closing others just to get a tax benefit.

What it has done, though, with its new rules on actuarial surpluses (explained on pages 246–7), is provide a way in which the employer can make a substantial gain by taking a refund of the scheme's surplus. This is called 'pension stripping' and is common in the US. It has happened occasionally in the UK, but has not yet become a fashion. The court decision in the Courage case (explained on page 181) made it a less attractive tactic for predator companies.

What Happens to Your Rights

The trust deed and rules always have a section spelling out what is to be done on discontinuance. Usually this will have a list of priorities – that is, who has first call on the funds available. A scheme that has been properly funded for discontinuance (explained on page 248) ought to have enough money to pay all the outstanding claims. If there is not, then the money is divided up in the order given in the deed and rules.

Pensions in payment will have the first priority; then come the GMPs in a contracted-out scheme, and any left-over payments from the old State Graduated scheme get priority. Then come the members' benefits in general. After the top priorities have been met, the money will be divided up, if there is not enough to go round, so that everyone has the same proportion of his/her full entitlement.

If there is enough money to pay the full entitlement, the trust deed usually says that any extra goes back to the company. It is possible, though, for a deed to be amended to say that any extra is used to increase the pensions of people who have retired, and the deferred pensions of existing members, right up to Inland Revenue limits. This is not often done, but it is worth trying before a company gets into financial difficulties. It is also a useful protection against a predator trying to take the company over.

Guaranteed increases in pensions will be covered under the wind-up rules, but one-off increases at the trustees' discretion will not. This is a good reason for making sure that there are guarantees.

It's rare for employers to try to wind up their schemes when they are still in existence, unless it is to put in an improved one, but it does happen. Reasons might be:

- To get at the surplus;
- Because they want people to move into Personal Pensions, or so many people are leaving to go into their own Personal Pensions that they feel it is no longer viable; or
- Because they want to create a new scheme on a different basis, such as a COMP scheme (explained on page 38).

None of these reasons is acceptable, and they should be resisted. If the members understand that they are losing substantial rights, they will probably be very willing to fight, even if normally you cannot get them interested in pensions.

Hoover, for example, tried to close down its pension scheme, and move the members into a 'money purchase' scheme, after they were taken over by the US firm Security Pacific. The stewards took legal advice, collecting money around the workplaces to pay the fees, but then decided that a campaign of union action would be the better approach. Their main weapon was publicity, embarrassing the company by contacting the national and local press. They also kept the members well informed about events, especially since the company quickly agreed to talk. They got substantial concessions from the company. The old scheme was still closed down and a new one started, but the existing members were given much better terms, and the new scheme as a whole was improved. They got half a loaf, but without taking strong action they would have had nothing.

If the company says it is closing the scheme because it wants people to move into Personal Pensions instead, try to persuade it of the problems of PPs from its point of view. These are covered on pages 59–60, in Chapter 7, so turn back to that for details of the arguments to use.

If the scheme has already lost people to Personal Pensions, closing down and giving up is defeatism. It would be better to try to recruit them back into the scheme, both by improving the benefits and by communicating better. If the scheme was any good, almost certainly those who are leaving do not realise what they are giving up. Creating a package of improvements, and running a large communications exercise, will be a much better bet than closing the scheme. It could be cheaper as well, given the dangers of uncontrollable costs in PPs explained on page 59–60.

When a Company Closes Down

If the company closes down altogether, the scheme will be wound up, and the rules governing this (explained above) come into force.

In a contracted-out scheme, if there is not enough money to go round, then GMPs or protected rights, and the premiums to cover them, must have priority.

If the scheme is winding up, and therefore going out of business, the pensions due to people cannot be preserved within it. So either:

- There must be a transfer to another scheme of the money that's built up for your pension; or
- The money must be used to buy a deferred annuity from an insurance company, and they will keep this for you until you retire.

In either case, you lose your rights to a further transfer when there is a wind up. Wherever the money goes – and this will usually be at the pension scheme's choice rather than yours – it must stay until you retire.

In a liquidation, the duty of the person put in by the creditors (the receiver) is to get as much money out of the company as possible to pay the debts due to the creditors. The receiver's duty to the pension fund members, therefore, is to give them only the minimum under the rules, so that as much as possible is left over.

In the dying months of a company before a liquidation, there may well have been a period during which the contributions to the scheme were not being paid. They might have been collected by the employer but not handed over to the insurance company or the scheme administrator. Under the Social Security Pensions Act, any employees' contributions deducted but not passed over for the last four months, and any employers' contributions for the same period, are a preferential debt in liquidation. That is, they rank with the tax people and the DSS, and before any business creditors.

What to Do if the Worst Happens

Move quickly. You'll have a lot of other things to think about as well as your pension rights, but they are important too. If you think a crash is coming, make sure that you have all available information about the scheme, including a copy of the rules, and check what they say about winding up. You have a legal right to this information (see Chapter 24).

Arrange a meeting with the receiver and ask him/her what the position is. Is there going to be enough money in the fund to pay all the benefits, or will there be a shortfall? If s/he says s/he doesn't know, because no proper actuarial review has been carried out, ask how long it will be before this is done, and ask to be kept informed.

You may then have to wait some time for things to be sorted out. The company's documents ought to include a list of the members' names and addresses. Since they may be in some chaos, make your own. Give a copy to whoever is dealing with the winding up, and then hang on to your own copy. Include on your list the members' dates of birth, whether or not they are married, and how long each one has been in the scheme. Give a copy to the full time union official, or the legal officer. All the shop stewards may have emigrated by the time it is finally settled.

Keep in touch with whoever is doing the work. It may be a bank, or a local solicitor, or the pension fund manager. Often tying up the ends takes one or two years, but don't let them forget you are waiting for news.

Ultimately, the ex-members should be sent individual notification of the amount of benefit that they have frozen for them, and the name of the insurance company with whom the policy has been bought. Check that this has gone to everyone; this is why keeping a list of those involved is important.

There are cases where, although a receiver is put in by the creditors, the company is given permission to continue trading and parts of it are sold off as going concerns. In that case, although you might not be able to do anything with the existing company, you might be able to persuade the new one to treat you reasonably. See the section in Chapter 21 on takeovers for information on this.

23

Additional Voluntary Contributions

What You Must Have

Every employer's scheme must have an Additional Voluntary Contributions (AVC) arrangement. The only exception to this is when the employer runs more than one scheme for the same group of workers, with a free choice about which they go into; then there need only be one AVC scheme altogether.

If you belong to an occupational pension scheme, you also have the right to go elsewhere and buy a 'free standing' AVC (an FSAVC). You can only buy one scheme each tax year. If you stop belonging to an occupational scheme, your FSAVC must stop too, but if you are transferring to another employer with a scheme that you join, you'll be allowed to continue.

What the Inland Revenue Allows

The Inland Revenue allows an individual to contribute up to 15% of earnings to a pension scheme, and this can be either a basic contribution or an ordinary rate plus the extra contributions through an AVC. Employers can contribute to their own AVC scheme, though not to an FSAVC. You are entitled to tax relief on AVC contributions, just as on the ordinary ones. The 'minimum contributions' in a contracted-out FSAVC, though, will not get tax relief.

In the past, once you started paying in, you could not reduce the contribution unless you could show hardship. You also had to pay for at least five years, or to retirement if that was sooner. Now schemes can change their rules to allow you to start and stop contributions when you like, and to pay extra money in odd years when you get a windfall – so long as you do not go over that 15% limit.

The Inland Revenue has also imposed a series of restrictions on what can happen to your contributions. They come under the same preservation rules as the ordinary contributions. If you have to take a frozen pension or a transfer on your basic contributions, you will have to do so on your extra ones as well.

The Inland Revenue's top limits on benefits, explained on pages 36–9, apply to the main scheme and the AVC benefits put together. This means that a person who starts paying into an AVC scheme early in their working life, and whose main scheme is a good one, can find they've got too much pension due. It's possible to use 'excess' contributions to improve the other benefits, like those for a spouse or dependant, or to increase the pension year by year once it's paid. If after that there is still money in your AVC fund, it can be returned to you as cash, minus 35% tax.

Anyone who started paying AVCs after 7 April 1987 can only use them for pension benefits, and cannot give up that pension in return for a tax free lump sum. If you'd already been paying, you can increase the amount without losing the chance of a lump sum, and you are not affected either if the organisation running the scheme alters – for instance, if the employer switches the contract from a building society to an insurance company. But if you change jobs, or if you want to start paying in now, you can't take the AVCs as a lump sum.

There's a special exception for schemes which provide a pension and a lump sum in fixed proportions – like the public sector schemes. Their 'added years' system can carry on as it did in the past.

You can also buy extra death or dependants' benefits, up to the Inland Revenue's limits, with AVCs.

Typical Arrangements

The best sort of AVC scheme is one where you buy extra years of pension. These are called 'added years' schemes. They are not very common except for people working in the public services or in nationalised industries. If you can fulfil a number of detailed conditions (too many to go into here) you can buy extra years of pension, so that where before you had perhaps 10/80ths, you now have 15/80ths. The extra benefits you've bought are treated in the same way as the ordinary benefits. They are inflation proofed, both before and after retirement. Since there are not many investments like that, they're well worth having. In order to guarantee the benefits, the employer, as well as the member, must put something in.

In private sector schemes, 'added years' are very uncommon. A few companies do have such arrangements; Lucas Industries, for instance, did so until recently, but closed it to new entrants and is now using a building society to run their scheme.

More often, you buy a 'money purchase' pension, of the sort explained on pages 27–8. This means that how much you get depends on how well the investments do. Putting money in a scheme like this is usually going to give you a better deal, though, than putting the same amount into shares or a building society on your own. This is because you get tax relief for AVCs, but you don't for your own savings. But you can't get the money out again until you retire, so it's a place to put your long-term savings, not the cash for your next holiday.

AVC arrangements can be administered as part of the main scheme, though they should always be separately accounted for, so that you can be sure that no-one else is getting the benefit you are entitled to. Alternatively, the employer can make an arrangement with an insurance company or a building society to run a scheme for them. Then each person has their own account, and probably gets a statement each year about how much has built up there. Building society AVCs are easy to understand, because they simply add compound interest to your contributions, at a rate linked to the mortgage rate. But they've done less well over the last few years than the insurance companies.

In the past, if you wanted to pay AVCs, you could only do so by paying into the employer's scheme or to the arrangement the employer has set up. But since October 1987, you have been allowed to pay in to any other scheme you like, under the new FSAVCs.

There are not many cases where this is going to be worthwhile. The only real advantage is that it gives you an extra choice of investments. A number of different schemes, with different investment policies, will be available. You'd be able to choose one that suited you if you did not like the way the employer's AVC scheme was run. But this could be an expensive choice, as you would pay administrative charges and commission to the commercial firm you went to, but not to the employer.

Should Members Take Out AVCs?

Where the employer's pension scheme is not very good, AVCs with the employer's scheme are a good bet for people who are coming up to retirement and know that their pension will be less than they would like. By the age of 50 or 55, you should be considering one of these schemes. Even if you have only a few months to go, it's worthwhile because of the tax advantage. Alternatively, young people doing a lot of overtime could pay in AVCs for a few years, while the money still has plenty of time to build up interest.

For negotiators, AVCs create some problems. If at some point you succeed in improving your scheme to anywhere near Inland Revenue limits, the people making the additional contributions will not be able to get full benefit from them. They will, though, be able to get back any excess money from them.

But because the most pension-minded of your members will be paying in to your scheme to get a bigger pension, there could be less steam than before behind attempts to get the pension scheme improved for everyone.

Especially if you are looking for improvements on past service, an AVC scheme can cut the ground from under your feet. Your argument that people with long service get pitiful pensions when they go could be countered by management saying 'Well, if they mind so much they can always join the AVC scheme.'

The Chancellor, though, has actually been some help in our arguments here! The big attraction of a pension scheme to many people is the lump sum. So you can stress the fact that they can get this out of the main scheme but not out of an AVC scheme. The bigger and better the main scheme, the more room there will be for turning pension into a lump sum (remember that you must keep the GMP, or the 'protected right' in a COMP scheme, as pension).

Other points, once you have an AVC scheme, are:

- Don't let management oversell it;
- Make sure that the implications are fully explained to anyone thinking of paying into the scheme;
- Make clear that you don't regard it as a substitute for a decent scheme;
- Keep an eye on the people running the scheme for you, if you go outside the company. There are league tables available to show which providers have done best. The insurance company with the best performance in the past, Equitable Life, does not pay out commission to brokers, and so it probably won't be recommended by them. Make sure the pension scheme manager has looked properly at what is on the market.

Anyone who thinks about taking out an AVC policy with a commercial provider, rather than sticking with the company, should be advised to look carefully at the small print. The big money promises could be so much fairy gold. Suggest to the member that s/he checks out how much is actually guaranteed, and finds out what the past record is; it's the best guide to likely performance in the future. People should always get more than one quote. They'll get better value for money, and also have much more freedom to shop around, if they pay 'single premiums' each year rather than signing a contract to continue to pay to the same people for good. This is because the broker will get commission of 3% of the single premium when you pay it, so 97% of the total will go into the FSAVC fund; but if you agree to pay regular premiums, the first 25 years' worth of them are rolled up into 'initial payments' to the broker, who gets 72% of the first two years' money. So pound for pound, more of your money is invested by the insurance company from a single premium than from a regular premium policy. But of course the broker will want to sell you the regular premium scheme, and won't tell you this!

24

Information to Scheme Members and to the Unions

What the Law Says

The laws on what information must be given to members of pension schemes, and to their trade unions, apply in principle to all types of schemes. But there are variations in what is required, because certain pieces of information are not relevant, or can't be provided in the same form.

There have always been some rights for members to have information about their pension schemes. The fact that schemes are set up under trust law (explained on pages 227–30) means that the beneficiaries of those trusts – that is, the members – are entitled to know what is going on, but this right is difficult to enforce. The Inland Revenue also lays down rules about the information that must be given to members when a scheme is set up, and the Employment Protection (Consolidation) Act 1978, Section 1, said that the details of the pension scheme had to be given to new employees, along with much other information about the company, within 13 weeks of starting work.

The Social Security Act 1985

In 1985, however, the government finally brought together all these requirements in one place, and also gave some new rights. This was under the Social Security Act 1985, which laid down the principles of disclosure. The detailed regulations came out in June 1986, and were gradually brought into force from November 1986 onwards. The full rights only operate, though, from 1989 onwards.

The new rules cover:

- Basic information about the scheme;
- The documents which lay down the constitution of the scheme;
- Information to individual members about their own entitlement; and
- Annual reporting by pension schemes.

Basic Information

This must be given to new members, automatically, within 13 weeks of joining the scheme. It must also be given to recognised trade unions, and to members and prospective members, their spouses, and the beneficiaries, if they ask for it. But the administrator does not have to give it to you, if you have already been given it within the last three years.

The main points of what they have to tell you are:

- Who is eligible to be a member of the scheme;
- What the conditions of membership are, the amount of notice you must give if you want to opt out, and whether you can re-enter the scheme and on what conditions;
- What happens to your benefits if you drop out of the scheme;
- How members' and employers' contributions are calculated;
- Whether the Inland Revenue has approved the scheme;
- Whether the scheme is contracted out;
- What the benefits are, and how they are calculated;
- Whether any of them are paid at the discretion of the employer or the trustees, and whether the scheme is properly funded, or covered by insurance policies;
- Whether the employer has an obligation to pay the benefits, if there is not enough money in the scheme itself;
- Whether there's power to increase the pensions in payment, who does so, and whether this is discretionary or not;
- The arrangements for transfers and refunds;
- An address to which enquiries about the scheme generally, or about the individual's benefits, must be sent.

If there are 'material alterations' to the scheme, the trustees must take reasonable steps to draw this to the attention of the scheme members. It's not specified what is 'reasonable', but probably letters to the members, or a statement in the company newspaper, would do. There's no time limit for meeting this requirement.

If the company wants to meet this requirement by putting up notices on the board, the question to ask is, 'Are they read regularly by most of the workforce?' If the answer is no, then they need to make more effort than that.

If the address for enquiries changes then all members and beneficiaries have to be told within a month.

All these are details which should be in the scheme booklet. Many employers, though, don't keep this up to date, or don't make sure that everyone has one. Check this point, and if there isn't a copy on the stewards' files, or in the union office, make sure you get one.

The Constitution of the Scheme

Every pension scheme of any size will have a trust deed that lays down the powers the trustees have, and the rules they must follow. The most recent rule changes may not yet be in the main trust deed, but they will be either in a supplementary one, or in letters between the employer and the trustees.

Members and prospective members, the spouses of members, beneficiaries, and independent trade unions, all have a right to ask to see all these documents, at a time and a place which is practical for them. They can do so once every 12 months. They can also have a copy to take away, though the employer can make a 'reasonable' charge for doing this. What's reasonable in these circumstances is not laid down.

There has to be an actuarial valuation at least every 3.5 years. This is the long-term forecast, done by an actuary who estimates whether there is enough money in the funds to pay the benefits that are promised, and is explained in more detail in Chapter 7. A brief statement about this has to go into the annual report (covered on page 201), but the full report also has to be available for inspection, on request, to the groups of people entitled to see the trust deed.

This valuation must be written in such a way that the expected future funding levels of the scheme, and the contribution rates being asked for, can be understood by ordinary people. It must say whether the actuaries' own rules have been followed in preparing it, or where there have been changes.

You have a right to see this only once every three years, but again, a 'reasonable' charge can be made if you want a copy to take away. You also have a right to see back-copies of previous valuations, though not those done before November 1986.

Details of Benefits

You should be given full information about what you are getting, and how it is worked out, either before or shortly after a benefit becomes payable. You must also be told about the conditions of payment, and any provisions under which it could be altered. So, for instance, a widow receiving a pension for the first time must be told if she could lose it by remarrying.

New details must be given if the amount of pension changes, unless it is simply being uprated in line with an annual formula.

When anyone leaves the scheme, s/he must be given details of his/her rights and options.

When a scheme is being wound up, details of the amount of benefit due, and who will be responsible for paying it, must go to every beneficiary, and every member who has an entitlement. If there's a shortfall because there's not enough money to go round, they must be told how much this is.

Current members of any scheme have a right to know about their benefits if they ask, but not automatically. If they've already been told within the last 12 months, they need not be told again, but otherwise they have a right to know:

- The amount of benefit that has been built up, based on their current earnings. As an alternative, the employer can give enough information to allow the members to do the calculation themselves. The figures can be based on one of two sets of assumptions – either that the member would leave tomorrow, or that s/he would stay in the scheme until due to retire;
- Rights and options on the death of the member or the beneficiary;

- The provision for benefit increases; and
- Information about leaving service benefits, along with the transfer value (see Chapter 19 for an explanation of these). There must also be a written statement that further information is available, with the address to which requests should be sent.

The Annual Report

All sets of trustees now have to draw up an annual report for the members, in the same way that a company has to for its shareholders. This has to be 'made available' to scheme members – in other words, you can have it if you ask – and their attention must be drawn to the fact that it exists. There's an exemption for 'public service' schemes.

Most members won't be very interested in the details of this document – even if we think they should be. So the best policy is probably to produce a short 'pop' version, perhaps a couple of pages or a well illustrated leaflet, which can be given out widely, and say on that that anyone who wants the full version can have it.

The first year that had to be covered is the 'scheme year' that started on or after 1 November 1986. Schemes then have to issue the report within 12 months.

These reports have to include:

- A report from the trustees;
- The audited accounts;
- A statement from the actuary; and
- An investment report.

It's the trustees' responsibility to see that it is done.

The report from the trustees has to give:

- The names of the trustees, and the arrangements for appointing and removing them. This, though, could be a very general statement, perhaps just that 'the company appoints from time to time those it considers most suitable, and has the power to remove them.' But if the unions or the membership have a role in the appointment, it should be made plain there;
- The numbers of members and of beneficiaries;
- Information about the increases in pensions and preserved benefits, and about transfers;
- A statement that the proper contributions have been paid by the employer, and if not, a note on what is being done to put things right; and
- The names of the investment managers, and details of what powers are delegated to them. If the cost of employing them is carried by the scheme, there must also be a statement of how (but not how much) they are paid. For instance, if they get all their money from commission on buying and selling the scheme's stocks and shares, this part of the report should tell you.

The accounts have to be pretty detailed, but will not be very easy for the lay person to understand. Information must be given about:

- Whether the scheme is funded or not (but they almost all are);
- What happened to the scheme, in financial terms, during the last year;
- What the scheme's money is invested in, broken down into a number of categories of investment, like shares, property, or money in insurance companies. They don't however have to tell you which shares the fund owns, except where there are 'concentrations of investment' or investment in the employing company of more than 5% of the value of the fund;
- Specific details of any investments held in overseas currencies.

If you look at a scheme's accounts, you'll see that there are two main tables. These are:

- The revenue account – that is, an explanation of what money has come in and gone out over the last year. This will have to include details of what contributions the employer and employees have paid over the last year and, if there has been delay by the employer in paying them over, the auditor will have to say so;
- An analysis of the assets held by the scheme. This is not quite the same as the balance sheet that you'd see in the company's accounts, because the liabilities – the amount that the scheme expects to pay out in due course as pensions – are missing. They're dealt with by the actuary, in his statement.

There must also be an explanation of changes in the assets, where these don't show up in the revenue account. For example, this section has to show how the market value of the shares has gone up or down.

If the scheme pays for an assessment of how well the investments are performing in the 'league table', it must say so. It won't be enough to make a vague statement, as has often been done in the past, about 'above average' performance when in fact you come number 49 out of 100.

If any of the assets would be difficult to sell, the investment manager also has to say so. One accountants' guide to the regulations (see booklist for details) suggests that South African investments should be reported on here, as it's difficult to get the money out if you sell shares in a company based in South Africa.

The other important item in the annual report is the actuarial statement. But this is very limited in what it shows; to know how healthy the scheme really is, you have to go to the full report, and check out a good many details (explained in Chapter 27).

The statement has to say, first, whether the actuary thinks there is enough money in the scheme to cover the liabilities that have built up so far. This is on the assumption that the scheme closes down tomorrow, and all the members are treated as early leavers. Since that's the last thing you want, having enough money to cover that crisis is no reassurance!

In the second half of the statement, the actuary has to say whether he or she thinks that:

> the resources of the scheme are likely in the normal course of events to meet in full the liabilities of the scheme as they fall due.

This is more useful, because it's saying whether enough's going into the scheme to meet the benefits promised, as people get longer service and the pension each one has builds up. There's then a summary of the contribution rates expected from the employer and employee, and details of the assumptions being made. These are covered in Chapter 27, since the whole question of how an actuary costs a scheme is important for negotiating purposes.

Where You Still Don't Have Rights

There are still some items that you don't have a right to know:

- If there are different benefits for different groups, there's no obligation to tell one group of members about another group's benefits. This clause was put in so that employers could carry on keeping quiet about the 'top hat' benefits they often give senior staff. You may be able to find this out from the trust deed, if the 'top hat' benefits are still within the same scheme. Your rights here are to the whole trust deed, not to edited extracts;
- You don't have a right, under these regulations, to see the minutes of trustee meetings. Under the much older trust law, though, it's arguable that you could at least claim to see minutes about decisions that affected you. You'll never get the right to see confidential material about other people – or them about you;
- The accounts have to give figures for category of investment, and whether it's in the UK or overseas, but not which companies' shares the pension fund owns or in what countries. Again, some lawyers would say that under trust law you have this right, and if you want to pursue that, the case to quote is called Re Londonderry's Settlement, dated 1965.

What Should Unions Look For?

One problem with these rules is that they are full of words like 'reasonable' and 'practicable', which are not defined. If you have difficulties with the employer about this, take a common sense approach and think about what has been regarded as 'reasonable' elsewhere. A rule of thumb is that you should not have to wait more than a month for a bit of information that ought to be easily available from the records anyway, or more than three months for something that will have to be extracted specially. If it's a matter of where you have to go to see something, it would be reasonable to ask you to go to a particular office on the site where you work, or which you visit regularly, during normal working hours. It wouldn't be reasonable to ask you to make a special journey elsewhere – unless the employer were willing to pay for your time and expenses in doing so.

Although the regulations also say that the employer has the right to make a 'reasonable' charge for copying things like the trust deed, we should resist this – members, and the unions, should have a right to the information about their own scheme for free. If you have to accept that there is a charge, it should be no more than the amount you'd pay in a high street copyshop, say 8p or 10p a page.

Overall, these legal rights are less than the unions have looked for in the past, and we should build on them rather than stick dutifully to them – though there are quite a lot of companies where just getting the legal rights would be a start!

The guiding principles should be that:

- All material should be easy to understand;
- Members should have a right to go to someone and ask for more details or more explanations;
- Full information should be given to recognised trade unions, without them having to ask; and
- The material that ordinary members will find useful – like a statement of their benefits – should be given to all members automatically. Where they're likely to find the full details intimidating or simply rather boring, a simplified version or a summary should be given automatically, with anyone who wants being allowed a full copy.

Understandability

Try to be involved in drawing up benefit statements or reports. Test them on a few of your members who know less about pensions than the negotiating committee will. Some employers have tried quite hard to produce material for their members, and still ended up with something that you have to be a pensions expert to understand!

If you are involved in a working group, or trying to persuade an employer that your way of doing things is practical, try to collect a few examples from other companies. Ask the other participants on a course, or people at the union branch or trades council meeting, for copies of theirs. Then before you meet the employer, go through these and pick out what you like best about each, and put together a rough draft that can be polished with the help of the experts. Though they'll know the law and the technicalities better, you'll be more aware of what language the ordinary member will understand and what will go above his or her head.

Automatic Information

Many schemes already give annual benefit statements to everyone, without waiting to be asked. This is what the unions should aim for.

If the employer refuses, it would be extremely easy – and painless – to organise industrial action over the issue. Duplicate a letter saying something like:

> Under the terms of Regulation 6 and Schedule 2 of the Occupational Pension Schemes (Disclosure of Information) Regulations 1986, I am writing to request that you provide me with details, as soon as practicable, of my benefits under the XYZ Pension Scheme; I would like to know the following ...
> [and then add the four points listed on pages 200–1]

Take this round to all the pension scheme members, get them to sign a letter each, and then deliver it to the pensions manager. Offer to get the members to withdraw their requests for statements, if the company will agree to sit down with you and work out the details of one that will be issued automatically to all members within the next financial year.

Many pensions committees, drafting benefit statements, have thought it right to give the details of a member's entitlement if he or she stays with the firm, but to say that if the member wants to know about the transfer value if s/he left, that must be a specific request.

This seems fair enough. It may be a little patronising to say so, but it is true that members could be bemused by the large figures that turn up as transfer values, and think that they would be money actually in their hands. As explained on page 166, this isn't so – it's the money that would be paid over to another scheme, a Personal Pension, or an insurance policy if you left the existing scheme, to buy you pension there.

Access to Further Details
The law only gives people the right to send a letter with further queries, and doesn't say that the pension scheme manager has to answer them. The union aim, though, should be that anyone who wants to know more has the right to see someone – with their union representative accompanying them, if they want – who can explain both about the scheme and about the individual's entitlement. This could be the personnel officer or welfare officer, but they are not specialists either, and for anything complex there should be a right to see the pensions manager, or whatever outside firm is running the scheme. With a widely scattered workforce, you might have to accept that this should be done through a telephone hot line in most cases, but where someone is particularly concerned, or has special circumstances, it should be possible to see the people actually dealing with the pension, in works time.

Sometimes a group of people will have a particular decision to make – whether to take early retirement, or to move between schemes because one company has taken another over. As part of the discussions about this, the unions should ask that everyone is offered the chance of a face to face interview with someone from the pensions department, but without pressure being put on them to decide one way or the other. Not many people will take it up, but it will be a reassurance.

Try to agree a time limit for queries being answered. Fourteen days would be reasonable in most cases, unless there is a particular difficulty. In that case you could allow a month. The pensions department will probably claim that it is understaffed – and many are – but in answer to that you can say:

- It takes no longer to answer a letter that came in a week ago than it does one that came in a month ago; and
- It will give them a good reason to go to the board with a request for extra staff so they can do their jobs better.

Union Records

Aim to build up a file in the union office of all the main documents, kept up to date. This should include:

- A copy of the scheme booklet, and any booklets for other schemes within the company. These could be the schemes for other grades of staff, or those for other subsidiaries. They'll be useful for comparisons;
- A copy of the trust deed, and any amending documents. If it's difficult to understand these, ask for a meeting with the pension scheme's solicitor to have them explained, and draw up a table of contents yourself. (At the same time, ask the trustees to set about getting a 'plain English' version done);
- A copy of the latest actuarial valuation, and any previous ones you can lay your hands on;
- A copy of the full annual report and accounts, and previous ones if you can get hold of them;
- Details of the share portfolio, how the fund is managed, and how well it has performed over the last few years.

Making Use of the Material

The point of having all this material is not to do the pensions department's job for them – they're paid for that. It's for the twin purposes of equipping you to negotiate better for the members, and helping you monitor the way the scheme is being run.

For example, a member may be in poor health, and want to know about retiring early. You can give him/her a rough idea of his/her entitlement, but send him/her to the pensions department for the details. At the same time, check in the booklet and the trust deed how the decision is made, and whether there's any discretion to increase the pension above the amount strictly laid down in the rules. Then you can decide whether, and how, to fight the member's case for a better deal.

Again, if you want better benefits from the scheme, having the actuary's report will help you to see how well financed it is, and what the employer is putting in. If you've got back copies, you can see whether they are being more or less generous than they were in the past. In many actuarial reports, there'll be a breakdown of the costs between the different benefits, and this will give you the chance to assess roughly how much you are demanding from the employer.

The actuarial report will also give details like the numbers of early retirements or deaths over the last few years. If there are a lot of deaths in one plant, or a group of management early retirements, you might well want to know why, as negotiators. It could alert you to a health and safety problem, for instance.

The annual accounts, and the investment report, will tell you if the scheme is being properly run. If, for instance, the accountant says that contributions haven't been paid, or been paid late, you want to know why. That's your money, and all the time it is being kept by the company, it's not earning interest and dividends for you. If you see that the people managing the scheme's investments have links with the company in other ways, you might ask whether your money is being used in other ways too. For instance, some merchant banks have been known to use the pension fund to help with a takeover deal the company is involved in. If you have more information on the investments it will also show how far the fund is fitting in with trade union policy on them. Is the fund invested in building up UK industry, or is it in speculative investments overseas, for instance?

Communicating Changes

When changes are being made to your scheme, the negotiators need to think about how to tell the members. Very often, the letter announcing them is written by the pension scheme administrator, and is in terms which the ordinary member won't understand. The scheme booklet is often not changed for a long time after the actual change is made in the rules, and so anyone who wants to check what his/her rights are has to find out by wading through the booklet plus various other odd bits of paper. With the new Disclosure of Information Regulations, what was always good practice is now a legal duty. Members have to be kept up to date, and so it may as well be done properly by clear, straightforward announcements and proper updating of the scheme booklet.

This applies also where the scheme rules are changed by law. There's a legal duty to tell people about the changes. It's good practice also to make the change in the booklet as well.

When schemes started contracting out in 1978, and to a lesser extent with the upheaval over Personal Pensions in 1987–8, many scheme managers set up extensive programmes for communicating the benefits, giving all the members a chance to attend meetings to discuss the changes being made. This has been seen by them as very worthwhile, but it may be forgotten again as soon as the upheaval is past.

It is worth having a 'briefing' for all the members every few years, and automatically when new people join, because one does forget quite quickly. Aim also for an agreement that:

- Any change, however minor and technical it looks to the administrator, should be discussed with the appropriate negotiating body and agreed before being announced;
- Not only the content, but also the wording, of any announcement should be discussed with the negotiating body, or a subgroup, to ensure that it can be understood by ordinary people;
- Where a major change is being made, details should be given to members via meetings in working time, either of the members themselves or their representatives, depending on the size and geographical spread of the membership. People should be able to ask questions and clarify issues as much as they need to at these meetings;
- Any amendment, even a minor one, should be issued as soon as possible in a form that means it can easily be added to the ordinary pension booklet – by slips of paper that can be gummed in, or by a leaflet that can be slipped inside; and
- After changes are made, the booklet itself should be reprinted as soon as reasonably possible, incorporating all the changes made, and should be kept up to date.

Possible Arguments and Responses
Generally, bad communication about changes in the scheme will not be deliberate, but because the administrator feels that:

- Since the members don't seem very interested in the scheme, there's no point in taking a great deal of care about how they are informed of changes; 'they won't read it anyway';
- S/he must be careful to keep the small print legally correct. S/he'll be worried about the possibility of claims from people which will have to be allowed although not strictly legitimate, because of loose wording.

On the first point, you could suggest that it is a 'chicken and egg' problem. If people can't understand their pension scheme, or the changes that have been made in it, they are naturally not going to be very interested. Worse than that, they are likely to be suspicious of changes announced in obscure language, and so regard the pension scheme as a management ploy for taking their wages back off them.

Clear wording need not mean loose wording. Professional communicators, on television or in the newspapers, can get over complicated ideas simply. The pension schemes that have tried hard have succeeded, but it is more difficult than writing in jargon. Mecca Leisure, for instance, produced comic strips about their pension scheme when they revamped it, and had a very good response from their members.

A statement that the booklet is only a general guide and that the trust deed contains the full rules should be enough to safeguard the scheme against any danger of paying out more than was intended.

Personal Pensions

You also have rights to information from a Personal Pension scheme. It will be much less use to you since there is no possibility of negotiating with the people running these schemes – all you can do is vote with your feet and leave.

On joining a PP scheme, members must be given details of the management and the investment policy of the scheme; the benefits being provided; their rights and options on leaving; the benefits payable on death; illustrations of the charges being made, and of how much pension would be preserved for you if you gave up the policy shortly after starting it (usually, very little).

On request at any time, 12 months or more after the last request was met, you can have details of your protected rights, and of the accrued rights from anything extra you have paid.

For each scheme year, there must be an annual report, a copy of which must be made available to each member on request. What this covers will depend on the type of PP scheme. Thus, it must spell out:

- The scheme's investments, for unit linked schemes, including a statement of the rates of return, and of any changes in investment policy;
- The bonus declarations over the last five years for with profit schemes; or
- The interest rates for the last five years for deposit schemes.

The OPB have said that this is a minimum requirement, and there is nothing to stop providers giving more information. Nor are there any restrictions on the form in which it is given. The chances are that it will be used heavily as a sales document, to tell people how wonderful the scheme is, and how much more money they should put into it.

Part III

25

Making a Claim

Negotiating for pension scheme improvements is like negotiating for any other sort of benefits from the company. You put in for what you think is reasonable, you argue for a while about money, and in due course you reach a settlement which is the best you can get out of the company at the time. But there are certain points which make pensions negotiations look different. For instance:

- You are more closely bound up with a legal framework. No power on earth will persuade a pensions manager to agree to a change in the scheme that means losing Inland Revenue approval or the contracting out certificate, so it's not worth trying. You're doing very well if you achieve the Inland Revenue maximum limits – though that doesn't stop people from putting in a claim based on those top limits;
- There will usually be more involvement of 'experts' than in wage negotiations, on one or both sides. The company experts – pensions manager, consultant, or insurance company – may well be on your side quite often, since they want the business. But the outside firms will want it at a profit. So you need to take care over what goes into the small print;
- Pensions negotiations tend to take longer, and be conducted at a more leisurely pace than wage negotiations. If things run on, you tend to adjourn till the next time. There will often be homework to be done outside the meetings, such as getting the actuaries to recost a particular element, or drafting a form of words to cover special circumstances. Actuaries and lawyers can be very slow, so you may need to put pressure on them to get negotiations finished at all. Insurance companies and brokers can be even worse, unless they see a straightforward profit coming out of it for them, as they would in a brand new scheme;
- It's not easy to achieve a retrospective pensions agreement, partly because it's incorporated in a legal document, and partly because all the time people are retiring, leaving or dying, and it will be difficult to treat them fairly after the event. So you need to start negotiating well before the 'anniversary date' when changes come into force. If things drag on too long, you may have to agree to wait until the next anniversary date for the changes to be put into effect. If the scheme is computerised, the deadline could be even earlier, because the computer programme will have to be amended.

Industrial Strength

Though it's very rarely spelt out, both sides are usually conscious of one general point in negotiations. You don't have much muscle on pensions. People will very rarely take industrial action about the pension scheme. Sometimes it can be linked to other items, or annoyance about the management attitude will be the final straw when a lot of other things have gone wrong – but never bank on it.

This puts the unions in a permanently weak position, and the employer in a strong one. You need to counter it by:

- Showing you know as much as they do, if not more, on the subject (not too difficult with many company managers!);
- Appealing to their common sense; and
- Appealing to their 'public relations' sense. It is partly in order to prove what a good employer it is that a company will set up a pension scheme, and want to keep people in it now that they have the chance to leave. You can show that, on the contrary, it is showing them up as a bad employer because the scheme is misleading or giving lousy benefits. You can go on to suggest that they are currently wasting the money they are putting into the scheme, and could get much better value out of it by putting in a little more.

Comparisons with other companies will often be useful. But there is a very wide gap between the best and the worst pension scheme, and there would be little point in comparing a struggling light engineering company with ICI, for instance. When you are doing your research before drawing up the claim, look at other companies:

- In your industry, and roughly your employer's size; or
- In completely different industries, but competing in the same labour market. You could argue, for instance, that a firm in Derby which tried to keep its wage rates comparable to Rolls-Royce's in order not to lose workers, ought also to keep its pension benefits comparable for the same reason.

Compare the staff and works benefits in your own company, and look also at the benefits that senior managers get, if you can find out about them. But 'top hat' schemes are usually kept pretty secret.

For national comparisons, the most useful publication is the *Survey of Occupational Schemes*, published each year by the National Association of Pension Funds. This is an organisation to which the majority of pension scheme managers belong. Every year the NAPF issues a questionnaire to its members, and then publishes the answers. The last survey covered 705 schemes. As it's voluntary to complete the questionnaire, it's probably the better scheme managers who do so. For our purposes, though, the survey is representative enough. The address of the NAPF is in the list at the back.

The government also does occasional surveys. Although you can be sure that they are statistically correct, they take too long to be published to be much use. The most recent was *Occupational Pension Schemes 1983; Seventh Survey by the Government Actuary*, which came out in 1986, and it's available from the Stationery Office (address on page 263).

Organisations such as Labour Research and Incomes Data Services, and some of the magazines about pensions, also do their own studies about pensions. So do some unions – APEX for instance have published a detailed analysis of the schemes their members are involved in.

Various employers' organisations do their own research, often on a regional basis. They can be extremely useful, but may be difficult to get hold of.

It will also be helpful to have with you in any negotiations a copy of the 'Practice Notes' (see page 263) from which you can quote if the company says something can't be done.

One place to find this material would be in a business library, either in the central reference library run by the council for your city or county, or in a polytechnic or university. Another would be the trade union studies department in the nearest further education college or polytechnic, especially if they have people who teach on trade union courses on pensions. If you don't know where these could be, ask the TUC's regional education officer for information about tutors in the area.

The Costs of Benefits

As with most negotiations, you're most unlikely to get everything you ask for. So in constructing the claim you need to think about what is really important and what is there to keep the issue open, but you don't really expect to win this year. As the different items cost very different amounts, it's useful to do a 'shopping list' which includes a mixture of high and low cost items. Some examples of high cost items would be:

• Improving the accrual rate substantially;
• Providing for past service at a reasonable rate;
• Reducing the retirement age by several years;
• Providing automatic increases in pensions payment; and
• Removing the integration factor.

You could expect a worthwhile improvement in any one of these to cost, very roughly, 3% or 4% of payroll. If the company claims it costs a lot more, ask them to justify their figures in detail.

There are small improvements in these items which would cost much less. Reducing the retirement age by only one year, for instance, would be a moderate or even a low cost item.

Moderately expensive items (roughly 0.75% to 2% of payroll) would include:

- Improving the definition of final pensionable earnings;
- Improving the spouse's pension from an accrued to a prospective basis;
- Improving the leaving service provision; and
- Giving a better deal for early retirement 'at the member's own request';
- Giving an extra year's earnings as a lump sum death benefit;
- Creating a Permanent Health Insurance scheme (PHI), or a good deal for ill-health early retirement from scratch, if you currently have only very limited provision.

How expensive these are will depend considerably on what your current benefits are. They'll also depend on the sort of industry you are in; ill-health early retirement or PHI is much more expensive for manual workers in the old heavy industries than for white collar people in sedentary jobs.

Cheaper improvements, costing under (and often very much under) 1% of payroll would include:

- Extending widows' pensions to widowers at more than the minimum amount required by law;
- Giving dependent children's pensions; and
- Improving temporary absence provisions.

Extending the scheme to new groups of people costs money on a different basis. It brings more people on to the pensionable payroll, so that the employer has to find an extra contribution for each one. Introducing member participation doesn't cost anything, except time and energy. Additional Voluntary Contributions normally only cost the company administrative time.

It's useful also to divide the items into those that stand by themselves, and those that have a 'knock on' effect in improving others, where you improve not only the pension, but also the early retirement pension, the spouse's pension, and the life assurance. Those that 'knock on' are:

- Improving the accrual rate;
- Providing for past service;
- Removing the integration factor; and
- Improving the final earnings definition.

That's one reason why these are expensive items. The ill-health retirement provisions, on the other hand, will be very important for the person who has to retire early, but have no effect on anyone else. Again, a balance has to be struck.

Finance

Normally in these discussions you will expect the issue of cost to be part of the overall discussion of the package of change sought. In the last few years many schemes have been improved without any extra money coming from the employer or the employee, because there have been surpluses in the fund. What an actuarial surplus is, and how it arises, is explained on page 246.

Improving the scheme out of the surplus is an easy option, and makes it look as if the improvement is 'free'. But it's important not to get caught on the idea that schemes can only be improved when there are surpluses. They can disappear as quickly as they appeared, if there is a recession or serious inflation. It's better to argue that the improvements are good in themselves, and that the existence of a surplus makes it temporarily easier to finance it, but that in the long term, the improvement will mean the employer paying more.

Negotiating Bodies

Over the last few years some companies have developed formal procedures for negotiating on pensions. Others bring together a group specifically created for the purpose when they need to, and have no national level meetings on a regular basis. But even a good scheme needs renegotiation when conditions change, and the many poor ones certainly need frequent discussions on improvements.

The argument for negotiating rights is that pensions are deferred pay, and should be subject to negotiation like any other item of pay. The legal position is that pensions are one item covered in the Employment Protection (Consolidation) Act, under which an independent recognised trade union may seek negotiating rights, and take the company to ACAS if it does not get them. These legal powers are not often used, because the unions are afraid that, once the lawyers begin to argue, definitions may be so narrowed down that they are useless. The unions have tended to rely on activities other than court action to get negotiating rights (see *Rights at Work* by Jeremy McMullen, Pluto 1983, for details on recognition).

The last section covered the differences between pension claims and other sorts of claims. In this section we deal with specific issues of setting up negotiations, including:

- The level at which you negotiate; and
- The role of full time officials.

Whether the company is centralised or has autonomy at plant level, the pension scheme is almost always centralised, and controlled by people reporting to the main board. Subsidiary companies normally have no independent powers to take decisions about the pension scheme. Even in the few cases where the parent company has deliberately broken up its pension scheme, and claimed to devolve control to local level, local management still rely on the 'advice' of group management, and follow policy made at the centre.

In any pensions negotiation at plant level, therefore, local management can be no more than messengers back to the employer. Even if the group pensions manager is present, major issues will usually have to be taken back to the group board for decision. What happens will therefore depend partly on the views of other managers at other plants. Local negotiations on pensions, except on issues that only affect that plant (such as the method of collecting contributions) are usually a waste of time. Central negotiations, at group level, with all interested unions involved, are far more useful.

This approach contradicts a lot of ideas, however, and could be resisted by several different groups:

- The company may dislike it, because it fears that there are possibilities of a pensions negotiating body being the forerunners of a combine committee. Even if the unions give assurances that this won't happen, the company will – probably correctly – assume that useful information will be swapped between stewards at different plants over lunch.

- It is out of line with policy in a number of unions. In practice, the unions have generally accepted, at head office level, the need for centralised pension negotiations, but for them it tends to mean full time officials being involved, rather than shop stewards or convenors.

- For this reason, centralised negotiations are often viewed with suspicion by shop stewards as well, as they see it as a method by which power can be removed from them on an important issue. So indeed it can be, if the procedure agreed allows it – which is why getting the structure right is important.

Pensions tend to be surrounded by an air of mystery, and people are therefore more conscious of their ignorance than on other subjects. You may be afraid of making yourselves look fools in front of management, and rely on the full time official or the expert. But on other subjects, you would be perfectly ready to handle the discussions yourselves. Your goal should be to build up member involvement in negotiations, while retaining the expertise of the full timers for when it is needed.

This is not easy, especially since more than one union, and often quite a large number, may be represented in a company. So if you simply add lay members to a negotiating committee, you may find it getting so big as to be unworkable. Rather than leave it all to the full time officials, however, it might be better to set up a procedure where you elect a small number of representatives on to a negotiating committee, along with an arrangement for reporting back.

One engineering company, for instance, has a procedure agreement which says:

1. A pension scheme delegate conference will be established which will meet at least once per calendar year. Each of the operating companies will send representatives to this conference.

2. The employees' representatives will be chosen domestically via the existing domestic negotiating/consultative bodies so as to give one representative from each recognised union for each operating

company. The representatives must be members of the general pension fund.

3. Executives nominated by ABC Engineering will also attend the conference, and there will be an agreed number of full time trade union officials ... present if they so wish ... one for each recognised union with members in the pension scheme.

4. Items for the agenda of the meeting will be invited and these will be circulated to those due to attend, 3 weeks before the conference takes place.

5. The principal purpose of the conference will be:

  (a) initially to formulate an agreed mechanism for appointing a number of trustees from members of the scheme;

  (b) to receive and discuss any reports of the trustees on the operation of the general pension scheme; such reports will be circulated with the agenda;

  (c) to reach agreement with the company concerning the future operation of the scheme.

6. If no acceptable agreement to any proposed alterations put forward by members of the scheme is reached (either at the conference or within 4 weeks afterwards) a negotiating subcommittee meeting may be called by the national officials or the nominees of ABC to discuss further the issues in dispute.

7. The negotiating subcommittee will consist of full time national union officials and lay members chosen at the annual delegate conference, and nominees of ABC Engineering. There will be a maximum of 12 people present at this committee, of whom no more than 4 will be members of ABC.

8. If agreed to be necessary, then at an appropriate stage the results of the meetings of the subcommittee may be reported:

  (a) to the operating companies and hence their negotiating/consultative bodies in the form of an agreed statement;

  (b) by the national officials at the resumed meeting of the delegate conference (which would not be attended by representatives of the company) if they deemed such a meeting necessary.

9. (a) The cost and the responsibility of organising the annual delegate conference would be that of ABC.

  (b) In the case of a delegate conference to discuss negotiations on changing the pension scheme, the travel costs of the delegates would be paid by the appropriate operating companies and the agreed paid leave of absence granted. The cost of any overnight accommodation would be the responsibility of the trade unions.

You wouldn't need this sort of elaborate arrangement in all cases, though. Where a joint negotiating committee exists, it can elect some of its members on to a pensions body. Or if there are only a few sites, all the convenors or senior stewards could be involved. You could ask one or more of the experts from the larger unions' head offices on to the committee to provide specialist advice. If several unions represented in the company employ experts, you could agree among your-selves which to invite. If none is available, you could employ a professional from a firm of insurance brokers or pension consultants to do the job. Be careful, though, because:

- It will cost a lot of money. Find out how much first, before com-mitting yourselves;
- They may try to push their own pet scheme, rather than what you want, and may be earning commission by doing so; and
- They may know less than they imply to you. Someone dealing with individual pensions may know very little about group pensions.

There can be difficulties in getting all the unions to sit down together, especially if you have long-standing differences of opinion over other things. It is vital, though, that you work out ways of doing so on this subject, so far as you have a common pension scheme. Otherwise the company won't hesitate to exploit the differences for its own ends.

If there are separate schemes – for instance, staff and works – there may not be any need actually to negotiate as one group. But you should still keep in touch, so that you are not putting forward contra-dictory arguments. This will be particularly important for the works representatives, even if harmonisation is a very long way away. You'll need to make sure that you don't ask for an improvement in a form that takes you further away from the staff scheme.

You cannot dictate who attends from the management side, but try to get the people who actually deal with the scheme, as well as those you normally negotiate with. The industrial relations or personnel manager is not likely to know much about the scheme, and you will waste a lot of time while s/he adjourns meetings, and goes off and gets advice from somewhere else. Try to get the pensions manager or, if the scheme is administered by a firm of consultants (there are several of these, mainly subsidiaries of big firms of insurance brokers) one of their representatives. You might also want the actuary (see pages 237–40 for an explanation of what s/he does), and if the scheme is insured, someone from the insurance company as well, especially if you are being told you can't do things because of them.

In deciding what sort of structure you want for negotiations, think about:

- The size of the company, and the geographical spread.
- Are there too many plants for a representative of each to sit on a negotiating body? If so, how are you going to select the negotiators?
- Is one plant much bigger than the others? If so, how are you going to stop the smaller ones from feeling left out?
- How many unions are involved? The majority union will nor-mally take the chair at negotiations. How will the others be represented?

- The occupational spread. It's usually crucial, in a joint scheme, to ensure that both staff and works are represented. But the same applies with craft and process workers, or indeed people who may be in completely different industries, in a large conglomerate. Their terms and conditions may be quite different. This can make things complex if, for instance, sickness is differently treated.
- The role of officials. How far do you want them to be involved? If they are doing the negotiating, how can you be sure that there is an adequate reporting-back mechanism?

Sometimes, rather than a negotiating structure being worked out in detail and then put into effect, it will just develop gradually. If once you can get people together to talk to management about something to do with pensions, you can always find something else to talk about. So another meeting has to be convened, and a strictly 'one-off' delegate conference can make demands which involve reporting back for a further conference.

Management itself may be engaged in an internal negotiating process. Those at the centre may have to break down the desire for autonomy and fear of joint union action among local managers. Underlying their resistance may also be their own ignorance, and a dislike of the unions getting to know about something, even the pension scheme, that they don't know about. Being pragmatic and taking it step by step may bring dividends in this situation.

Possible Arguments and Responses
When the Labour government's White Paper came out on member participation (see page 226) all the big employers' organisations decided they were in favour of participation; what they were against was trade union involvement. It's that issue you have to win on.

Trade unionists believe that participation should be via the unions, because pensions are deferred pay. If the money was not going into the pension scheme it might be going into the pay packet. So we have as much right to negotiate on it, and be involved in the administration of it, as on any other item. While wages are a matter for joint negotiation, items like sick pay, bonus schemes, overtime, and so on are (or should be) matters for joint negotiation and control . Pensions are another item on this list, as the Employment Protection Act recognised. There's no hope of a group of unorganised people succeeding in negotiating and controlling anything. So it must be the unions.

Management's response tends to be:

- Since the scheme includes non-unionists, it would not be right for the unions to negotiate, or appoint trustees, on their behalf. This will be said particularly when the scheme includes senior managerial staff. You could answer that, first, all the non-unionists are free to join a trade union, and secondly, that the company and the non-unionists seem happy enough to allow the unions to negotiate on their behalf when it comes to wages, so why should they be suddenly concerned now? As far as senior staff are concerned, they will anyway be adequately represented among the management trustees.

- It would be impossible to have proper negotiations or trustee bodies, as there are too many unions concerned. It is remarkable how often management will produce this reasoning, in all seriousness, believing that having more than one union makes them unique and that getting the unions to sit down together is therefore obviously impossible. But it is certainly not true. Most companies of any size in the UK have a number of trade unions involved. The record, so far as anyone's counted, was GKN during the negotiations on contracting out in 1977, when there were 34 unions with membership in the company. There would be fewer today, because many of the small craft unions have amalgamated with others.

Management may then fall back on arguments about 'management's right to manage' and assertions that it does not consider pensions a negotiable item.

It will be a matter for your judgement how far you want to push the issue, if faced with this. You can take it to ACAS, or you can take some form of action. But people will not often take industrial action about pensions, as management are well aware; that's why they take this stance. You may need to leave the question on the table and return to it later. If necessary, you might accept a body that has only advisory powers as a 'foot in the door'.

26

Member Participation

Introduction

This issue is closely linked with that of negotiating rights, covered in the last chapter. A member trustee is not in a negotiating role. But the fact that s/he is there on the board of trustees is part of an extension of the scope of collective bargaining. Just as the job of a health and safety representative often differs substantially from the job of a shop steward, so the job of a trustee or the member of a pensions committee will differ from that of a shop steward. But they are all part of collective bargaining in a broad sense.

There has been a tremendous growth in the number of companies with member trustees in the last few years. In most cases, the members are able to perform a useful role – though more limited than the unions would like – but sometimes the company, having appointed someone, gives them no real power to intervene in the affairs of the pension scheme.

There are also many companies with 'advisory' or 'consultative' committees. Some of these are doing a good job, but others are just talking shops. They were accepted by the unions originally either because it was the best they could get from the company or because they were new to dealing with pensions, and not too sure of the way to move. Now that there's been some time to test them out, and there is more knowledge and involvement in pensions among shop stewards, many of these arrangements need reviewing, and bringing more firmly within the control of the unions.

Trustees

Except in the public services, almost every pension fund these days is set up as an irrevocable trust. This means that it must have a trustee, or more than one, to control the trust.

A pension fund can also have a large amount of money in it. The Ford scheme, for instance, had over £800 million in 1987. So it's important that these funds are kept legally separate from the employer's accounts. If they weren't, then if the employer went into liquidation the money saved up for pensions could be used to pay all the other debts.

Technically, the owners of all the money in the pension fund are the trustees. But they hold it on behalf of the members, not for themselves. The name says it all; they are being trusted with other people's money. So they have to act in the interests of those other people – the scheme members – both in the way they run the scheme, and the way they invest the funds. There are considerable disputes between the unions, employers, and the City about what that really means, and this is covered in more detail in Chapter 28. The trustees cannot run the scheme just as they want; they must follow the rules laid down in the trust deed, a legal document signed by the employer when the scheme is first set up or altered. This is binding on the trustees, even if they don't like what it says.

The trade union view is that half the trustees of any scheme should be scheme members; they can be elected by the membership as a whole, or they can come through the trade union structure, depending on the circumstances in any scheme. But it's also important, in pressing for this, that we ensure that the trustees are given real powers and not simply made figureheads. Anyone can be a trustee provided s/he is capable of performing the duties, and competent to carry them out. This means that the trustees must be UK residents, and they must not be minors or of unsound mind. A company can be a trustee, and non-UK residents can be directors of that.

The job of a trustee is to look after the fund in the best interests of all the members, not to negotiate changes in the scheme. Wearing different hats, the same people who sit on the trustee board may also be negotiating on pensions, but when meeting as trustees they should not do so.

In an average sized fund, the items that might come to a trustee meeting would include:

- Deciding on investment policy, and monitoring its carrying through;
- Supervising the administration of the scheme;
- Satisfying themselves that the legal duties, for instance on reporting to the Inland Revenue, are being complied with;
- Receiving and studying the accountants' and actuaries' reports;
- Preparing and publishing the annual report to all the scheme members;
- Taking decisions on what happens to discretionary benefits – death benefits, for instance; and
- Interpreting the rules, and deciding whether particular cases – for example, requests to retire early – come within those rules or not.

So the job is one of supervision. Usually there will be paid staff to do the actual administration, or else the work will be contracted out to a specialist firm, and it's for the trustee to check that the work is being done satisfactorily.

But even so, the trustees have a legal responsibility which they cannot delegate. It is always their duty to check on what is happening, and satisfy themselves that things are going well. They have to take steps to put them right if they are not. This is as much the case when an insurance company is running the scheme for you, as when you are doing it directly.

This at least is the legal theory. If ever a case is brought to court for breach of trust (which is very rare), it's what the court will say. In practice, things have been very different. There has been a great deal of negligent, and downright bad, trusteeship, and a good many skeletons are waiting in the cupboards of pension schemes to be pulled out. For instance, both before and after the reforms on the Stock Exchange – the so-called 'Big Bang' in October 1986 – many investment managers set up very peculiar charging structures, which gave them fat fees without their making any real effort. The trustees, and hence the members, have been ripped off in many cases – because they've assumed that things are all right when in fact they are not.

Given that the job is limited to supervision, why do we want member trustees? There are divided views on the subject in the trade union movement itself. Some people argue that activists should refuse to get involved, because of the danger that we will get sucked into the system and start playing capitalism's game better than the capitalists. Here are some of the counter-arguments:

- It's our money. Since management bears some of the risk if things go wrong, because of the company commitment to 'pay the balance of the cost' it is fair enough that they should have some part in the administration, but we should at least have an equal share;
- If you are going to take a 'more socialist than thou' attitude about pension fund money, the time to do so is before the scheme ever starts. Once there is a fund, it will be several million pounds and it will grow fast. You can then either ignore it or get involved in it. It won't go away if you pretend it's not there, any more than will a piece of new technology you don't like.
- Someone is going to control the funds, and with them economic power. If it's not us, it's management. The pension funds and other institutions are now the most important buyers and sellers of shares and government stock. They've taken it upon themselves before now to change government policy – for instance, by refusing to lend to the 1974–9 Labour government until it did what they were asking.

The appointment of member trustees is no guarantee that things will change. Many of those in place today are simply acting as rubber stamps. But at least if we are in there we can try to change things.

The opposite argument against having member trustees also comes sometimes from trade unionists – that we ought to leave it to the experts, that it's management's job to manage, and ordinary shop floor workers are not competent to do the work, because they don't have the knowledge. Against that view, the arguments are:

- The 'experts' are not the trustees, they are the people whom the trustees employ – the pension fund manager, actuary, merchant bank, insurance company. There's a lot of evidence that these people haven't been very effective at doing their job, and so no-one need feel diffident about supervising them.

The trustees' job is to supervise and to be a watchdog. You don't need to be an expert yourself to see when the experts have got things wrong. But you do have to be willing to question closely, and not take things on trust. On that basis, an active trade unionist can do at least as good a job as someone from the personnel department, who is no more knowledgeable about pension funds than you are.

Many member trustees have been rather uncritical about what their advisers tell them. The reasons for this are understandable. A member trustee is sitting as an equal on the board with management. People from the City, trained in public relations, spend a great deal of time convincing you that their view is the only reasonable one. It's extremely easy to get sucked into the cosy world of pension fund management, and to find yourselves rapidly accepting the orthodox City view of what is in the 'best interests' of the member. There's not space in this book to go into the whole question of an alternative investment policy. All that can be said here is that there's no reason in law for speculative property investment to be acceptable, when the funding of a cooperative making socially useful products is not. But to fit in with the requirements of trustee law, the trustees must show that they are likely to get a rate of return on either investment which is reasonable and safe.

The TUC has published a handbook for member trustees which goes into the subject in much more detail than can be done here (see booklist for details).

The Legal Position

There's no legal obligation on companies to appoint member trustees. When they do, the legal power of appointment, even of member trustees, usually belongs to the company. This is because they set up the trust to start with. The technical term is that they are the 'settlors' of the trust. It's possible to add a clause to the trust deed spelling out that there are member trustees. For example, the British Leyland Hourly Paid Trust Deed, drafted originally in 1976, said:

Rule 25. Appointment of Trustees
A. The statutory power of appointing a new or additional trustee or trustees shall be vested in the principal employer which shall have the power by deed to remove any trustee from office and appoint another trustee or trustees in place of any trustee so removed;
B. The power vested in the principal employer by paragraph A of this rule shall be exercised only after consultation with the relevant trade unions;

C. ... The number of trustees of the scheme shall not be less than 4 and the following provisions shall apply:
a. those of the trustees who are participating members are ... called 'member trustees' and those who are not participating members are called 'management trustees';
b. the number of member trustees and management trustees shall be equal.

The employer may say that this is unnecessary, because he's making an agreement with you in good faith and does not intend to break it. However, the print unions at News International found it very useful to have a clause of this sort in the trust deed, after the employer tried to dismiss the trustees and appoint his own, and they were able to threaten him with legal action.

An alternative is to have a signed agreement referred to in the trust deed.

Structure and Powers

The exact structure of a board of trustees can vary a lot, depending on what is set out in the trust deed. So too can the powers. You need to be very careful that a company does not appear to be conceding member involvement while at the same time moving control away from the trustee board.

In the Ford schemes, most of the powers that would usually be with the trustees are actually kept by the company. So if the company were to agree to member trusteeship (which it shows no signs of doing) the unions would still not have achieved very much.

There are three main types of boards of trustees:
1. Groups of individual trustees, each appointed as a named individual. The procedure for doing this is rather cumbersome. Each time a trustee is changed, there has to be a variation in the trust deed, and each new trustee has to sign a legal document, countersigned by a representative of the company, to give him/her his/her formal position;
2. Directors of a trustee company. Here, there's legally only one trustee. It could be a legal entity on its own, or it could be a subsidiary of the main company. Then the people carrying out the formal trustee duties are legally directors of this company, and they get their powers from the articles of association of the trustee company. They take up their position once their names have been added to the company's register of directors, which is a much easier procedure than varying the trust deed.

At Swan Hunter, for instance, the pension scheme is run by Swan Hunter Pension Trustee Ltd, whose directors are nominated by Swan Hunter and the Confederation of Shipbuilding and Engineering Unions in equal numbers.

3. A professional trustee company. The banks, big insurance companies, and insurance brokers, run these. The company setting up the pension scheme buys the services of, for instance, Barclays Bank Trust Co, who then carry out all the duties for your pension fund alongside a lot of others. The legal responsibility for doing the job properly then falls on them. If the company insists on maintaining this arrangement, then in order to get member involvement here you would need to have a management committee with member representatives, with powers of decision formally delegated to it by the trustee company.

Some pension schemes have one of these professional bodies as 'custodian trustee'. This means that they look after the share certificates and deeds for the property the scheme owns. They may also have some special duties if the scheme is ever wound up, or if there is a takeover. It's a convenient arrangement, so long as it is not a disguised way of taking away power from the unions.

Boards of trustees in themselves may not be all that they seem. For example:

> BOC's board of pension trustees consists of four individual trustees from the company, and four from the membership. But there is also an extra trustee, BOC Pension Trustee Ltd, of which all the directors are management people, and a representative of this body also sits on the trustee board. All the fund's investments are held in the name of BOC Pension Trustees Ltd.
>
> There is a separate Pensions Investment Committee, chaired by the finance director, with the other members coming from the company's main board and an outside investment house. None of the member trustees sit on this committee, although the trustee board does receive quarterly reports from it.

This is a good example of the sort of structure we should not be accepting. Where we have been trapped into it in the past, we should aim to change it. It means that power is diverted away from those who ought to control it.

TUC policy is 50% member representation on all controlling bodies. This may not always be attainable. More usually, the company insists on holding the balance of power, with 50% of members other than the chair, so that there is a 3–4 or 5–6 split. If you have to agree to this, try again in one or two years' time, when you're in a position to point out that disaster has not yet befallen the fund.

Another point to look at is the method by which people are to be appointed. This will vary a lot according to the size and complexity of the company.

A ballot among all the members of the fund is one way. In a small company with only a few sites, where everybody on each site knows each other, this is the obvious method. You need to ensure, though:

- That the unions can keep control of the ballot; and
- That the people who go forward for election understand what the job of a trustee is, and especially that it is not a negotiating job.

In a large company, you may need a rather more complicated electoral structure to get a fair balance between sites and employment groups. You may not be able to have as many trustees as you have sites, if the committee is to be of a workable size. You'll also have to perform a balancing act between, say, the large site in Manchester and the small one in Gloucestershire, or between process and craft workers, to make sure that they will all feel fairly treated. Including all this in an electoral structure may be just too complicated.

An alternative is indirect elections, perhaps via a delegate conference, or appointment by the combine committee, national joint committee or a special pensions committee if you have one. The people you appoint need not be members of the committee – though they could be. You'd need to get your nominations from the plants, and perhaps to bring into your discussions someone with experience of appointing trustees. This could be a union pensions specialist, if one is available, or possibly the consultant employed by the company on pension matters, if you are sure you can still keep control in your own hands.

The Lucas Industries works scheme has a central consultative committee of nominated representatives from shop stewards' committees.
The constitution says:

Representatives
1. Principles. The following general principles will regulate the nomination of Trade Union representatives:
    (i) Each representative shall represent approximately 2,000 members;
    (ii) Each representative shall, if possible, represent members whose places of employment are in the same geographical location;
    (iii) each representative shall, if possible, represent members within the same manufacturing group of the Lucas group of companies;
    (iv) each representative shall be a member of the Lucas works pension fund.
2. Nomination. Senior shop stewards' committee or the appropriate shop stewards' committee with representation constituencies shall choose their representative or representatives in such a manner and in accordance with such procedures as are applicable in those constituencies...
4. Nomination of directors for Lucas employees of the Lucas Works Pension Fund Trust Ltd;
    (a) there shall be three Lucas employee directors;

(b) the employee directors will be nominated by the members of the Lucas works pension fund consultative committee. To be eligible for appointment a person must be:

(i) a contributing member of the Lucas works pension fund and able to complete three years with the company before normal retirement date;

(ii) age 23 or over and have been in the employment of a participating company for at least 5 years and during 4 whole years of such employment, have contributed to a pension scheme operated by a participating company;

(iii) a member of the Lucas works pension fund consultative committee;

(iv) supported in his or her nomination by 3 members of ... the committee ... and receive the votes of a simple majority of the entire number of such members of the committee.

(c) In the event of the provisions ... above being inconclusive, the final choice will rest with the members of the works pension fund, through a ballot.

A third alternative, which has been widely used in the past, is joint selection. Here, appointment is done by interview by both company and union full-time officials.

At engineering company GKN, for instance, nominations are asked for from the different sites, and each must be supported by at least 10 members. These are then forwarded to the company. Interviews and selections are done by a joint panel of company representatives and union full-time officials.

The arguments that have been used for this type of procedure are:

- It tends to be easier to obtain from the company than other procedures. As any decision should be unanimous, the unions can still veto people they do not like.
- It means you can appoint 'the best person for the job'. Since the role is not the same as that of a shop steward, that person might not be elected in a ballot.
- It enables you to do a 'balancing act' between plants, areas, and bargaining groups, without needing to draw up a complicated electoral system.

But the arguments against are stronger:

- It goes very much against the democratic basis of the trade unions, and the practice of electing (and recalling) the holders of other posts in the collective bargaining structure.
- The joint procedure should apply to all trustees or none. Since the management trustees are never chosen this way, why should the member trustees be?
- The trade union members of the selection committee will have their hands tied on the sort of questions they can ask (for

instance, on political involvement) by the presence of senior company management.
- There's a limit to how far you can find 'the best person for the job' in a 20 or 30 minute interview anyway.

Some very good member trustees have been appointed by a joint selection procedure; and there will be many cases where a company will not agree to anything else, and you have to compromise. But generally the principle that should be followed is that the appointment of member trustees should be under union control. Selection should not be ruled out. In a smallish company without a strong joint union committee, it may be the only practicable procedure. The members themselves may not be sure enough that they know what pension trusteeship involves, the first time round, to feel confident that they would pick the right people in a ballot. But it should be union selection, for instance by union pension specialists, not a joint procedure with the company. Before entering into it, you also need to get clear agreement from the company that they will appoint whoever you select, and not use their legal powers to veto your choice.

Other Points

- Once trustees are appointed, legally they are all equal. All have the same powers and responsibilities. Member trustees should not allow themselves to be treated as second class citizens. The management trustees should not have special places on the investment committee, nor should the member trustees let themselves be pushed into a purely 'welfare' function. The research by Tom Schuller (see booklist) shows that this does happen quite widely.
- Any facilities given to management trustees – like places at conferences, travelling arrangements for meetings or discussions with the 'experts' – should be given to member trustees as well.
- Training should be given, preferably before the trustees ever take up office. Several unions, and the TUC regional education service, run courses for trustees. In-company training can also be useful, as it will teach you about the details of the scheme you're working with, and the administrative procedures the company uses.
- Don't allow the company to dictate that the trustee should not be a shop steward, or that s/he must give up union jobs if appointed a trustee. It's a matter for discussion with the members whether the trustee should be a shop steward or not. The advantage of having a shop steward is that s/he is already part of the union structure, and in close touch with the members. The disadvantage is that stewards are generally overloaded with work, and they might find it difficult to step out of the negotiating role and into the administrative role.

- You need to establish a mechanism, again under union control, for regular discussion of how the trustees are getting on. An occasional slot on a combine committee agenda, or a meeting with the unions' full time officials and the site convenors, are two possible ways to do it. If there is a pensions negotiating body, then the member trustees should be expected to attend these meetings, though not take the lead in negotiating.
- There needs to be a clause saying specifically that acting as a trustee will not lead to any penalties in terms of the work allocated, or promotion prospects, and that all time spent on trustee duties (including reading up in advance) will be paid at average wages. Member trustees can be very vulnerable to petty annoyances from their local managers, who may resent the fact that they are sitting on a board with top people from the company, and possibly getting to know them a great deal better than the local manager does.

Possible Arguments and Responses

The arguments for member trustees are the same as the arguments for negotiating on pensions. It is the members' deferred pay, and they have a right to share in its control. Management may well try to draw you, though, into an argument about competence. Don't get into a position where it looks as if you are criticising the existing management trustees, unless you have solid facts to go on. Otherwise, it will only put their backs up. Instead, you could say that:

- Trustees are not meant to be experts. They are meant to supervise the experts, and for that straightforward common sense, together with additional training, is the best quality;
- Members will be given confidence that the problems that may arise on their death, for instance, will be considered by someone whose lifestyle is similar to theirs, and who appreciates what it would be like to live on State benefits. Managers are much better off, and with the best will in the world, have had their experience in a very different environment.

You will also, inevitably, have to say reassuring things to the effect that:

- You do realise that it is not a negotiating role, and that the trustees' responsibility is to act in the best interests of all the members, not only those in his/her particular trade union;
- You do appreciate that there is a definite, and often quite arduous, legal responsibility; and that you know there are certain matters which will have to be kept confidential, such as the personal circumstances of individuals.

When you have won on this issue in negotiations, the people appointed may find that they have to fight the battle all over again at the trustee board. Many of the people who sit on boards of trustees at the moment, the company secretaries and senior directors, will not often meet trade unionists and will frequently be quite naive in their views. The new member trustees will probably have to spend the first two or three meetings proving that they are human. So you need to add patience to the list of the trustees' necessary qualities.

Pension Schemes in the Public Services

In the public services, superannuation schemes – some of them very big – do not have trustees or a trust deed. Instead, they were created by Acts of Parliament, and then sets of regulations on top. Nor do they all have funds, though what they do instead varies:

- In the Civil Service, the money goes straight out of the tax-payer's pocket into the pensions; it goes through the payroll. This happens also with the armed forces, judges, and Members of Parliament;
- For the Health Services, the teachers, and some other groups there is a 'notional' fund which is really just a piece of book keeping. The government works out what the value of it would be if it puts money into it each year, but it doesn't actually do so. But the rules are laid down by statute, after agreement with the unions.

  Here you won't be able to get the right to trusteeship; but you can still have consultative rights. In practice, these tend to stay with full time officials through the national negotiating structure, and it may be difficult to find out what is going on. You may need to put pressure on the national officials through your annual conference, if there are no reports coming through.

- In local government, the rules are laid down by statute, and are identical for every council, but there are real funds, run by the county councils, or by one metropolitan borough on behalf of several others. So there are 90 different funds altogether. This means that power and control is fragmented, and is probably the reason that it has stayed that way. The council as a whole acts in the role of trustee, though it is not legally appointed in the same way as in the private sector.

  Here, the unions at local level are able to get 'observer' or 'consultative' status on the council committees which run the investments, though they cannot affect the benefits. NALGO has been very active in doing this in many areas, but the manual unions have been much less so. If you want to know what is happening in your area, the best place to start asking is in the NALGO branch.

The nationalised industries have funds and trustees as if they were private companies although in some cases the changeover is fairly recent and they are still paying off debts from the days when they were run like the Civil Service scheme. This is one of the issues that has to be considered when a nationalised industry is privatised.

Advisory and Consultative Bodies

In addition to member trustees, many employers have set up pensions advisory committees or pensions consultative committees. These vary a lot in intention, and in the format. They are often set up outside, and with no proper connection with, the union structure.

BOC has a pensions advisory committee of 28 drawn from its different divisions. The divisional management committee decides on the method of appointment. In the case of BOC Gases it's by ballot. In other divisions the procedure is not formalised.

You can find that these committees are being used by the employer as a method of giving token member participation and defusing the demands for real involvement. Thus another company in the chemical industry, when it had a request for negotiations on improving the scheme, replied that:

Consultative machinery has been set up in the divisions, and a group pensions advisory council (GPAC) was formed, with trade union and other members from all the divisions. This body, which is chaired by a main board director, is free to discuss all matters concerning pensions, pensioners and the pension fund, and is enabled at regular intervals to put forward to top management proposals for change ... We believe that the members of GPAC and of the pension scheme as a whole are well pleased with these arrangements ... the pension fund trustees include trade union members.
   In view of the comprehensive and successful joint arrangements already in force we see no advantage in a further meeting at national level to discuss pensions.

In a large company, some sort of formal communication structure is necessary if the trustees are going to keep in touch with the members. You do not, though, need a special committee. The work can just as well be done by the shop stewards' committees, if they feel they can cope. The unions, not the company, should decide whether they want to have a separate organisation for pensions.

The important point is to have a channel of communication both up and down. Members will feed in problems, queries, things they don't understand and points where they believe improvements are necessary. These can go up, according to what they are about, either to the trustees, for matters of administration, or to the negotiators, if it is a rule change that is being asked for. From those bodies, in the other direction, draft scheme booklets, other written material, suggested rule changes, and information on the progress of the fund, should be coming for comment. A consultative body at plant level can also send lay representatives to a central negotiating body. Thus the Ransome Hoffman Pollard agreement says, for instance:

Consultative Committees

To contribute to the effective participation in the running of the pension scheme there will also be established:

1. A local pensions consultative committee, membership of which is open to contributing members of the pension schemes who are also members of their appropriate trade unions. The nature of the representation and the number of members will be determined in detail by local agreement. In general it will reflect union membership at the location.

The function of the local committee is:

(a) to provide a forum for the election of one or two of its members to the central pensions consultative committee;

(b) to provide such assistance to the central committee as the latter considers necessary for the successful conduct of their responsibilities;

(c) to provide a channel of communication between members of the fund and the pension administrators.

2. A central pensions consultative committee. Membership of this committee will be drawn from senior management, local consultative committees, and the full time national officers or their nominees from the appropriate trade unions. Its function will be to play a major role in communication, consultation and negotiation of pensions matters. Changes in the pension scheme will be negotiated by the committee, and not through the normal site negotiating machinery.

The member trustees sit in on these negotiations, but take no part when the company is there, although they do take part in the trade union side of discussions.

Again it is important that any consultative bodies are clearly part of the trade union structure. If one has been set up that is not, then clear links need to be made, even if you change nothing else in the structure. A conference of consultative committee members, trustees, convenors and full time officials, on a regular basis, would be one method.

Any advisory body can be turned into a mere bureaucratic talking shop, with everything interesting being referred somewhere else for decision. It's important to see, therefore, that:

- Those on the local committees get some proper training, preferably from the unions rather than the company;
- If something goes up to the next level, whether it came from them originally or was initiated at local level, a decision is reached reasonably fast and the local committee are told what it is. It is very frustrating to see your good idea disappear in a mass of paperwork, never to appear again; and
- There is a mixture on the committee of people whose main interest is in pensions, and people whose interest is in the more day-to-day problems of the workplace.

If it is clear that the company is trying to make it into a talking shop, it may be better to threaten to pull out if it doesn't improve, rather than to struggle on.

27

How Pension Schemes are Financed

Introduction

Schemes in the private sector which are approved by the Inland Revenue and therefore get tax relief, are almost all funded. This chapter looks at what funding means, how the cost of a pension is calculated, and how there can turn out to be a 'surplus' on the fund.

What Funding Means

Each year you are a member of the scheme, you and the company put contributions into the pension fund to cover the pension you've earned in that year. This then builds up interest payments, and if the arithmetic has worked out well, there should be enough in the fund when you retire to meet the cost of paying your pension, for as long as you live.

To see how it operates, we'll take a very simple example of a single person, and assume that there is no inflation and no wage rises.

MacGregor and Co agree to pay £100 a year for ten years into a bank account for their employee Peter Rabbit's pension. P. Rabbit adds £50 a year. Interest rates are steady at 5% a year, so the first year's £150 accumulates compound interest over ten years, and becomes £233. The second year's accumulates over nine years, and so on. In the end, when P. Rabbit reaches 65, a lump sum of £1,887 is waiting to be turned into pension.

(Compound interest means that each year interest is paid not only on the basic money, but also on the interest already paid in previous years. So the first £150 becomes £157.50 at the end of the year, and the next year's interest is paid on the £157.50.)

P. Rabbit knows that the average life expectancy of a 65 year old man is 13 years. So he decides to arrange for his pension to last for 13 years. But this does not mean he must simply divide £1,887 by 13. The money that he draws out last will have been accumulating compound interest each year while it is waiting for him to draw it. So he can be a little more generous. He decides to draw his money out at £170 a year to live on.

However, P. Rabbit knows that 13 years is the average life expectancy – but he has no way of knowing whether he is going to match the average or not. He may live one year, or he may live 30.

238 The Essential Guide to Pensions

If he lives one year, there will be money left over. If 30, he'll run out of cash.

This is why the majority of pension schemes are group pension schemes. The new Personal Pensions are too; the group is all the other people who have bought pensions from that company. Though Peter Rabbit cannot be sure that he will match the average, he can be pretty sure that, taken as a whole, a large group will. The money that is saved on those who don't draw their pension for long can be spent on those who draw it for many years.

In an employer's scheme, the money is put in not for any one person, but for the group as a whole. The average employer's contribution of 10% or so could equally well be calculated as a much higher contribution for the older person and a much lower one for a young person. There may be no need at all for a contribution from the employer to cover the benefits of a person under 30 – the member's own contribution may be enough.

Inflation

The basic framework of funding is complicated by the fact that we have inflation. Very few schemes now pay fixed sums of money. It would be far more likely that MacGregor's were paying in 10% of P. Rabbit's earnings, and Peter himself 5%, and that it was agreed that he'd have 10/80ths of his final earnings when he retired. Those earnings might be £1,500 when he started, but with 5% wage increases they'd be £2,440 when he retired. With annual increases of 10%, they'd be £3,890, and with annual increases of 20%, as we had for a few years in the 1970s, it would be £9,280.

It may seem impossible for pension schemes to cope with this, but what enables them to make promises that they can pay a pension based on final earnings is that, when inflation is high, normally interest rates are too. Over the long term, interest rates have averaged out at a percentage point or two above the rate of earnings increases. If earnings increases were running at 5%, for instance, you expect interest rates to be 7% or so, so that people can earn a 'real' rate of interest on their money. This means that the money they have in the bank is actually increasing in terms of what it will buy, not just in money value.

Over the last two decades, this hasn't always been so. In the 1970s, interest rates did not keep up with the high rate of inflation. So money was sitting in stocks and shares losing purchasing power, even though it was gaining large amounts of dividends and interest payments in money terms.

Then in the 1980s the reverse happened. Inflation fell, but interest rates didn't. The stock market also boomed, and the prices of the shares were pushed up and up because there were more and more people chasing after the same number of bits of paper. So pension funds were making large amounts of money (at least on paper), while wages were not going up very fast. So there was more money in the funds than was needed to pay the benefits so far promised.

Why bother to put the money away at all? The alternative would be to 'pay as you go'. This means paying pensions to the people who are already retired from the income being created today, and relying on future workers to pay our pensions when we in turn retire.
The problems with this are:

- What happens to the pensioners if a business goes bankrupt?
- What happens if a whole industry disappears, for instance because of new technology? In 20 years' time nobody might be reading printed newspapers any more. It might be all on the television screen, and where would the print workers get their pensions then?
- People might rebel against paying high contributions and taxes for the benefit of pensioners.

These arguments have some force, but they'd have much less if the government either took over the pensions industry, or regulated it more heavily, so that for instance it could act as a back stop in cases of bankruptcy. Other countries that are more economically successful than we are manage without funding pensions in the way that we do. France and Germany have quite different systems, and on the whole their pensioners are better off.

It's an open question whether funding or 'pay as you go' is more beneficial. But funding is deeply entrenched, and many pension professionals become nearly hysterical if someone suggests moving away from it. Changing it, unless done gradually, would cause a considerable upheaval.

Pension funds are now huge; there's round about £300bn in them, though no-one knows exactly how much. They own a third of the shares on the stock exchange, but ownership and control are very different things. The control has stayed with a small group of City institutions – merchant banks, stockbrokers, and others – who manage the funds for many companies. Member trustees have hardly begun to wrest control away from these 'high priests'.

How the Cost of a Pension is Calculated

Having seen what funding means, we now need to come down to detail and look at how the cost of a specific pension scheme is calculated. This is the job done by a professional called an actuary, whose job is to make a long-term budget forecast for the scheme. This is drawn up to look like a balance sheet, and is called an actuarial valuation. But only part of the money on that balance sheet is actually there at present. The rest is what is assumed to be coming in over the lifetime of the scheme, and what is assumed to be paid out.

Actuaries have a highly specialised mathematical training, but a lot of their work is really making informed guesses. They are very well paid, and have some of the toughest restrictive practices around.

Going back to the example of Peter Rabbit, the actuary there could simply have been told by MacGregor and Co what pension they wanted to give Mr Rabbit, and for how long. S/he could then work backwards, calculating the compound interest, and could in due course tell them how much they and P. Rabbit have to put in to get that answer.

But when s/he is dealing with the real world, with larger schemes and problems about the rate of inflation, the actuary has a more difficult job. Instead of a straightforward mathematical calculation, s/he has to make assumptions about:

- How many people are going to die before retirement and therefore get a lump sum, rather than a pension;
- How many of them are married, so that there is also a spouse's pension due;
- How many people are going to leave the company;
- How many are going to retire early, and therefore start drawing their pensions before they would normally be expected to;
- How long people are going to live after they've retired;
- How fast earnings are going to rise between now and the date people retire; and
- How fast prices are going to rise, and whether scheme pensions will be increased;
- What is going to happen to interest rates, dividends, and stock market values, in the future.

How many people are going to die, and how long the pensioners are going to live, can be estimated fairly accurately. There are tables, drawn up from the experience of many years, showing for any particular age group how many people can be expected to die in the year. For early retirements, and for leaving service, it will be a combination of guesswork based on the 'feel' of the scheme, and what management tells the actuary about the future of the company.

The last two estimates are more difficult, because they involve making predictions about the political and economic situation many years from now. It is possible to make predictions which at least give you a basis to work on, for two main reasons:

- The two factors tend to interrelate. Interest rates have usually been a little higher than the rate of inflation, and what matters most is the relationship between them. So if the actuary decides that the rate of interest is going to be 11% and the rate of wage increases 9%, he is predicting a 2% 'real rate of return'. It doesn't matter all that much if the rate of interest is 13% and the rate of wage inflation is 11%, as the real rate of return is still 2%. But it matters a lot if the rate of interest is 11% and the rate of wage increases is 10%, because that means the real rate of return is drastically cut to only 1%.

- Even if an actuary gets the figures wrong, any one set of predictions does not have to last very long. By law, an actuarial valuation has to be done at least every 3.5 years, and some companies even have them done every year. Actuaries tend to stress in their reports that if they get their figures wrong once, they can always correct them next time.

Valuations can take a very long time, though they are always done 'as at' a certain date. The Government Actuary's valuation of the Health Service scheme, for instance, has been known to be five years late! The employer will usually blame the actuary for delay, but in fact it may be the employer's own fault, if the facts aren't supplied quickly.

Before a valuation can start, all the information needed has to be collected together and checked for accuracy. This will cover the ages of the people in the scheme, their pension rights, what the rules really mean, the scheme's holdings of stocks and shares and property. It will often take the scheme administrators a very long time to get all this together.

A formal actuarial report is usually made to the trustees of the scheme – though the actuary will often be in close touch with the company about what to put in it. If the scheme is fully insured, there will be a routine valuation done for the insurance company, but the trustees can – and should – still see it in full. The report will be a bound pamphlet, anything up to 40 pages long. The valuations can be written in any number of ways, and there is no standard or model form, though the actuaries' professional body have done a lot in the last few years to see that at least the same words are used to describe the same things in different reports. There is also now a 'Guidance Note' (GN9; see details in booklist) which requires valuation reports to include certain information.

The unions have a right to see any valuation report done after November 1987, and you ought also to press to see earlier ones. If there are member trustees, they should aim to meet the actuary face to face, both before s/he starts writing the report and when it is presented.

If the trustees have a particular set of improvements to the scheme in mind – or know that the unions have – it is sensible to ask the actuary to calculate the cost of making these, and include it in the overall report.

What the Report Should Contain

This section goes into the points you should look for in your report, and also points to some of the questions to ask. If the report of your scheme doesn't contain all the items of information that are dealt with here, ask why not.

The examples are all taken from an imaginary valuation of the 'ABC Ltd Staff Pension Fund'.

The first major item will be information about the scheme. This will cover:

- Details of the membership, which will come from the pension scheme's own records, and the employer. It will probably be set out in the form of a table like the one shown:

Summary of Membership Data at 6 April 1988

Category	Number of Cases	
Contributing members		Total annual earnings £000
Men	470	7,350
Women	520	2,800
Total	990	10,150
Deferred pensioners		Total annual deferred pensions £000
Men	220	287
Women	148	89
Total	368	386
Pensioners		Total annual pensions £000
Men	300	692
Women	402	505
Children	12	30
Total	714	1,227

If the figures here look different from what you would expect, ask for an explanation. This is the basic material of the valuation, and if something is wrong here, the whole thing will be wrong.

Then there will be an outline of the main benefits (which can be worth using elsewhere, since it is often clearer than the scheme booklet). There will be a brief note about when the last valuation was done, and what the results were. So in the ABC report, this section says:

The previous actuarial valuation was carried out as at 6 April 1985 and the results were presented in a report dated 30 October 1985. As a result of this valuation the company continued to contribute at a rate of 14% of members' pensionable earnings.

If there have been changes in the scheme benefits, or in the numbers of people covered by the scheme, details should be given here. So you will be able to see, for instance, how many plants have been sold off or bought, or how many early retirements at the employer's request there have been. There'll also be brief details about any recent changes in the law – like that on early leavers' benefits – and perhaps an explanation of the effects this will have on the scheme.

- Then there will be a summary of the fund's assets, though not in any great detail. The ABC summary, for instance, looks like this:

ABC Limited Staff Pension Fund – Distribution of Investments at 6 April 1988

		Market Value £000	Percentage of Total
1.	Directly invested assets		
	Fixed interest securities	6,287	15.8
	UK Equities	27,402	68.9
	Overseas equities	5,225	13.1
	Cash and deposits	464	1.2
	Net current assets	389	1.0
		39,767	100.0
2.	Managed Fund Units		
	XYZ Assurance Society	8,000	
	Total	47,767	

The next section should cover details of the assumptions. The actuary goes through saying what guesses are being made about the future. He starts off by saying what he thinks will happen to interest rates in the long term. This need not bear much relation to what is happening at the moment – in fact, it should not, because all the money coming in from the interest payments will have to be reinvested, at whatever rates are available at that time. Really, the actuary just thinks of a number, though s/he can relate it to past experience about what interest rates have been over recent decades.

Next comes a set of estimates about the money currently in the fund. This is what the ABC fund valuation says:

We need to put a value on the assets which is consistent with the assumption of a long term investment return of 9% per year [because that's what they've already assumed]. Their market value is not necessarily appropriate for this purpose because market values can fluctuate widely over short periods of time, reflecting short term considerations not affecting our long term assumptions. We have, therefore, adjusted the market value of the assets so as to reflect average market yield levels over the three years leading up to the valuation date. The value thus obtained amounts to £39.4m, equivalent to 82.5% of the market value.

The Stock Market crash of October 1987 showed why stock market values were not suitable. They could be drastically cut overnight. If the pension fund did not need to sell its investments overnight, this did not matter, so long as the values were going to recover before the date when they did want to sell them. But though actuaries think they are very cautious people, this example shows that they have often not been cautious enough in the last few years. The Stock Market fell by over 30% in a few weeks, so writing the values down by just 17.5% was not enough.

- The next item is wage increases. In the ABC scheme, the actuaries assume that wages will increase by 7%, which is 2% less than the rate of return they have assumed. Since it includes staff and there will be a lot of people on incremental scales, they've also added in a figure for increases related to age.

Again this is simply guesswork; it doesn't mean the company is committed to paying you this much over the years – though if it is more than they are offering, you could always try this on as an argument.

They'll then say what they are assuming pensioners and deferred pensioners are getting as an increase. This will be based on what the scheme has actually done over the last few years, plus the actuary's assumption (often as a result of a conversation with the employer) about how generous they will be in the future. Challenge them if it looks as if they are planning to be mean to the pensioners.

If the scheme is contracted out, and/or integrated with the State scheme (see page 22 for an explanation of this) there'll also be assumptions about how far the Lower Earnings Limit and State benefits will increase.

A second group of assumptions will concern the future of the people in the scheme. One important one will be on the numbers of people leaving. Schemes (except those with a money purchase underpin) tend still to make a profit on early leavers, because their benefits don't increase as fast as those for stayers. So if the actuary has assumed that there won't be any early leavers, there is a 'hidden reserve' available because the fund will benefit every time anyone does leave.

Then there'll be material on the mortality rates of pensioners and scheme members, and details of the numbers of people who are married when they die (which will mean that dependants' pensions have to be paid). There could be a statement about the future numbers of early retirements. This is something the actuary has probably got from the company, and it could give you a useful insight into the employer's plans for reducing staff in future years, so it is worth checking.

A further section will be about what has happened since the last valuation. Often this is called, in the jargon, the intervaluation experience.

This will say how the fund has done over the last few years, and how this compared with the actuary's predictions last time. So the ABC valuation says:

The principal factors affecting the Fund during the period 6 April 1985 to 6 April 1988 were the very high investment returns achieved on the assets of the fund – an average of about 22.3% per annum – coupled with a relatively modest rate of wage increases of about 7% per annum.

It might go on to say, as well, that there have been more early retirements, or more deaths, than expected, or that a large number of people were early leavers because of redundancies.

The most important section is the one giving the results. This usually looks like a balance sheet, with a final result showing whether the scheme is in actuarial surplus or actuarial deficit. The figures may be broken down in some detail, with costings for past and future service separately, and a split between the different benefits such as death in service and retirement pensions. Alternatively, there may be only one set of totals. Some actuarial firms give these figures both in terms of millions of pounds, and percentage of payroll, while others show only one. And finally, some firms put the employers' contribution, at its current level, in as part of the whole equation, but others make it only the 'balancing item' at the end. The actuary will usually also make a recommendation about what is to be done with any surplus. In many cases, you'll find that the employer has nobbled him and the recommendation is for a reduction in his contribution. But the trustees could ask for recommendations also on improved benefits.

All this should be on the basis that the firm is going to continue to exist – what is called an 'ongoing' valuation. As an extra check, there is usually also a 'discontinuance' valuation, which is to say that there is enough money in the fund to cover the benefits if the company were to close down tomorrow. This valuation is used in the 'actuarial certificate' which has to go in the annual report (see page 201). If the scheme is so poorly funded that it could not pay you if it closed completely, you need to be very worried. But apart from that, it is the ongoing valuation that should interest you.

The more detail you can get included in the valuation balance sheet, the more useful it will be for the unions. If the costs of the different benefits are given, then deciding how much an improvement is going to cost is much easier. The split into past and future service is also helpful, as it shows what effect a retrospective improvement will have.

There can be useful information in the valuation, for negotiators on subjects other than pensions. It's likely to include, for instance:

- Details of average earnings levels at different ages;
- Details of the percentages of men and women in the organisation, and possibly also their gradings, which could be useful to the people dealing with equal opportunities;
- Forecasts of the likely level of early retirements at the employer's request over the next few years, and so some idea of how the employer is expecting to reduce the workforce; and

- Details of the levels of mortality and ill-health retirements; the health and safety representatives ought to be informed, if it seemed as if there was a particularly high level in one plant.

The Inland Revenue's Requirements

Since April 1987, there has also had to be a valuation done on standard terms, laid down by the Inland Revenue.

This is because there are new rules, laid down in the Finance Act 1986 about actuarial surpluses. Every scheme must now have a valuation done, at least once every three years, according to the Revenue's guidelines, which are rather different from those used by many actuaries. These guidelines are fairly pessimistic, and they allow so much leeway that in many cases they do not show a surplus even when the ordinary valuation does. But if the Inland Revenue surplus is 5% or more above what is needed, the 'administrator' of the scheme has to decide what to do about it. This can be the employer, or the trustees, depending on the terms of the trust deed. They have the choice of:

- Improving the benefits;
- Increasing the pensions for pensioners and early leavers;
- Giving employer and/or employee reduced contributions;
- Giving employer and/or employee a contribution holiday – that is, saying that they need not pay contributions at all – for up to five years.

If having done all these things, or considered them all and decided not to do them, and there is still a surplus, then the administrator can either pay over the extra money to the employer, or keep it in the fund and pay tax on that part of their investments. If the money goes to the employer, there is a tax charge of 40% – regardless of the employer's tax position.

These new rules have put many employers off the idea of taking refunds of surpluses, although a few have done so, sometimes as the result of taking over a company with a rich pension fund. More often, though, they have reduced their contributions, or cut them out altogether, instead. In some cases they have reduced the employees' contributions as well. Often, also, they have 'split the difference' and given some of the benefit of a surplus to the members in improved pensions, while pocketing the rest.

What We Should Ask For

The starting point in discussion of a surplus is normally to say that it is all the members' deferred pay, and so it should all be used for their benefit. Though this is a reasonable point at which to start, it's not very realistic, and we have to expect that the employer will want some benefit from it.

A major reason for actuarial surpluses, in many companies, is that the pensioners and deferred pensioners have had very small increases, while the money that was set aside to cover their benefits has been earning interest at a much higher rate. So logically and morally, they should have first call on any surplus. Their benefits should be increased up to the level of the increases in the Retail Prices Index since the last increase was given. This is something the trustees can decide on, but beyond this, it should be a matter of negotiation with the unions, on their own 'shopping list' of benefits.

The employer may be wary of offering improvements that have a permanent cost-effect, if he feels that the surplus is only temporary. So he may be more willing – especially if it fits in with his other priorities anyway – to offer something like a special early retirement scheme running for one or two years and then being reviewed. You may have no option but to take this, if it's the only thing on offer. But try to trade it off against something you really want, assuming that the employer is going to be keen enough to give you that improvement anyway.

Contribution Holidays

One of the ways in which surpluses get reduced is by the company or the members going on 'contribution holiday'. This means that for a few years, you simply stop paying in. The members see the results in their pay packets, the company in its annual accounts. Its overheads are less, and so its profits, and/or the amount available for investment, are larger.

Since about 1985, contribution holidays for the employer have been increasingly common. They are much less so for the employee. Though it's tempting for the unions to ask for equal treatment with the employer, and simply to share any contribution holiday that they are taking, it is usually a mistake. This is because:

- It creates all the disadvantages of a non-contributory scheme, explained on page 80. You'll lose control, and your members will lose interest;
- You create a very difficult situation when the holiday finishes. All of a sudden, the members have to start paying again. If the contribution is very large, this could eat up all of a pay rise in that year. The most likely thing is then that members will become disgruntled about this, and vote with their feet to move out of the scheme altogether, perhaps into much worse Personal Pensions.

During any years when you are not paying, the union and employer should both be clear that this is a temporary arrangement, and the reasons for it. That should lessen, though it won't eliminate altogether, the shock when contributions start again.

If you do accept a reduced contribution, or none at all, for a few years, make sure you still get your proper wage increase! Some employers have offered 'contribution holidays' as a way of giving less of a pay rise, or none at all. Phillips Industries, for instance, did this in 1987. Not surprisingly, the members were highly annoyed and took industrial action. In effect, they were being asked to pay for their own wage increases.

The employer, though, should not have a contribution holiday either. In principle, any surplus on the scheme should go into improved benefits, and the first call on the money should be for the existing pensioners, as it was built up over the years when they were working for the company, and they have probably not kept up with inflation in the past. Second, for the same reasons, are the people who have already left the company and have frozen pensions. As explained on pages 165–70, frozen pensions do not remain the same size, as they used to, but they do not keep up fully with price increases, and so a 'catching up' exercise is needed every so often. After that, you should look at improvements to the benefits, and only when they are as good as you want them should you talk about reducing contributions.

That, of course, is in the ideal world. In practice, it will usually be impossible to stop the employer taking some of the benefit of a surplus by reducing his/her payments. If s/he promises to use the money to create jobs by putting in new machinery, you may not even want to. In many cases, unions have felt that a 50/50 split is acceptable. But it should be a matter of discussion and agreement, not unilateral action by the employer.

Actuarial Deficits

We have not seen actuarial deficits for the last decade, but they were widespread in the 1970s, and could appear again. These are where there is not enough money forecast to go into the fund to meet the benefits promised. Under the rules of almost every scheme, if the trustees are convinced that the money is not sufficient, they must reduce the benefits or close down the scheme. But that is a last resort.

The trustees' first step should be to ask the employer for proposals about how to make up the deficit. This could be done by a special single payment, or by extra payments over a number of years. If the employer makes clear that s/he does not intend to make up the deficit, then the unions involved should be told, as it is clearly a negotiating matter. The member trustees ought also to safeguard their own position, by having their views recorded in the minutes.

Sometimes it's necessary to put up with a deficit, because the company is in such a poor financial position that making any extra payments might push it over the edge into bankruptcy. If this is the case, then it needs to be closely monitored, and treated as purely temporary. Don't allow this to happen if the deficit takes the scheme below its solvency level on a discontinuance basis; if the company does then go bust you will have lost a great deal.

28

What Happens to the Money

When pension contributions are collected, they are not just put in the bank. The money is invested in stocks and shares, and anything else that is believed to provide a reasonable rate of return.

The legal responsibility for this will be with the trustees, or sometimes with a separate 'corporate trustee company'. Usually the trustees give this work to the fund manager, which can mean someone directly employed by the pension fund (or the company) to do the work, or it can be a contract with a merchant bank, stockbroker, consultant, or insurance company. Many schemes have a pensions manager who runs the scheme day to day, but hands all the money over to someone else to invest. Even when the pensions manager is doing the investment, s/he probably gets advice, on a fee-paid basis, from one of these bodies.

Types of Investment Administration

There are many variations on the mechanics of dealing with the money. Which one is chosen will depend on the size of the fund, its history, and how far the trustees want to have their own 'headquarters staff' – which itself often depends on the company management's own philosophy.

Whatever type of investment management you use, the trustees' responsibilities stay the same. Even in schemes where all the money, and the administration, is handed over to an insurance company, the trustees are still legally responsible. But often it's only when member trustees are appointed that the company trustees realise that they have serious legal duties which take up a fair amount of time if they are dealt with properly.

Schemes Run by Insurance Companies

Apart from those run by the employer, the biggest category of pension schemes with outside involvement is those run by insurance companies. But whereas originally these were simple, with the employer buying a pensions policy to cover his or her employees, in the same way as an individual might, today insurance companies offer a whole range of different services and it's not always clear just what they are doing.

The assets of some pension schemes are partly invested in a policy with an insurance company, and partly invested direct in bonds, shares, and property. Other schemes have an insurance company simply managing their funds along with a number of others which are all pooled together, and still others are just using the insurance company as an investment manager, in the same way as they would a bank. Having an insurance company involved, therefore, does not necessarily make the money any safer, or give any extra guarantees to the benefits.

The next section goes through the various types of management available from insurance companies.

Traditional Insurance

Insurance companies first went into the pensions business because there was a series of risks that people wanted to insure against. Someone might die, so that a lump sum needed to be paid out at a time when it didn't suit the company's cash flow, or someone might live longer than the average, so that the pension had to be paid for longer.

Life insurance companies specialised in setting up 'annuities' which are contracts to pay an annual income in return for a capital sum. The more the insurance company can make, either by buying shares on which it can make a lot of money, or by putting money into something with a high interest rate, the higher the annuity it can give for the same amount of capital.

So it is gambling first on its investment expertise – that it can make a bigger return than others in the same field, by buying and selling investments at the right time, so that it needs to ask for a smaller lump sum to start with. Secondly, it is guessing about the length of time the pensions will be paid on average. If it insures a group of people who all live to be over 100, the insurance company will probably be bankrupted. On the other hand, if it insures a group of 66 year olds whose bus falls over a cliff on the way back from an outing, it will make a profit. The larger the number of lives the insurers can cover, the better the chances that overall, they will live the average length of time.

An ordinary insurance contract, therefore, guaranteed that, in return for a certain amount of premium each year, a pension would be paid out to the insured person for as long as they lived, whether that was one year or 40. The simplest form of contract was 'non-profit'. This meant that the employer paid in a certain amount which the insurance company invested. If it did better on those investments than it needed to finance the benefits it promised, it hung on to the profits.

After a few years, the competition between insurance companies became rather keen, and employers began to resent the large profits that were being made at their expense. So some insurers began offering 'with profits' schemes, which meant that some – but by no means all – of the profits were passed back to the policy holders, usually in the form of bonuses on the premiums. There are two sorts of bonus – 'reversionary' which are added each year and cannot be taken away, and 'terminal' which are only added to contracts which are coming to an end in that year. In the last few years, bonuses have generally been going up, but at the begining of 1988, after the Stock Market crash, most companies held them at the same level as in the previous year, and one had to cut them because it was in financial trouble.

With both these types of policies, there is a guarantee of benefits written into the contract. Under the 'with profits' policy the benefits may well be higher than the guaranteed amount, but will certainly not be less. Again, though, competition among insurance companies led to the invention of yet more new forms of contract, which had very little insurance element in them. These are the 'unit linked' contracts where the guarantee is that the capital will be put into investments, and you'll get the profits – or losses – from the sales of those investments. Usually with a pension contract, at the time when you retire the fund that has accumulated will be used to buy an annuity, at the best rate that is available on the market.

So if you retire when the Stock Market is high, and interest rates are high too, you can do much better out of a unit linked contract than out of a with-profits one. But if – as happened at the end of 1987 – the Stock Market crashes and interest rates go down too, there's no cushion, and the amount of benefit you get will fall. In a scheme run by an employer with a unit linked contract, normally you'd expect that the employer would pick up the bill so that the member did not suffer. But in the new Personal Pensions, people who take out unit linked contracts are taking a considerable risk.

Managed Funds

These are run by insurance companies, but are really nothing to do with true insurance. Over the last 10 or 15 years, as pension schemes have grown in size and coverage, managers began to look hard at the charges the insurance companies were imposing for running schemes, and at their rather poor performance. However, when they started thinking about changing the method of investing their funds, they often found themselves locked into the insurance contract. Hidden away in the small print was a heavy penalty for 'surrendering' the policy – that is, for taking the business elsewhere.

The insurance companies argued that their investment policies were geared to the need to sell their investments at the point when people are expected to retire. If they had to sell earlier, they might not be able to get so much for them. But people found this rather unconvincing, and threatened to take their business away, even with this penalty. So to hang on to the business, the insurance companies started offering rather better terms if the scheme managers let them continue managing their investments, at least for a while. Since then, managed funds have also been marketed as a good way to invest money anyway. If you invest in this way, you normally buy 'units' in the fund. Legally you own those units, rather than the stocks and shares which give them their value, and which carry on belonging to the managed fund. In this way, the funds are very similar to unit trusts in which pension schemes also have quite a lot of money.

More recently, insurance companies have also offered entirely separate or 'segregated' funds, where the pension scheme trustees can know exactly what investments they have. There's also been a development of very specialist managed funds and unit trusts – for instance, in order to invest in Japan or US property. The argument is that this allows a small pension scheme to enter into a new area, without needing to acquire investment expertise there. But the management costs can be considerable. If the specialised fund is run by the same people as are managing your main fund, their opportunities for making money by swapping your investments around between funds are also considerable.

Very few pension schemes have their funds totally in one managed fund or unit trust. If they are not fully insured, though, they may well have part of their money in one or more of them. Particularly in the case of the specialist overseas unit trusts, they may buy into them for a short time when the return looks good, as part of their overall investment strategy.

Many funds that are generally self administered have part of their money in insurance policies. Even large funds find it useful to insure their death benefits, because the risks are too great to carry on their own. If a whole group of highly paid people were killed at once, the lump sum that had to be paid out at once could be very large. But since the risk of this happening is small, the premium to be paid to an insurance company would also be small, and the scheme can get a better rate for insuring a whole group than individuals could on their own.

Self Administration

This means that the scheme does the investment itself. But complete self administration is very rare, and could only happen with companies that were in the financial services industry anyway, as otherwise they would need to go to a stockbroker or a bank to do the buying and selling of investments at least.

There are any number of firms in the business of managing pension fund investments, ranging from stockbrokers to estate agents. A fund can buy a package of services from these people and the larger the fund (and therefore the more keen they are to acquire the business) the more likely it is to be able to dictate exactly what terms it wants. So it could specify, for instance, what reports are made to the trustees and what discretion the investment managers have.

There are also a number of ways in which investment advice can be provided to a self administered fund. It's often combined with management by outsiders, to act as cross-check. For instance, there can be an 'investment panel' or an investment committee, perhaps meeting quarterly with all or some of the trustees, or possibly only the investment manager, to discuss the fund's policy. The composition of these panels varies enormously, from a large group of stockbrokers, independent advisers and trustees to a small team of one stockbroker, one outside adviser and the fund manager. They can be very cumbersome. Since investment managers are in many cases sitting on other people's investment panels, it means there's a somewhat incestuous network within the industry, especially since the various financial institutions each manage large numbers of funds.

The next section covers the different sorts of organisation doing fund investment. They all have their disadvantages and operate within the same closed circle, so there's no recommendation of the 'best' sort of manager – that must be for trustees to decide.

Full Time Investment Manager

A large fund will have its own investment manager, responsible for buying and selling the stocks, shares, and other investments. Usually, he or she is given a considerable amount of discretion on day-to-day matters, but has to report on policy to the trustees or to a subcommittee.

Merchant Bank

These are the 'wholesale' banks, responsible for shifting very large amounts of money around the City. For a fee, geared to the size of the investment portfolio, and (except for giant funds) probably less than that involved in maintaining a full scale investment department, merchant banks will sell the service of an investment manager, for instance:

- Keeping the investments under review, and buying and selling when they think the time is right;
- Advising the trustees about developments in the market;
- Giving reports, valuations and performance tables;
- Taking decisions on how to vote on important issues at companies' AGMs.

The merchant banks are at the centre of a vast financial network. They offer investment advice, negotiate takeovers and privatisations, float new companies on the Stock Exchange and raise cash for new ventures. They also now – since the legal changes in the City in October 1986 – tend to own other financial institutions like stockbrokers. They can be involved in so many things that conflicts of interest are inevitable. For instance, the merchant bank could be advising one side or another in a takeover battle, or could be in charge of floating a large issue of shares or a privatisation. They'll be tempted to use the investment power of the pension funds under their control, to make sure that their other ventures are a success. At the very least, it's difficult for an employee to say, 'Don't buy the newly issued shares of company X, they're not a good investment', when it's a colleague in that office who is advising on the terms on which the shares are offered. The banks, though, claim to deal with this potential conflict by setting up what are called 'Chinese walls' between departments – meaning that information is not passed between them – and that each investment manager has independence and is not required to act in the same way as his colleagues at the same time.

Stockbrokers

There are now very few independent stockbrokers – they are usually owned by banks, either British or foreign. The larger firms offer the same sort of investment management service as the banks. They make money out of commission on the stocks and shares they sell, or by buying at one price on their own account, and selling on to you at a slightly higher one. So it can look as if the cost of their services is much lower than that of merchant banks. But there's a danger that they will deal too often, so as to make extra money.

Specialist Investment Managers

There are a good many of these 'boutique' services around, and it's a growth area. These are firms – some of them very small – who only manage investments, rather than having their fingers in other City pies as well. They can be linked to others who do, though. Often they have particular views about what type of investment is best, and so if you buy their services, you are buying a whole philosophy. Some, for instance, put a much higher amount of money than usual into over-seas investments.

The Trustees' Role

The duty of a trustee is to see that the funds are invested in the best interests of all the members. The trustees have a right to appoint whatever professional advisers they feel they need to assist them in carrying out their job. But it is still the trustees who have the legal duty, and who have to decide what is in the best long-term interests of the members. There is a lot of evidence that trustees, including member trustees, allow themselves to be used as rubber stamps for the professional advisers' doings.

The law is that trustees must put the interests of their members first, ahead of their own interests or wishes – this is what they are being 'trusted' to do. This usually – but not invariably – means their financial interest. So if the trustees want to avoid doing something, such as South African investment, or to do something specific like putting money into an enterprise board, they must find a financial reason for doing so. The moral or political reasons can underlie the financial one, but they must not be taken on their own. Nor can trustees be mandated by their union conferences or branches about investment (or anything else). They've got to make their own decisions, and act, in the legal phrase, as 'reasonable and prudent people'.

What the Funds Invest in

This is only a very brief summary of the main areas of investment. It's not intended to cover everything. The TUC guide for member trustees goes into the subject in much more detail, and there are other books listed in Appendix One which also cover it.

There are three main areas where it is standard practice for funds to invest:

- Shares in companies;
- Lending money to the Government;
- Buying property.

Shares

These are also called 'equities', and what you buy is actually a share of the ownership of the company. If it pays a dividend out of its profits, you receive a share of it.

The larger companies have shares which are 'quoted' on the Stock Exchange, which means that on any one day you can find a published price for them, and a stockbroker who will sell or buy them for you. Pension funds tend to concentrate on fairly large blocks of shares in the larger, well known companies, which means that it can be difficult for the smaller, less familiar company to find finance.

If there is more demand for shares to buy than there are shares available, the price goes up. If there is less demand than shares for sale, the price goes down. But the shares sold on the Stock Exchange are claims on the resources of companies that were set up long ago. You're passing pieces of paper, giving you these claims, 'second hand' from one company to another. The fact that your pension fund, rather than someone else's, now has a right to the dividend of XYZ company, does not have any direct effect on the company. But a high share price can make it easier to raise capital for new things, while a low one makes a company vulnerable to a takeover bid.

New capital is only raised on the Stock Exchange when new shares are issued, either in an existing company or a new one. The most common way of raising new capital for existing companies is by a 'rights issue', which means that current shareholders are given the 'right' to buy new shares at a lower price, before they go on sale generally. Pension funds have in the last few years got very involved in 'underwriting' new share issues and rights issues. This means that they guarantee beforehand that if any shares are left in the hands of the people – usually merchant banks – who are issuing them, the fund will take them for an agreed price. In return for this, they get a fee. Many share issues are over-subscribed, but every so often an issue goes wrong and then the underwriters find themselves left with these shares, which they can't sell without making a short-term loss. This happened on a huge scale with the BP sale in the autumn of 1987, for instance, and was estimated to have cost the pension funds about £300m.

Providing Venture Capital

This is one way in which pension funds can actually create new investment, rather than swapping round second hand paper. It means taking shares in – or sometimes giving a loan to – new or expanding companies that don't yet have a quote on the Stock Exchange. This can be done directly by the fund, but it's time-consuming and needs specialist skills, so it's more often done by an outside body. There are now a large number of these, often linked with the banks or insurance companies, or occasionally public bodies like the Scottish and Welsh Development Agencies.

There is more risk in these investments than there is in buying the shares of a company like ICI, but they are genuinely about economic growth, and the returns – even if they are long term – can be higher. But there are a lot of criticisms to be made of the organisations operating at present:

- They tend to be obsessed with the company that can show some sort of track record, needs between £0.25m and £1m, and has above average prospects. High technology products were a fashion a few years ago – more recently it has been specialist retailers like Sock Shop, or 'management buy-outs' where the local managers are helped to buy the plant from the parent company. Real start-ups tend to be avoided, and companies that want 'too little' money can find it difficult to obtain;
- They want a quick return, and so can force the company to develop too fast, and float on the Stock Exchange before it is really ready to;
- Companies which are sound, but whose capital base has been eroded over the years, find it very hard to obtain new money to help with restructuring – they don't fit into the City image of a 'good investment'.

Some of these venture capital firms have a 'hands-on' approach, while others are 'hands-off'. A 'hands-on' firm intervenes actively in the management of the companies it invests in, including hiring new staff to provide technical knowledge and perhaps also offering things like marketing skills. A hands-off one will make the investment, and then leave local management to get on with it – until it decides to pull the rug out because the money is not coming in fast enough.

Local Enterprise Boards

These have been set up by various local authorities, especially the old Metropolitan Counties and the GLC before their abolition. They're venture capital firms with a difference, looking for long-term returns and capital gains rather than short-term payment of interest or dividends.

So for instance GLE, Greater London Enterprise, sees itself as filling a gap in the venture capital market, and doing so in a special way. The gap is for 'hands-on' investments in the £50,000 to £250,000 range. It's interested in long-term equity investment in medium size companies. It has had a number of referrals from City firms who do not want to turn people down flat but cannot themselves offer help. GLE can afford higher overheads than a purely commercial firm, because there is an element of public sector subsidy, and because the boroughs that have put money in are not looking for dividends, but are willing to plough back the returns from their investments into further schemes.

GLE is now providing a bridge between the public and private sectors. It can work closely with the public sector, but mobilise private funds. It offers investees a 'company secretary' service, and helps with training and recruitment, as well as the advice, consultancy and practical help so often needed by small businesses. Some services are charged for at full rate, others come from separate grant budgets or outside sources such as the Manpower Services Commission. All this involvement reduces GLE's risk of losing its investment, as they will have early warning of problems, and opportunities to put them right.

Most of GLE's funding now comes as loan finance from the banks. But in 1987 it also set up a London Enterprise Venture Fund, which successfully approached pension funds for investment, including some in the private sector.

Some investment managers have discouraged funds from investing in Enterprise Boards, or even refused to put the possibility on the agenda, because they have said they are not appropriate investments. This has to be something for the trustees to decide, not the manager on their behalf.

Government Stocks

These are also called 'gilts' or 'gilt-edged securities' because it is assumed that there is no risk to them and they are therefore as safe as gold. The Treasury issues 'stocks' which are promises to repay so much in x number of years, and to pay x rate of interest meanwhile. It is these that the fund can buy, both from the government itself, and 'secondhand' from other funds.

The government borrows the money to cover a budget deficit, and also, along with other public bodies, to pay for capital spending. The amount that the government needs to borrow in this way, at any one time, makes up the Public Sector Borrowing Requirement (PSBR) which politicians and economists talk about.

Any government can normally rely on the financial institutions lending it any money it needs, by buying up all the stocks it offers. Every so often, though, the institutions decide that the price is not right. Then †hey refuse to buy stocks for a few days or weeks. When this happens, a government that wants to carry on borrowing is forced to adjust the price, and this means that the rest of its economic strategy will have to change. There is thus enormous power in the hands of the pension funds. It was used against the Wilson government in the 1970s for instance, to force them to bring in the IMF. But they have not used it against Mrs Thatcher's economic policies.

Property

This is the third major way in which pension funds invest. The larger ones buy complete buildings, such as office blocks in the City of London or shopping centres or warehouses in the provinces. The smaller funds go into 'property unit trusts' run by other financial institutions. Some of the very large funds also finance redevelopments directly, in partnership with property development companies.

The funds tend only to look at the 'best' sites and prospects, concentrating heavily on the South East. It's an area where there are huge conflicts of interest, with the same small group of estate agents advising on buying, valuing, managing and finally selling the properties for large numbers of funds. It's difficult to find an objective valuation, and you may not be able to find a buyer when you need one, which makes the property 'illiquid', in the jargon.

In theory, property should be a good 'hedge against inflation'. That is, its value should go up in line with prices overall. To some extent it's done this, but the rates of return have been rather lower than on other investments, so over the last few years pension funds have been putting less money into property, and more elsewhere, especially overseas.

Other Investments

Funds invest in a number of other things, in a small way. Forestry, farmland, commodities, and gold coins have taken people's fancy at different times. The British Rail Pension Fund put about £20m into paintings and art objects in the 1970s. When it sold them, some barely covered their costs, while others made large profits. As this shows, all this sort of investment is more or less speculative and a fund should not have much money in any of them.

The Inland Revenue may decide that a fund that is investing outside the more normal areas is 'trading' and therefore must pay tax.

Overseas Investment

This has grown in popularity since in 1979 the Tory government removed exchange controls. In some years since then, more money has gone overseas than has been put into new investment in this country. In 1979, just under £2bn was overseas, but by 1985, according to the CBI, it was £22.6bn – just under 16% of all pension fund money. It is put into shares, lent to foreign governments, and spent on real estate in cities like Washington and Paris. The argument used by the financial institutions doing this is that it gives them investment opportunities which are not available in the UK, and that it helps to spread the risks.

Most trade unionists are very wary of overseas investment, particularly in companies which are competitors of their own. But because of the limits of trust law, there must be good financial reasons for restricting the amount of money overseas. The TUC considers that no more than 10% of any one fund should be overseas, because:

- It's going to be more risky than investing in the UK, because on top of the possibility that the investment itself can go wrong, the pound can move the wrong way against the foreign currency at the time when you need to get the money back home. Pensions, after all, have to be paid in pounds and not in dollars or yen.
- As we saw in October 1987, investing on a lot of different stock exchanges exaggerates the risks rather than spreading them. All the different stock markets fell sharply at the same time, though they bounced back at different rates afterwards. The big financial institutions now 'think global', which means that if something goes wrong in one country, the effects are felt very quickly in others;
- The rate of return in UK equities has actually been higher over much of the last decade than overseas, and the costs of investment are much less.

The financial institutions are very keen on overseas investment, partly because many of them are parts of multinationals themselves, and partly because they can make big fees on it. For instance, when a pension scheme puts money into a managed fund, it normally pays a management charge, and the first units bought are valued at a lower rate to cover the costs of selling them. Managed funds specialising in overseas investment often make a higher management charge, and then charge you directly for the cost of transactions overseas as well.

There's evidence that the managers of overseas investments buy and sell them more actively than they do UK ones – so making even more money.

Pension Fund Accounts

As explained in Chapter 24, there is now a legal duty on all pension schemes to produce an annual report, including accounts of the scheme, and a legal right for the unions to be given copies. The union negotiators, and members of any sort of pensions committee, should have copies as well. Ask for someone involved in preparing them to come along to your meeting, to go through them with you.

The difference between the accounts, and the actuarial valuation explained in Chapter 27, is that the accounts are a snapshot of the position at the end of the financial year, and an explanation of what has been going on over the last year. The actuarial valuation is a forecast of what's going to happen in the future, based on the past experience. This means that you cannot compare the two sets of figures with any real meaning. For instance, the fact that more money is coming into the fund this year than is going out in payments to pensioners does not mean that the fund is making a profit or a surplus. It shows that it is building up resources in order to be able to pay the pensions of the current workers in the future. To find out if there is going to be a future surplus, you have to look at the actuarial valuation.

What has to go into those accounts was summarised briefly on pages 201–3. There is quite a lot of useful information in them. Some of the questions to raise are:

- What is the company's contribution? Has it gone up or down in the last year, either in actual cash or as a percentage of the payroll? Why?
- How does it compare to the members' contributions? What's the ratio between them? Has it gone up or down? Why?
- What is the money invested in? How is it split between the main categories of investment, compared with other schemes? Why?
- How many companies has the fund got shares in, and in what sectors of industry? Is too much concentrated in one sector? (If there was a very large amount of investment in breweries, for instance, a bad summer when people drank less beer would harm the fund.) How much is overseas and what is the justification for this?
- If part of the fund is in property, who decides what to buy and sell, and who values it?
- Does the pension fund own shares in the employing company? (This is called self-investment.) The law is being changed to limit this, in the Social Security Bill going through Parliament in 1990. It is anyway not a good principle to invest much money – more than perhaps 5% of the fund – in your own company;
- Has there been a lot of turnover of stocks and shares in the last year? Buying and selling costs money because you have to pay the cost of doing so. How much has been paid? Did the new purchases have a better rate of return after the cost of buying and selling has been taken into account?
- How is the fund manager paid? What are the fees and how are they worked out? They could be a flat rate, a percentage of new money, or a percentage of the fund;
- Does any part of the fund manager's income come from buying and selling stock? If so, this would give him an incentive to do this as often as possible;

- Where does the fund come on the various 'league tables' prepared by the specialist firms to show how well you're doing compared to others? How are those league tables worked out? You shouldn't place too much faith in them, though – they are only as good as the information that goes into them;
- Who makes policy for the fund? For instance, who decides whether to sell shares in a particular company so that a takeover bid can go ahead? How did they come to that decision, and who did they consult? Who attends the AGMs of companies in which the fund holds shares, and how do they vote on controversial issues?

According to the CBI, over half the pension fund managers never take any interest in what's being done by the companies in which they invest. If they wake up and don't like something that is going on, they simply sell the shares. The TUC, and many union activists, consider that since the pension funds are the owners of these companies through the shares they hold, they should exercise some control as well.

Many workers whose money is going into pension funds are asking questions about the use of their money in more radical terms. For instance, how far is it being used for socially responsible investment? Since this is intended to be a handbook, it is not the place to discuss these more political issues, but there are books listed in Appendix One which do so. But don't underestimate the difficulties of making progress here. The people managing your pension fund may be willing now to give you information since they have to by law, but they will regard it as a public relations exercise. Any attempt to go beyond information to taking power will be met with great hostility – because it will be challenging their own control.

And that's a very good reason for doing so.

Appendix One:

Useful Publications and Addresses

1. The Relevant Acts of Parliament

Social Security Pensions Act 1975
Social Security Acts 1985, 1986, 1989
Finance Acts 1986 and 1989
Financial Services Act 1986
Finance (No 2) Act 1987
Sex Discrimination Act 1987

In most cases the clauses in the Acts are 'skeletons' giving power for regulations to be made. There are over 30 sets of regulations under the Social Security Act 1986, for instance.

All obtainable from Her Majesty's Stationery Office, 49 High Holborn, London WC1V 6HB, or (by post) PO Box 276, London SW8 5DT.

2. Official and Semi-Official Publications

Employer's guide; occupational pension schemes and contracting out , NP23, DSS
Technical guides available from DSS (S Guyon, Room 419, Friars House, 157–68 Blackfriars Road, London SE1 8EU) on:
Contracted out money purchase (COMP) Occupational Schemes and Incentive Payments to Newly Contracted out Schemes
DHSS payments to Appropriate Personal Pension and Newly Contracted Out Occupational Pension Schemes
New Pensions Choices, a General Guide to the pensions changes, NP40, available from DSS local offices.
Information for Employers NP41
Information for Employees NP42
both with detailed further fact sheets from Leaflets Unit, PO Box 21, Stanmore Middx HA 1AY
Equal Treatment in Occupational Pension Schemes, Ann McGoldrick, Equal Opportunities Commission, December 1984
Model of Equality, a consulting actuary's report on the methods and costs of equalising the treatment of men and women in occupational pension schemes, Equal Opportunities Commission, March 1985
both available (free) from EOC, Overseas House, Quay Street, Manchester M3 3HN
Inland Revenue Practice Notes (IR 12) and SFO/OPB Joint Office Memoranda, available from Joint Office, Lynwood Road, Thames Ditton, Surrey
Institute of Actuaries' Guidance Notes on actuarial valuations (GN9) and on transfer values (GN11) available from the Institute, Staple Hall Inn, High Holborn, London WC1
Contents of Pension Scheme Accounts (SORP no 1), available from CCAB Ltd, 399 Silbury Boulevard, Milton Keynes, MK9 2HL (£1.50)
Pensions Advice and Management Authorisation under the Financial Services Act, Securities and Investment Board, 3 Royal Exchange Buildings, London EC3

3. TUC and Union Material

Guide for Member Ttrustees in Occupational Pension Schemes, TUC Publications, 1984
Law of Trusts and Pension Schemes; Note of Guidance, 1980
TUC Guide to Occupational Pension Schemes, 1983
Equality in Occupational Pension Schemes, 1988
Pensions Bulletin nos 1–15, and *Pensions Briefing* nos 1–10, available from TUC
Pension Fund Investment and Trusteeship, July 1983

You can be put on the TUC's mailing list for pension scheme trustees by writing to them at Congress House, Great Russell Street, London WC1B 3LS.

APEX Pensions Guide available from APEX Partnership, Thorne House, Ruxley Ridge, Claygate, Esher, Surrey; free to members, £1.50 to non members
Apex Pensions Survey, 1985 (same address)
A Young Person's Guide to Pensions, BIFU, 1B Amity Grove, London SW20 0LG

Most unions have also produced material about Personal Pensions; ask your full time official or Head Office.

4. Other Useful Material

Pension Funds and their Advisers (annual directory) lists all the major pension funds and advice firms. AP Information Services, 33 Ashbourne Avenue, London NW11 0DU
Pension Fund Trustees and the Law (free), Bacon and Woodrow, 55 East Street, Epsom, Surrey
Choose Your Pension, Consumers' Association/Hodder and Stoughton, 1989
A General Introduction to Institutional Investment, A J Frost and D P Hager, published for the Institute and Faculty of Actuaries, Heinemann, 1987
Pensions; The LRD Guide, Labour Research Department, 78 Blackfriars Road, London SE1 8HF, price £1.30 inc postage and packing
Investment Management; A Guide for Trustees, National Association of Pension Funds, 1986
Duties and Responsibilities of Pension Plan Trustees, David Nichols and Tony Williams, CCH Edition, 1984
Pension Funds and British Capitalism, Richard Minns, Heinemann, 1980
That's the Way the Money Goes; the Financial Institutions and Your Savings, John Plender, Andre Deutsch, 1982
The Money Moguls; the Inside Story of Investment Management, Alastair Ross Goobey, Woodhead Faulkner, 1987
Pension Scheme Disclosure, Teresa Seinkiewicz, available (free) from Touche Ross, Hill House, Little New Street, London EC4A 3TR
Age, Capital and Democracy; Member Participation in Pension Scheme Management, Tom Schuller, Gower Press, 1986
Socially Responsible Investment, Sue Ward, Directory of Social Change (Radius Works, Back Lane, London NW3), 1986 (£5.95)

5. Material on the 1986 Act and Personal Pensions

What are Personal Pensions?, Company Pensions Information Centre, 7 Old Park Lane, London W1Y 3 LJ (free)

Your New Pensions Choice, Bryn Davies and John Wilson, Tolley Publications (£2.95)

Stealing Our Future, 1986, Independent Pensions Research Group, 5 Goldspink Lane, Newcastle on Tyne, NE2 1NQ

6. Magazines

Occupational Pensions, IRS Eclipse Publications, 18–20 Highbury Place, London N5 1QP

Pensions, monthly, United Trade Press, Bowling Green Lane, London EC1R 0DA

Pensions and Employee Benefits (free), Linklaters and Paines, Barrington House, 59–67 Gresham Street, London EC2V 7JA

Pensions Management, monthly, FTBI, Greystoke House, Fetter Lane, London EC1

Pensions Service Bulletin, Incomes Data Services, 193 St John Street, London EC1V 4LS. They also publish, and will keep up to date in future, a Personnel Manual on pensions.

Pensions World, monthly, Tolley's, Tolley House, Scarbrook Road, Croydon, Surrey, CR0 1SQ

Most of the major firms of actuaries and consultants also publish quarterly newsletters or regular briefings, which are usually free. Ask to be put on the mailing list for the firm which your pension scheme uses.

The insurance company Legal and General also run a Pensions News Service, which is a sheet of press cuttings every week or so. You can be put on the mailing list for this by writing to Pensions Publicity, Kingswood House, Kingswood, Tadworth, Surrey, KT20 6EU.

7. Other Addresses

Company Pensions Information Centre, 7 Old Park Lane, London SW1H 9LL

DSS: Benefits Division, Newcastle Central Office, 091 285 7111

Contracting Out: 091 261 2341

London Office, Occupational Pensions Division, C2/3 Friars House, 157–68 Blackfriars Road, London SE1 8EU

Labour Research Department, 78 Blackfriars Road, London SE1

Independent Pensions Research Group (trade unionists, actuaries, lawyers, academics) c/o 5 Goldspink Lane, Newcastle on Tyne NE2 1NQ

National Association of Pension Funds, 14–18 Grosvenor Gardens, London SW1W 0DH

Occupational Pensions Advisory Service, Room 327, Aviation House, 129 Kingsway, London WC2B

Pensions Investment Resource Centre, 40 Bowling Green Lane, London EC1R 0NE

Pensions Management Institute, PMI House, 124 Middlesex Street, London E1 7HY

Trade Union Occupational Pensions Advisory Group (for TU members in Scotland), c/o Benny McGowan, Central College of Commerce, 190 Cathedral Street, Glasgow G4 0ND

Appendix Two:

List of Abbreviations

ACAS   Advisory, Conciliation and Arbitration Service
APP   Appropriate Personal Pension
AVC   Additional Voluntary Contribution
CEP   Contributions Equivalent Premium
COMP   Contracted Out Money Purchase Scheme
DSS   Department of Social Security
EOC   Equal Opportunities Commission
FSAVC   Free Standing Additional Voluntary Contribution
GMP   Guaranteed Minimum Pension
IMRO   Investment Management Regulatory Organisation
IR   Inland Revenue
LEL   Lower Earnings Limit
NAPF   National Association of Pension Funds
PHI   Permanent Health Insurance
PP   Personal Pension
OPB   Occupational Pensions Board
SERPS   State Earnings Related Pension Scheme
SIB   Securities and Investments Board
SFO   Superannuation Funds Office (of the Inland Revenue)
SSP   Statutory Sick Pay
TV   Transfer Value
WGMP   Widow/ers' Guaranteed Minimum Pension

Index